The Great Plains Guide to CUSTER

The Great Plains Guide to
CUSTER

85 FORTS, FIGHTS & OTHER SITES

Jeff Barnes

STACKPOLE
BOOKS

To Lucy

Published by
STACKPOLE BOOKS
5067 Ritter Road
Mechanicsburg, PA 17055
www.stackpolebooks.com

Printed in the United States of America

10 9 8 7 6 5 4 3 2 1

FIRST EDITION

Cover and title page photo: ***George Armstrong Custer in May 1865, at the end of the Civil War. Custer was probably the most photographed of the Civil War generals and this was his favorite likeness.*** LIBRARY OF CONGRESS

Cover design by Caroline M. Stover

All interior photos by the author or from the author's collection unless noted.

Library of Congress Cataloging-in-Publication Data

Barnes, Jeff, 1958–
The Great Plains guide to Custer : 85 forts, fights, & other sites / Jeff Barnes. — 1st ed.
p. cm.
Includes bibliographical references and index.
ISBN-13: 978-0-8117-0836-4 (pbk.)
ISBN-10: 0-8117-0836-5 (pbk.)
1. Great Plains—History—19th century—Guidebooks. 2. Indians of North America—Wars—1866–1895—Guidebooks. 3. Custer, George A. (George Armstrong), 1839–1876. 4. Indians of North America—Wars—Great Plains—Guidebooks. 5. Fortification—Great Plains—Guidebooks. 6. Great Plains—Description and travel. 7. Frontier and pioneer life—Great Plains. I. Title.
E83.866.B374 2012
978'.02—dc23

2011032307

Contents

Acknowledgments

There are many, many people who make a book like this possible and I need to thank them. Of course, first on the list is my wife Susan. She's endured this other love of my life by losing home space to books and boxes, taking repeated "vacations" to Great Plains sites, and listening to me muse about current and prospective projects. Patient and understanding doesn't begin to describe her!

I've known my friend Randy Garlipp for half my life now and he continues to ride along on the more challenging research trips. When the situation called for climbing Inyan Kara and Harney Peak on back-to-back days, he was there for both (that's about ten hours of mountain hiking for a couple of flatlanders). I wish we'd taken Bear Butte and pulled the hat trick though!

Since meeting Paul Hedren just before my last book came out in 2008, he has become a great friend and adviser. I can't begin to thank him for the connections, the insights, and the camaraderie. The only place I drink coffee is in Paul's basement, surrounded by his books and talking Indian wars, and that makes it one of the best places on Earth.

I need to thank five very important people in the "Custer community."

Robert Utley was kind enough to write a blurb for my forts book, and he gave me something else when I heard him speak at the Order of Indian Wars convention in Austin in 2009. "Write books about people who people know," Bob told us. I was set to write a book about forts on the southern plains, but by the time I returned home I'd decided to turn it into a book about Custer.

That OIW convention held another blessing in that James Donovan—author of one of the best books written on Custer and the Little Bighorn—was presenting there and I got to meet him. I stayed in touch with Jim and it was one of the smartest things I did. He's since become a trusted adviser and confidant, and he truly made this a better book.

Vince Heier has followed the Custer trail for decades and, after a recommendation from Paul Hedren, I asked Father Heier if he'd review this book to make sure I didn't screw it up too badly. There are thousands of stories about Custer, and it's fantastic to have someone in your corner who knows what's right and what's wrong.

Paul Horsted put together two amazing books on Custer's expedition to the Black Hills and I should be thankful for that alone. He went far beyond that, however, as a ready source of information for the Black Hills chapter and even as a personal tour guide for the hike to the summit of Harney Peak. The incredible view was matched by his generosity.

There probably hasn't been anyone who's moved more earth for Custer than Doug Scott. With his archaeological digs at Little Bighorn, Doug's work has almost certainly revealed more about the battle than anything since the 1879 Reno Court of Inquiry. He also knows an amazing amount of minutia about Custer beyond Little Bighorn, especially on the Great Buffalo Hunt, and I was thrilled to have my fellow Nebraskan's help.

Thanks again to my editor at Stackpole, Kyle Weaver, and assistant editor Brett Keener. I know my books are also their books, and their encouragement, insights, and hard work twelve hundred miles away get this project done. The occasional extension when I need it is also appreciated!

Belated thanks to my friend Liz Whealy. Back in 2005, we were commiserating over jobs that were petering out, and it soon turned to what we'd rather be doing. I said I'd love to write historical travel guides; when she said "Why *don't* you?" it finally clicked. I started on my first guide that month. (Liz, by the way, is living out her dream job as executive director of the Great Plains Zoo in her hometown of Sioux Falls.)

Thanks to my friends in the Omaha Corral of the Westerners, the Order of Indian Wars, the Custer Battlefield Historical and Museum Association, and the Little Bighorn Associates. I've enjoyed the camaraderie!

Many friends have offered their best wishes for this book, but I want to single out those who have taken a particular interest in helping develop it. My deep appreciation goes to John B. Seals, Holly Herman, Stew Magnuson, John Bryan, Beverly Bremer Johns, Tim Ryan, Sherri Bishop, and Terri Zapata. Some I've known for decades, others a very short time, but they all pitched in when it was truly needed. Thank you!

Sincere thanks go to the folks at the sites, museums, and organizations for providing the time and expertise needed to complete the book. It was a long trail, but one easily made with their guidance and goodwill along the way. My best to Stephen Allie, Amorette Allison, John Bromley, Jeff Broome, Sandy Brown, Frank Carroll, Connie Childers, Steve Dunkin, George Elmore, Don Fontenot, Steve Friesen, Dale Genius, Kathryn Harrison,

Wayne Heimbuck, Michele Janczak, Christopher Johnson, Beverly Komarek, Phoebe Kowalewski, Frona Lorimer, William McKale, Jim McNally, Crystal Mensch-Nelson, Pat and Bob Miller, Shirley Nelson, Ariel Overstreet, Matthew Reitzel, John Richardson, Reid Riner, Norbert Robben, Marijo Robben-Isbell, Ronette Rumpca, Bruce Schulze, David Seitz, Sharon Small, Towana Spivey, Ken Stewart, Blair Tarr, and Bob Wilhelm.

Finally, special thanks to Doug and Sheila Hunter for sharing a mountain, to Russ Talbot and John Mintling for sharing their campsites, and to Larry Ness for sharing his incredible collection.

The Custer Trail was long, sometimes grueling, sometimes frustrating, but always an adventure I'll cherish. Thank you to everyone I met along the way!

Introduction

More than three hundred thousand people visit the site of Custer's Last Stand at Little Bighorn every year. But how many visit his *first* stand on the Great Plains . . . or even know where to find it?

Or where Custer chiseled his name into stone in the Black Hills, not once but twice? And where's the site of his court-martial at Fort Leavenworth? Where did Custer hunt buffalo with the grand duke of Russia? Where did fellow officer Frederick Benteen allegedly dare Custer to horsewhip him?

There are about a dozen national or state historic sites commemorating Custer on the plains—but there are many more sites that also have a Custer connection. This book will tell you how to find them.

The most popular Custer site on the plains is where he died, which is somewhat ironic since he did so much *living* on the Great Plains. It's here that he marched through blizzards and blistering heat, chased and fought Indians, led countless buffalo hunts, climbed mountains, and found gold.

George Armstrong Custer was born, raised, and found fame and glory in the East, but once he crossed the Mississippi he became the West. It's here that he passed from boy general to legend. Even those associated with him were magnified: would Buffalo Bill and Sitting Bull be as well known today without their Custer connections?

Like my first book, *Forts of the Northern Plains,* this guide has background on the sites before Custer's arrival, what happened while he was there and after he left, and what you'll find at the sites today. Where available, I also direct you to contacts, related sites and attractions, and reading material. Admission prices and operating hours are also included and were current at the time of writing. They do change, so confirm them before you make travel plans.

Custer's strong personality contributed to conflicts with commanders, fellow officers, and even an animal. Those conflicts influenced what happened to him on the Great Plains, so I've highlighted those "personal battles" as well.

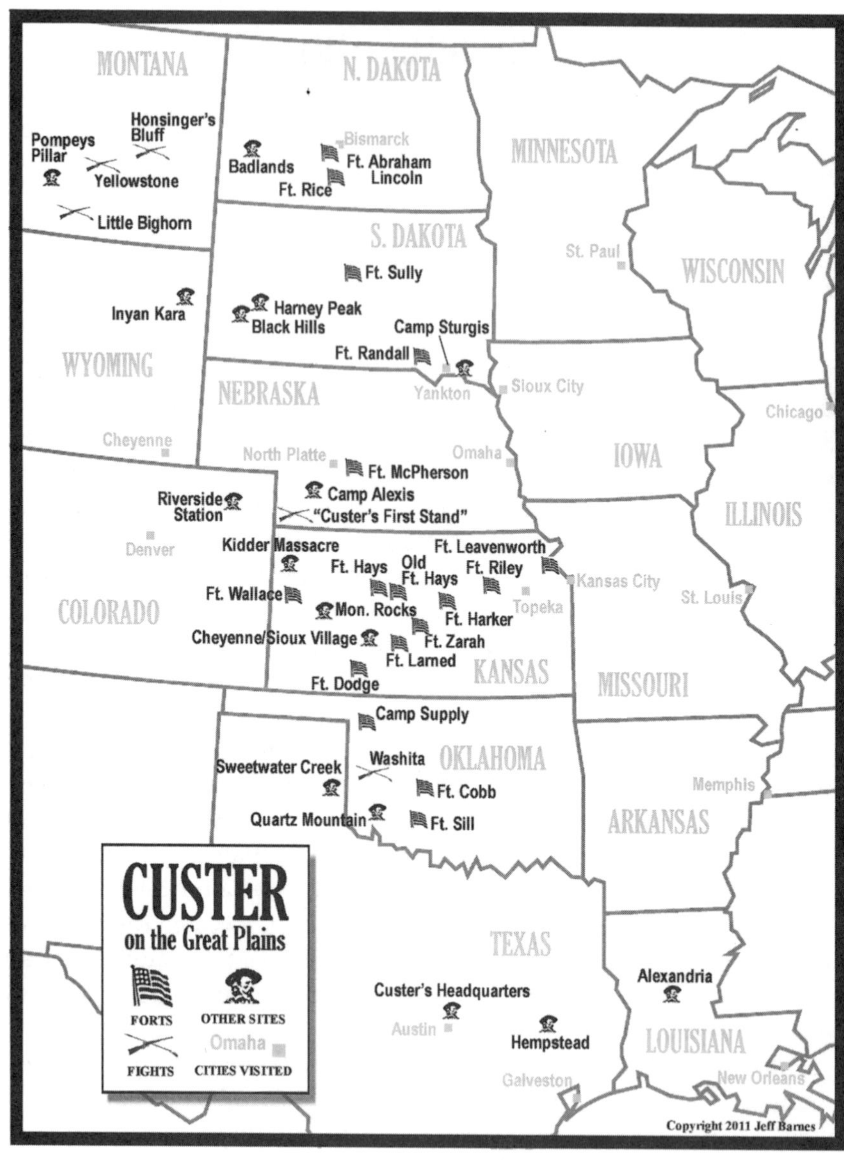

Putting the book together was a nonstop adventure, since I'm one of those guys who pauses at every historical marker and also enjoys the thrill of the chase. I find excitement in locating the marker for the Cheyenne and Sioux villages that Winfield Scott Hancock burned in Kansas. Seeing the porch on which Custer sat is a big deal, and climbing Inyan Kara and locating Custer's name at the summit is a high point in my life. I take comfort in knowing I'm not the only one who feels this way, and I hope this book finds its way into the hands of like-minded people.

The guide is presented in chronological order, beginning with sites related to Custer's post–Civil War assignments in Louisiana and Texas, through his disastrous involvement in Hancock's War in Kansas, the successful winter campaign in Indian Territory, the transitional years between plains campaigns, the transfer to the Dakota Territory, and expeditions to the Yellowstone River, the Black Hills, and finally, the Little Bighorn.

Some of these sites I've visited for decades (primarily due to my in-laws living in southwest Oklahoma), others I've frequented in the past decade, and some I visited for the first time in 2010. As with *Forts of the Northern Plains,* I put in thousands of miles to track down these Custer sites. In some places there are roads where there once were trails, or parking lots where buildings once stood. But many sites are preserved and restored, and many have the same scenery and terrain as in Custer's day.

In some cases, that scenery and terrain is spectacular. The two most difficult Custer sites to reach are the summits of Inyan Kara and Harney Peak in the Black Hills. These are mountains, and those who make the climbs are rewarded with amazing views—the same views seen by Custer.

There are hundreds of Custer books, and more and more are published every year covering his life, his battles, his associates, and his adversaries. As far as I know, this is the first comprehensive guide to the Great Plains sites associated with those stories. I hope it finds a place among those who know the stories or are learning them and now want see and enjoy the land that Custer walked.

If you do come, I hope you also visit the many related historic sites and museums listed—some of these locations would be thrilled to have one percent of Little Bighorn's visitation numbers. Many of these staffed sites have resident experts and the stories and information they share may inspire journeys of your own.

Happy trails!

George and Libbie Custer in 1864. LIBRARY OF CONGRESS

1865–66

Custer Crosses the Mississippi

At the onset of the Civil War, it didn't seem likely that George Armstrong Custer would emerge as one of the conflict's stars. Custer, born in Harrison County, Ohio, in 1839, had a spotty record as a West Point cadet, picking up enough demerits from pranks to continually put him on the verge of expulsion. He finished last in the class of 1861 and likely would have received a hardship assignment had the Union not been desperate for officers.

As soon as Custer was given a command, however, he displayed an aggressiveness and fearlessness that inspired his men and impressed his commanders. Detractors called him careless, reckless, and lucky, pointing to the number of horses shot out from beneath him (two in one day and eleven by the end of the war), but no one could deny Custer's ability to scout the enemy, determine their weaknesses, and then exploit them.

Fortune favors the bold, and Custer rose from first lieutenant to major general in less than three years. At twenty-five, he was the youngest general in the war, earning newspaper fame as the "boy general." He had the audacity to design a distinctive uniform for himself, featuring a wide-brimmed hat and a scarlet cravat to ensure that he was seen, and he had the additional pluck to bring along reporters in order to make sure their readers knew of his exploits.

In finding his fame and promotion, however, Custer engendered the jealousy and ill will of many fellow officers, especially those with more seniority. Like Custer, some hoped to continue their military careers after the war and they knew the competition for openings would be fierce.

The Civil War ended in April 1865, but in Texas there were still some elements of rebel resistance. There was also concern farther south in Mexico, where the French had propped up Maximilian I as emperor in hope of creating a new French empire in the Americas. The United States prepared to invade Mexico in order to drive out the European expansion.

Gen. Philip Sheridan was sent to New Orleans to organize an army of more than thirty thousand, and the commander he selected to train and head a unit of four thousand cavalry was George Custer. Sheridan was Custer's mentor in the final campaign of the war and each admired the other greatly—they even shared a management style of being impulsive, emotional, and exceedingly tough.

Missing the hometown hero celebration he would have received in Monroe, Michigan, Custer, his wife Elizabeth (known as Libbie), and their servant Eliza Brown left Washington by rail to Louisville, and then traveled by steamer down the Ohio and Mississippi Rivers to New Orleans. Custer had his first opportunity to rest in months on the trip and the party even met Confederate general John Bell Hood on one of the stops.

The Custers arrived in New Orleans on June 18, 1865, and were able to take in the French Quarter and other sights of city. Legendary general Winfield Scott also stayed at their hotel in New Orleans and the Custers paid a call. Scott was a hero of Libbie's father and she was stunned to see the old general as decrepit as he had become. "I was almost sorry to have seen him at all," she wrote, "except for the praise that he bestowed upon my husband, which, coming from so old a soldier, I deeply appreciated."

Custer would train his troops at Alexandria in central Louisiana. Before leaving New Orleans, he met with Sheridan to discuss plans for Texas and Mexico. In the last week of June, he, Libbie, his staff (including his brother Lt. Tom Custer), and their horses boarded a steamer for Alexandria. They went up the Mississippi and turned into the mouth of the Red River—and from that point on, Custer was forever linked to the West.

Alexandria and the Louisiana Mutiny

Alexandria, Louisiana

On the northern edge of Cajun culture and the south bank of the Red River is the central Louisiana town of Alexandria. As far back as the 1760s, Indian, French, Spanish, English, and American traders frequented the site. The town developed into a major shipping and warehousing port, and the fertility of the surrounding land made its planters among the wealthiest men in America.

In 1859, the Louisiana Seminary of Learning and Military Academy was established in Pineville, across the river from Alexandria. Its first superintendent, Col. William Tecumseh Sherman, resigned when rebels seized the United States Arsenal in Baton Rouge in 1861. Despite the enormous destruction caused by his 1864 "March to the Sea," General Sherman asked the Union commander of the district that included the seminary not to destroy its buildings. The commander honored the request and the buildings survived the war.

Alexandria itself didn't fare so well—most of it went up in flames when Gen. Nathaniel Banks and his Union forces evacuated in May 1864. The town of six hundred quickly rebuilt and the Confederates erected two

The Red River waterfront in Alexandria during the late 1860s. The large building on the right is a hotel; the Custers lived about a block or two behind it. LOUISIANA HISTORY MUSEUM

earthen forts on the Pineville side of the river in case the Yankees returned. The South surrendered in 1865, however, before the forts saw action.

During Custer

Custer arrived in Alexandria in late June 1865 from New Orleans with his staff and family. The Custers moved into a vacant house that had been occupied by General Banks during the war, only about one hundred yards from the Red River and the cotton docks.

Besides preparing the troops for Texas, the boy general came to Louisiana to suppress any residual rebellion from the Civil War as the Confederate soldiers returned home. Custer promoted peace and order with the citizens and newly freed slaves. It represented tremendous responsibility for him at only twenty-five years of age and still inclined toward impetuousness and pranks. Still, he proved himself an able statesman and impressed the local community with his civility.

Ironically, the most pressing conflict came from Custer's own troops. These were volunteers, angry at still being in uniform for a war that was over. What's more, the soldiers from the Union's western armies weren't accustomed to taking orders from officers—they saw officers as "equals" and certainly weren't about to accept discipline from them. This entirely contradicted Custer's Civil War experience. He'd had the respect and loyalty of his troops back east and dealt with disciplined soldiers; here soldiers challenged and threatened his authority for the first time. Where Custer sought peace from local landowners, his troops sought plunder. They were frequently absent without leave and many deserted their camp.

The Custers escaped the problems of his command and the shabbiness of Alexandria by riding every evening. Their rides often took them across the Red River to Pineville where they sometimes passed the Louisiana Seminary and its main building, by this time known as the Sherman Institute after its first superintendent. In *Tenting on the Plains*, her memoir of the early western campaigns, Libbie wrote of the earthwork forts along the river in Pineville that she and the general visited. He admired them greatly and pointed out details of their construction to her. Unknown to him at the time, the forts had been engineered by Lt. Alphonse Buhlow, a West Point classmate of his.

There was no escaping conflict with his men, however, which came to a head in August. Prior to Custer's arrival in Alexandria, two enlisted men had been convicted of military crimes: one a deserter and thief and the second a popular sergeant who petitioned for a colonel's early retirement so another officer could rise to the rank before the war ended. Both of the convicted men were ordered to be shot and Custer refused to remand the order. Protests came from the troops, and there were threats that Custer himself would be shot.

General Sheridan, commander of the military district and Custer's mentor, told him to "use such summary measures as you deem proper to overcome the mutinous disposition of the individuals in your command." Custer ignored the threats and became more resolute in the face of mutiny. On the scheduled day of execution of the condemned men, Custer had the forty-five hundred soldiers of the camp form a hollow square; he and his staff rode slowly around the square, almost in defiance of the assassination threat. When the two convicts were blindfolded and sat on their coffins for the firing squad, however, the sergeant was pulled to the side; he fainted as the first man was shot. When he awoke, the sergeant was told that Custer spared him, believing that he had been influenced by others.

By early August, the men had grudgingly accepted the discipline of Custer's command and soon were ready to march to Texas.

After Custer

Alexandria was one of the first Louisiana towns to rebound from the Civil War and has since grown to a city of more than forty-six thousand residents.

The Site Today

There is no remnant of the encampment of Custer's military post, his first west of the Mississippi. The home in which he stayed is long gone and there is no historical marker of his time there. According to staff of the Louisiana History Museum in Alexandria, the Custers' home was in the vicinity of Fisk and Third Streets, now the site of a civic center and parking garage.

The Confederate forts visited by Custer and his wife are still there within today's Forts Randolph and Buhlow State Historic Site. Located on the Red River in downtown Pineville, the site includes a visitors center with exhibits on the Civil War's Red River Campaign, an elevated boardwalk around the fort area, and an open field that hosts Civil War reenactments. *Address:* 135 Riverfront Street, Pineville, LA 71360. *Hours:* Wednesday through Sunday, 9 A.M. to 5 P.M.; closed on Thanksgiving, Christmas, and New Year's Day. Guided tours are offered daily. *Admission:* $4 per person; free for seniors (62 and over) and for children age 12 and under. *Phone:* (318) 484-2390 or toll-free at (877) 677-7437. *E-mail:* fortsrandolphbuhlow@crt.state.la.us. *Website:* www.crt.state.la.us/parks/iftsrandbuhlow.aspx.

Farther north and also along U.S. Highway 71 are the grounds of the Louisiana Seminary and the Sherman Institute, where George and Libbie

Whereas Custer and Libbie once toured Forts Randolph and Buhlow on horseback, modern visitors use an elevated boardwalk, with an overlook near Bailey's Dam. FORTS RANDOLPH AND BUHLOW STATE HISTORIC SITE

enjoyed horseback rides. (Incidentally, the seminary lost its main building to fire in 1869. The school resumed classes in Baton Rouge that same year and was later renamed Louisiana State University.) The original buildings are long gone, but ruins and historical markers are there to help interpret the site.

Related Attractions

The Louisiana History Museum in downtown Alexandria collects and presents history associated with the city and all of Louisiana. The museum maintains one of the foremost collections of historic objects in the state, including artifacts from the Civil War and Reconstruction. *Address:* 503 Washington Street, Alexandria, LA 71301. *Hours:* Tuesday through Saturday, 10 A.M. to 4 P.M. *Admission:* Free. *Phone:* (318) 487-8556. *Website:* www.louisianahistorymuseum.org.

Recommended Reading

Custer in Texas: An Interrupted Narrative by John M. Carroll (Sol Lewis/Liveright)

Liendo Plantation

Hempstead, Texas

Originally a Spanish land grant and one of the first cotton plantations in Texas, Liendo Plantation was established in 1853 by Leonard Waller Groce, a descendent of one of the state's original settlers. He made Liendo the social center of Texas, receiving the well-known and well-placed during lavish parties. During the Civil War, four Groce sons fought for the South and the plantation also hosted Camp Groce, used as a camp for Confederate soldiers and Union prisoners of war.

During Custer

Custer and his troops arrived and camped at the plantation in late August 1865. In spite of their wartime allegiance to the Confederacy, the Groces immediately offered their hospitality. When they found out Libbie was living in a tent, they invited her to stay in their home. She refused, in spite of the scorpions, tarantulas, and malaria-carrying mosquitoes common to the area. After Libbie took ill, the Groces insisted she stay with them and nursed her back to health.

Libbie and George Custer at Hempstead, Texas, on October 18th, 1865. LIBRARY OF CONGRESS

Custer frequently hunted deer with Groce and other planters who controlled their hounds by horns. After he got himself a horn and his host gave him five dogs, Custer nearly split his cheeks trying to duplicate their calls.

General Sheridan soon arrived with Custer's father Emanuel, who took on the role of forage agent to allow him to travel with his son. The condition of the men and horses pleased Sheridan—as did reports of no insubordination—and he placed Custer in command of all cavalry in Texas.

The reputation of Liendo for its warm hospitality served it well, and probably helped ensure its survival. When the time came for Custer and the troops to move on to Austin in November, he reemphasized that Liendo and all Texans and their property be treated with respect.

After Custer

Like most Southern plantations, Liendo fell on hard times after the Civil War and went through several owners. Among its better-known owners and occupants were the world-famous sculptor Elisabet Ney and her husband, Dr. Edward Montgomery. They made Liendo their home from 1873 to 1911 and were buried on the plantation grounds after their deaths. You can find her sculptures of Stephen Austin and Sam Houston in both the Texas and U.S. capitols.

Visiting Liendo Plantation

38653 Wyatt Chapel Road, Hempstead, TX 77445-4503
(800) 826-4371 or (979) 826-3126 • www.liendo.org

How to Get There: Located in Waller County in southeast Texas. Liendo Plantation is two miles east of Hempstead on FM 1488, then a quarter mile south on Wyatt Chapel Road.

Hours: Docent-led tours begin at 10 A.M., 11:30 A.M., and 1 P.M. Special group tours are available with some requirements and advance notice.

Admission: $7 (seniors, groups, and students $5).

Special Events: The Civil War Weekend (the weekend before Thanksgiving) includes battle reenactments and folklife demonstrations such as spinning, weaving, quilting, blacksmithing, and soap-making. Tours of the plantation are also available this weekend alone. For more information, call (936) 931-2811 or (979) 826-3126 or visit www.11texascav.org.

Liendo Plantation at Hempstead, a site visited many times by the Custers, is still a private residence, but remains open for public tours. WILLIAM J. BOZIC JR.

Liendo saw a reversal in its deterioration in 1960 when Carl and Phyllis Detering purchased the home and began a ten-year restoration. They traveled throughout the Deep South and Europe in search of period furnishing and décor, succeeding in restoring the home to its nineteenth-century prestige. Hempstead itself remains a small town today but is growing due to its proximity to Houston, less than an hour away.

The Site Today

A Texas historic landmark, Liendo Plantation is still owned and occupied by the Detering family, who open it for public viewing the first Saturday of most months.

If you happen to be at Liendo during its non-public time, you can always get a photo of the state historical marker near the Liendo drive's entrance, commemorating the "Gen. George and Libbie Custer Campsite."

Custer's Texas Headquarters

Austin, Texas

Several state-run asylums for the mentally ill and physically handicapped were built just outside of Austin, the capital of Texas, in the mid-nineteenth-century. Among them was the Texas State Asylum for the Blind, built by Abner Cook around 1858. The two-story, brick and limestone Italianate structure, featuring a large cupola, served as the asylum through the rest of the 1850s and early '60s, until it was temporarily closed during the Civil War.

A number of Austin citizens offered their homes to Custer as his column approached in November 1865, but they were declined. The provisional governor of Texas, A. J. Hamilton, offered the abandoned blind asylum at the city's edge to Custer as a headquarters, which the general accepted. Custer set up his camp at Shoal Creek on November 4 at the plantation of former Unionist governor E. M. Pease.

During Custer

The Custers moved into the former asylum on November 9, 1865. Libbie noted the considerable room for all of the staff, including a long salon parlor and dining room for entertaining. The headquarters offices were on the ground floor and the upstairs served as the private residence of the Custers. After being so long outdoors during the move from Alexandria to Austin, however, Libbie wrote that she found the building "suffocating" and was compelled to open the windows at night.

The lawlessness of postwar Texas required troops throughout Custer's district, yet they were instructed to avoid being seen as invaders. To that end, Austin served as a vacation of sorts for the Custers. He and his immediate circle enjoyed riding, hunting, and even a horse race between the locals and the Custer clan in which the general's horse lost. They hosted many dances in their temporary home and also allowed their servant Eliza to host a dance to return the hospitality showed her by Austin's black population.

Libbie reported that one of the favorite activities of the now twenty-six-year-old Custer was a ride south of town across the Colorado River to the Deaf and Dumb Asylum. "There seemed to be a fascination for him in the children, who were equally charmed with the young soldier that silently watched their pretty, pathetic exhibitions of intelligent speech by gesture," she wrote. "The children knew him, and welcomed him with lustrous, elo-

Tom, George, and Libbie Custer sit directly before the door of the headquarters in Austin, with their servant Eliza leaning against the frame and Custer's father Emanuel seated on the porch.

quent eyes, and went untiringly through their little exhibitions, learning to bring him their compositions, examples and maps, for his commendation." Through this charming interaction between Custer and the deaf children, the general learned sign language that later served him in communicating with the Plains Indians.

While Custer and the officers enjoyed their stay in Austin, it was bleak at times for the enlisted soldiers—cholera swept through the camp during the winter and a number of the men died and were buried in the meadow near Shoal Creek.

When the French threat from Mexico evaporated and with the state of Texas back within the Union, the need for army occupation ended. On January 27, 1866, Custer received orders to muster out his regiments; the orders relieving him and other generals of volunteers came a few days later. Gen. Samuel D. Sturgis was placed in command of the troops in and around Austin as Custer made plans to return east and to postwar civilian life.

Custer, Libbie, and his staff made stops in Hempstead and Brenham, where they picked up a train for the Gulf Coast. The Custers departed Galveston by steamer to New Orleans and were back in George's hometown of Monroe, Michigan, by March 3.

After Custer

The Asylum for the Blind eventually reoccupied the building. After the asylum was moved to a new home in 1917, a series of tenants expanded the main house and added several more buildings to the surrounding grounds. Among the tenants since the 1920s were the School of Military Aeronautics, the Central Texas State Fair, and the State Lunatic Asylum. The University of Texas used the building until the early 1970s, including as a dormitory.

Neglect took its toll on the house, however, and it was slated for destruction in the mid-1970s. A grassroots effort by the Texas Historical Commission, the Little Bighorn Associates, the Austin Landmark Commission, and the Travis County Historical Commission led to its protection and eventual restoration.

The Site Today

The Custer House, now officially known as the Arno Nowotny Building, is today the administrative offices of the Dolph Briscoe Center of American History, the historical research unit of the University of Texas. The building's wood trim is painted burnt orange, the school color; no one knows its original color.

Related Attractions

Custer regularly visited his cavalry encampment, located a little more than a mile west of his headquarters. Travel west on today's East Martin Luther

Visiting the Custer Headquarters

1 University Station D1100, Austin, Texas 78712
(512) 495-4684

How to Get There: Located on the eastern edge of the University of Texas campus at the southeast corner of Red River Street and East Martin Luther King Boulevard, west of I-35.

Hours: Monday through Friday, 8 A.M. to 5 P.M.; closed Saturday and Sunday.

Admission: Free. Metered parking surrounds the building; free parking is extremely difficult to find on the UT campus and is limited to spaces on the south side of the LBJ Library (Parking Lot 38).

The restored Texas Blind Asylum is today the Arno Nowotny Building on the University of Texas campus.

King Boulevard and you'll arrive at Pease Park, the site of the camp. The cavalry was camped at the park's north end; the area next to Parkway Street is called "Custer's Meadow." The soldiers who died of cholera are no longer buried there, as flooding in 1900 washed up the graves; they were reburied in Austin's Oakwood Cemetery.

Governor Pease's 1853 plantation mansion, Woodlawn (also known as Pease Mansion), still stands in the adjacent Enfield neighborhood at 6 Niles Road; like the Asylum for the Blind, it too was designed by Abner Cook and Custer visited it during his stay in Austin. It spent many years under state ownership and was once considered for the Texas governor's mansion, but state officials were not interested in taking on the extensive and costly restoration required. The state sold the home, and it's now in private hands.

One of the Custers' favorite spots to ride to in the surrounding countryside was Mount Bonnell, where they regularly picnicked and enjoyed the view of the Colorado River Valley on sunny December days. Mount Bonnell is Austin's oldest tourist attraction and at 785 feet, the highest point within city limits. Picnickers still come to the hill for the great view of the city and Lake Austin. Be advised: You'll have a long, hard staircase to face in getting to the top. *Address:* 3800 Mount Bonnell Drive, Austin, TX 78731. *Admission:* Free. *Phone:* (512) 974-6700.

While in Austin, Custer almost certainly made official visits to the Neill-Cochran House, which served as a hospital during Reconstruction. The Greek Revival mansion, built in 1855, has been restored to its original glory

Did Custer Visit the Alamo?

As close as Custer was to San Antonio while in Austin, did he ever visit the famous Alamo? The landmark was then used by the U.S. Army as a depot, and Custer would have had the opportunity to visit during his time in central Texas.

He apparently didn't, however. A letter to *The National Republican* in early 1866 accused Custer of public drunkenness and speaking at a rally for ex-Confederates in San Antonio. Custer answered the charge in the March 3, 1866, *Army-Navy Journal*. "There are several facts and reasons why the imputation is unjust, untrue and inapplicable," he wrote. "First I have never been nearer San Antonio than I am at the present moment (eighty miles). Second, the charge of drunkenness is wholly unfounded, whether at San Antonio or elsewhere, as I have abstained from the use of spiritous liquors for several years."

Stereoview of the Alamo. SOUTHERN METHODIST UNIVERSITY, CENTRAL UNIVERSITY LIBRARIES, DEGOLYER LIBRARY

under the ownership of the National Society of the Colonial Dames of America in the State of Texas. *Address:* 2310 San Gabriel Street, Austin, TX 78705. *Hours:* Tuesday through Saturday, tours from 2 P.M. to 5 P.M. *Admission:* $5; free to children 15 years old and younger. *Phone:* (512) 478-2335. *Website:* www.nchmuseum.org.

If you'd like more on the military history of Texas, take time to visit the nearby Texas Military Forces Museum at Camp Mabry. The museum features an extensive collection of artifacts from the state's military history, from the Alamo to current deployments in Iraq and Afghanistan. Visitors should enter at the security gate and have photo ID ready. *Address:* 3100 West 35th Street, Austin, TX 78703. *Hours:* Wednesday through Sunday, 10 A.M. to 4 P.M.; closed Thanksgiving and December 24–26. *Admission:* Free. *Phone:* (512) 782-5659. *Website:* www.texasmilitaryforcesmuseum.org.

For insight into the state's history in general, from pre-European exploration to modern times, visit the Bob Bullock Texas State History Museum. This state-of-the-art facility includes many rare and unusual artifacts, three floors of interactive exhibits, a special-effects show, a gift shop, a café, and Austin's only IMAX theatre. The museum is at the corner of MLK and Congress. You can't miss it: a thirty-five-foot-tall bronze Lone Star sculpture in front of the museum tells you that you are there. *Address:* 1800 N. Congress Avenue, Austin, TX 78701. *Hours:* Monday through Saturday, 9 A.M. to 6 P.M.; Sunday, noon to 6 P.M. *Admission:* Fee for museum; free to children under 5. Additional fee for theaters. *Phone:* (512) 936-4639. *Website:* www.thestoryoftexas.com.

Farther south at 1102 S. Congress is a historical marker for the Texas School for the Deaf. It was here, under the school's previous name of the Deaf and Dumb Asylum, that Custer learned sign language from the students.

Of course, the State Capitol is a must-see, but for all that Austin has to offer, stop by the Austin Convention & Visitors Bureau at 209 E. 6th Street, call 1-866-GO-AUSTIN, or visit www.austintexas.org.

Recommended Reading

Custer in Texas: An Interrupted Narrative by John M. Carroll (Sol Lewis/Liveright).

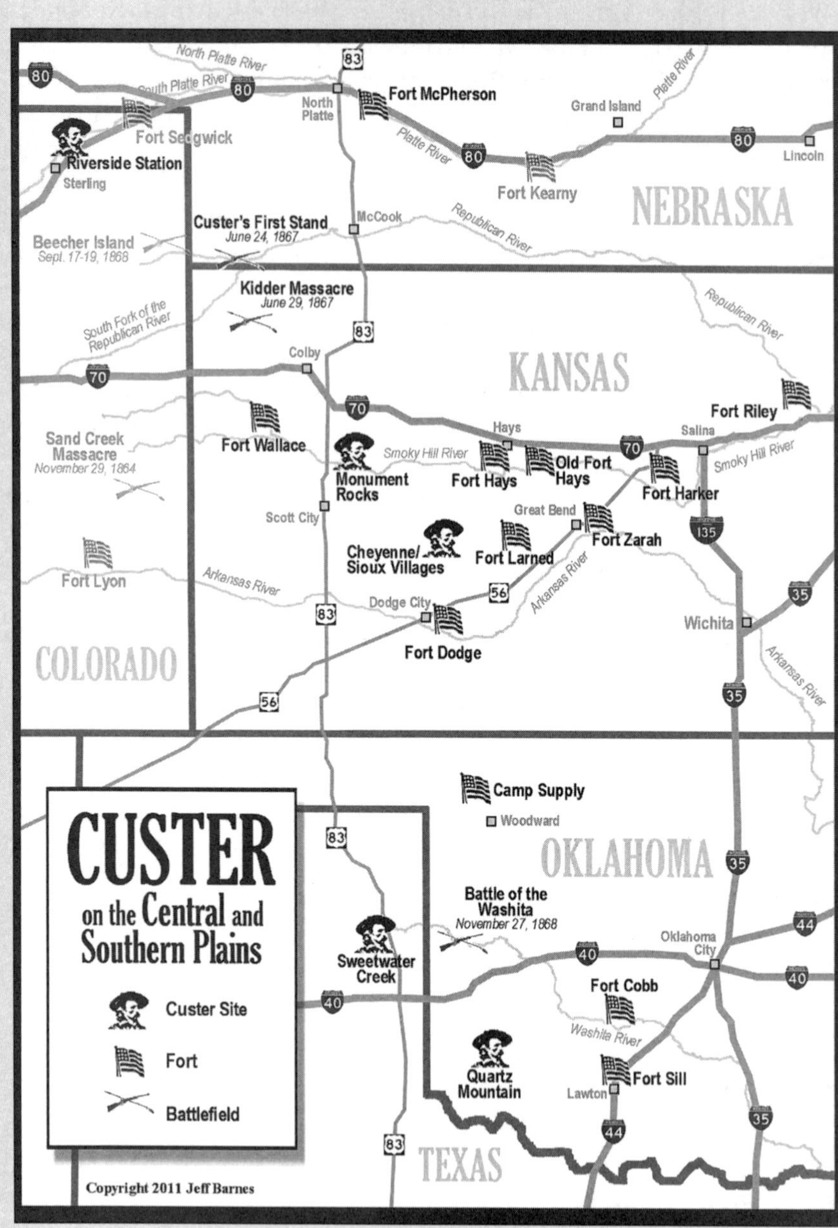
North Platte River
South Platte River
Platte River
Fort McPherson
North Platte
Grand Island
Lincoln
Fort Sedgwick
Riverside Station
Sterling
Fort Kearny
NEBRASKA
Custer's First Stand
June 24, 1867
McCook
Republican River
Beecher Island
Sept. 17-19, 1868
Kidder Massacre
June 29, 1867
South Fork of the Republican River
Colby
KANSAS
Fort Riley
Hays
Salina
Sand Creek Massacre
November 29, 1864
Fort Wallace
Monument Rocks
Smoky Hill River
Fort Hays
Old Fort Hays
Fort Harker
Scott City
Great Bend
Fort Zarah
Cheyenne/ Sioux Villages
Fort Larned
Fort Lyon
Arkansas River
Dodge City
Wichita
Fort Dodge
COLORADO
Camp Supply
Woodward
CUSTER
on the Central and Southern Plains
Custer Site
Fort
Battlefield
OKLAHOMA
Battle of the Washita
November 27, 1868
Sweetwater Creek
Oklahoma City
Fort Cobb
Washita River
Quartz Mountain
Fort Sill
Lawton
TEXAS
Copyright 2011 Jeff Barnes

1866–67

The Kansas–Nebraska Campaign

Following the end of his duty in Texas and his reduction in rank to captain in the regular army, Custer considered careers outside the military. Fortunately for him, a reorganization of the postwar army and an influential friend in General Sheridan got him a lieutenant colonelcy within a new regiment, organized on the Great Plains for America's expansion west.

Millions were headed west across the plains: emigrants, miners, railroaders, shippers, speculators, and settlers. Although many of the Plains Indian tribes had been subdued and moved to reservations, some of the stronger and more feared ones—including the Sioux, Cheyenne, and Kiowa—actively resisted the invasion.

Gen. Winfield Scott Hancock was chosen to head the army's 1867 summer campaign in Kansas, the purpose of which was to negotiate peace with the Sioux and Cheyenne. If the tribes refused, it was hoped a show of force would provoke them into war, in which case they would be destroyed by the army. Or so it was assumed. Hancock and the War Department entered the campaign without a strategy, fighting a new enemy the likes of which they had never fought before, using volunteer troops unfamiliar with army ways.

Compounding the troops' inexperience were their backgrounds of various ethnic origins, economic classes, and education. They weren't fighting for a cause, as during the Civil War—they were fighting for a paycheck, and many deserted when they got close enough to the Colorado gold fields. To the further detriment of the army, alcoholism ran rampant among enlisted men and officers alike.

The officers had backgrounds as diverse as those of their troops. Some were West Pointers, some were volunteers, and some were appointees. They often fell into factions, to the point where many felt no loyalty to a commander, especially to one as hard-driving and impulsive as George Custer. To compound matters, Kansas and other central plains states were being ravaged by a swift-moving cholera epidemic, which spread death and fear at the forts and other settlements.

Circumstances such as these made the campaign's failure almost a certainty, and—aided in part by his own actions—Custer became the campaign's best-known victim.

Fort Riley

Fort Riley, Kansas

Increased conflicts along the Oregon–California and Santa Fe trails in the early 1850s led the army to establish posts along the routes. They built Camp Center in 1852 near where the Smoky Hill and Republican Rivers merge in northeast Kansas to create the Kansas River. The post got its original name for its central U.S. location but was given its present name with the 1853 death of Maj. Gen. Bennett C. Riley, a Mexican War hero who led the first military escort down the Santa Fe Trail.

Fort Riley was caught in the middle of "Bleeding Kansas" during the 1850s, as pro- and antislavery activists poured into the territory and open violence became the norm. The fort was both an enforcer and pawn of the law; it tried to keep the peace even as the borders of its own reservation constantly changed based upon which side had the upper hand in government.

During the Civil War, many of the regular army officers resigned their commissions to fight for their home states in the South. The enlisted regular army troops were sent east to fight for the Union and volunteers filled most of the bunks at Fort Riley. After the war, the soldiers continued their escort duties along the trails and later provided protection for the Union Pacific Railroad's Eastern Division (soon to be the Kansas Pacific) construction crews.

Detail from an 1864 painting of Fort Riley. US CAVALRY MUSEUM

In 1866 the government authorized the creation of four new cavalry units to patrol the Plains—the Seventh, Eighth, Ninth, and Tenth U.S. Cavalry regiments. The Ninth and Tenth were both made up of black troops, nicknamed "Buffalo Soldiers" by the Indians they fought; the Seventh and Eighth were formed at Fort Riley on September 21, 1866.

Brevet Maj. Gen. (Major) John W. Davidson of the Second U.S. Cavalry was essentially the first commander of the Seventh, since he pulled officers from the Second to help form the new regiment. One of those officers was Brevet Maj. Gen. (Colonel) Andrew J. Smith, who took over the Seventh for a three-month period beginning in November; another was George Armstrong Custer.

During Custer

Custer, accompanied by Libbie and Eliza, reported for duty at Fort Riley on the evening of November 3, 1866. However, he left for Washington, DC, shortly after his arrival for an appearance before an examining board, missing much of the training of the Seventh. He returned to the fort just in time for Christmas.

Two months later, after Smith's promotion to head the District of the Upper Arkansas, Custer became the new commander of the Seventh Cavalry—a post he held from February 26, 1867, to June 25, 1876. He and his new regiment left for Fort Harker, southeast of Riley, on March 26 in the midst of a bitterly cold Kansas winter.

Custer returned to Fort Riley on July 19—without leave—to retrieve Libbie. He returned to Fort Harker on July 21 on General Smith's orders and was arrested upon arrival. Fearful of potentially exposing Libbie to the cholera rapidly spreading on the frontier, Smith sent the Custers back to Fort Riley; from there, the Custers went to Fort Leavenworth, where George awaited his court-martial (see page 74).

After Custer

Fort Riley saw a decline in importance as the frontier moved farther west. The end of the Indian wars in Kansas led many to expect Fort Riley to join other forts in closure in the 1880s, but General Sheridan recommended in his 1884 annual report to Congress that the fort instead become the "Cavalry Headquarters of the Army." Congressional approval led to a major expansion and renovation of the fort: New buildings went up, hills were removed, and the parade ground was leveled out. After years in the Dakota Territory, the Seventh Cavalry returned to its original home at Fort Riley in 1888; it embarked from there to participate in the last battle of the Plains Indian Wars at Wounded Knee on December 29, 1890.

State militia units joined the cavalry in training at the turn of the century, and with U.S. entry into World War I tens of thousands of men came

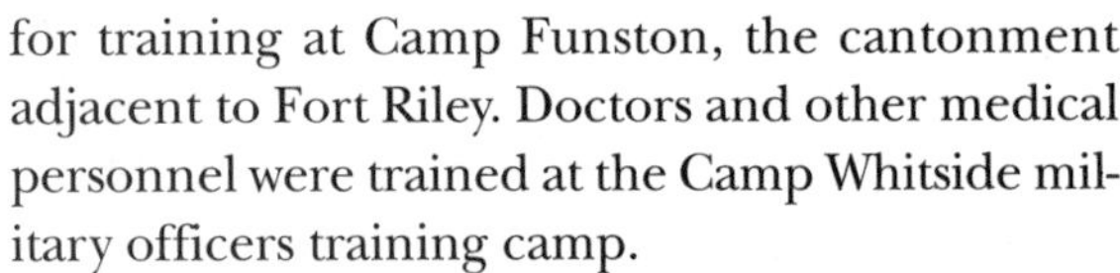

for training at Camp Funston, the cantonment adjacent to Fort Riley. Doctors and other medical personnel were trained at the Camp Whitside military officers training camp.

The Site Today

Fort Riley is one of *the* most historic army posts in the United States. It shouldn't be missed if you want to walk in the footsteps of names like Robert E. Lee, Jeb Stuart, and George Patton—as well as George Custer.

Nearly all of what you'll want to see from Custer's time is on Main Post West, the original site of Fort Riley. An exception is the First Territorial

The birthplace of the Seventh Cavalry, also the first Kansas territorial capitol. The building is adjacent to the Union Pacific tracks, appropriate to the cavalry's later role in protecting the railroad's construction in western Kansas.

Capitol State Historic Site, next to the Union Pacific tracks at 693 Huebner Road. This building was the capitol for only four days in 1855, but it played an integral role in the prewar struggle to determine whether Kansas would be slave or free. Of note for those with an interest in Custer: The army formed the Seventh Cavalry here in September of 1866. *Note:* At press time, the building was closed until further notice due to adjacent construction projects by the army and railroad. *Address:* PO Box 2122, Fort Riley, KS 66442. *Phone:* (785) 784-5535 or (785) 238-1666. *Website:* www.kshs.org/portal_first_territorial_capitol.

A walking tour of the historic main post should begin at Building 205, better known as the U.S. Cavalry Museum. This stately limestone building with a clock tower was constructed in 1854–55 and originally served as the

Visiting Fort Riley

U.S. Cavalry Museum
Building 205, Huebner Road, Fort Riley, KS 66442
(785) 239-2737 • webmaster@riley.army.mil
www.riley.army.mil/UnitPage.aspx?unit=dptms.museum

How to Get There: Located in Riley and Geary Counties in northeast Kansas. If you do not have a military/civilian ID for accessing Fort Riley, you must have a photo ID (driver's license), proof of vehicle insurance, and vehicle registration available. To get to the Marshall Army Air Field entrance from I-70, drive down Henry Drive, on which you will cross two bridges. Turn left at the small traffic island onto Marshall Drive and you will come to a three-way stop. Turn left onto Custer Avenue. Drive up Custer Avenue and look to your right. Approximately 150 meters up this road, you'll see an equestrian statue. Turn right at this point and the Cavalry Museum is located beyond the equestrian statue.

Hours: Monday through Saturday, 9 A.M. to 4:30 P.M.; Sunday, noon to 4:30 P.M. Closed New Year's Day, Easter, Thanksgiving, and Christmas.

Admission: Free, with donations accepted.

Special Events: Apple Days (usually first Saturday in October) features pioneer crafts, reenactors, modern military equipment displays, and homemade apple pie on the cavalry parade field. On the Sunday before Halloween, ghost tours are offered of the Main Post's "haunts." An annual Homes Tour of Army quarters in the historic district is given; call for information.

post hospital; it was converted to a museum in 1957. Budget at least an hour for its dozen amazing galleries telling the story of the United States cavalry from Revolutionary War days to 1950, and give special attention to its unique art gallery, which includes a Frederic Remington.

Before leaving the museum, pick up the brochure for the walking tour. The next stop is Quarters 24 on Sheridan Avenue, known to most as the Custer House. Because papers signed by Custer were found in the A-side of the duplex in the 1940s, caretakers assumed he lived there; they decorated it with period antiques and furnishings typical to those of an army officer of the mid-1870s. Researchers now believe the general and his wife actually lived in the west side of Quarters 21, destroyed by fire in the 1930s and later rebuilt. Quarters 21 is today a private residence and not open for public tours, but Quarters 24 is still the "official" Custer House and open for viewing and tours. *Phone:* (785) 239-2737.

Farther down Sheridan Avenue, at its intersection with Huebner Avenue, is the Wounded Knee Monument, dedicated to the men of the Seventh Cavalry that were killed in that 1890 fight.

Two other structures remain from Custer's brief time at the fort. North on Huebner is Quarters 123, built in 1855. The post chaplain originally lived in the house, and army officers Robert E. Lee and Joseph Johnston once heard court-martial testimony here. (*Note:* This is a private residence.)

Although researchers now believe the general occupied different quarters, the "Custer House" was long assumed to have been his home while at Fort Riley.

Built in 1861, St. Mary's Chapel was the post chapel and school during Custer's time at Fort Riley and is now used for Catholic services.

Make a right from Huebner onto Barry Avenue to reach St. Mary's Chapel, the smaller of the two houses of worship at the post. It is used for Catholic services. St. Mary's was built in 1861; it was also used as the post chapel and schoolhouse, and was an ordnance building during the Civil War. While stationed at old Fort Hays, Capt. Albert Barnitz of the Seventh would make reference to the chapel, writing to his wife that the Custers' personal tent was as large as this church.

Related Attraction in Lawrence

When the Seventh returned to Fort Riley in 1888, it also brought with it the "sole survivor" of Custer's Last Stand. Comanche was the horse of Capt. Myles Keogh and was the only horse not shot or taken by the Indians in the battle. Badly wounded, he was brought home to Fort Abraham Lincoln in North Dakota and nursed back to health. As the official mascot of the Seventh, he followed the regiment to Fort Meade in South Dakota and finally to Fort Riley, where he died in 1891 at the approximate age of twenty-nine.

Not wishing to completely say goodbye, the officers sent Comanche's remains to the University of Kansas in Lawrence to be mounted. Once completed, they decided that Comanche should remain with the museum at the university. The horse has undergone a couple of moves and restorations within the KU Natural History Museum, but he now resides—about two hours east of his last home—near the museum's front door wearing his Seventh Cavalry tack and saddle.

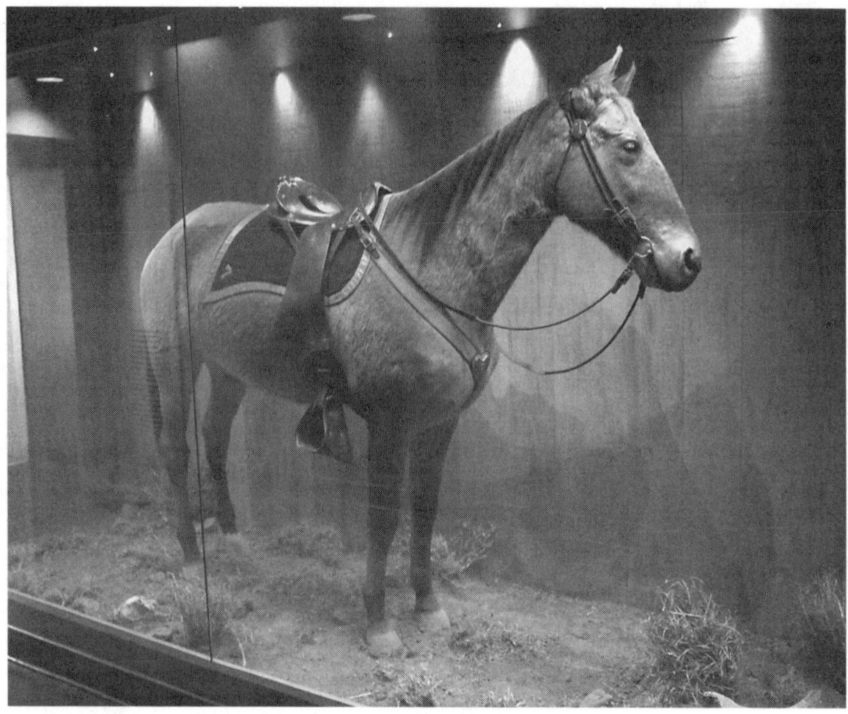

Comanche, now at the KU Natural History Museum in Lawrence.

Address: 1345 Jayhawk Boulevard, Lawrence KS 66045. *Hours:* Tuesday through Saturday, 9 A.M. to 5 P.M.; Sunday, noon to 5 P.M. Closed on holidays. *Admission:* Free (Suggested donation is $5 for adults, $3 for seniors and for children age six and older). *Phone:* (785) 864-4450. *E-mail:* naturalhistory @ku.edu. *Website:* naturalhistory.ku.edu.

Related Attractions in Council Grove

An hour south of Fort Riley is the Santa Fe Trail town of Council Grove, Kansas, and among its many historic sites are a couple of Custer places—maybe.

Local legend holds that Custer and the Seventh made camp under a shady elm grove here in 1867 while patrolling the trail. The problem is that the last wagon of the trail passed in 1866 and there are no official accounts of the Seventh camping here. Nonetheless, a large elm tree was revered as the "Custer Elm" for many years until Dutch elm disease killed it in the 1970s. A remnant of the tree is under a protective pavilion at Custer Elm Park, five blocks south of West Main Street on Neosho Street at its intersection with Elm Street. The south portion of the park is on land purchased by Custer in 1869, some say intended for his retirement.

The second Custer site is the Hays House restaurant, downtown at 112 West Main Street. It was constructed in 1857 by Seth Hays, a great-grandson of Daniel Boone and cousin of Kit Carson, and is claimed to be the oldest eating establishment west of the Mississippi. It's also claimed to have hosted Custer many a time while he was in the area—again, no documentation, but plenty of local legend.

The building lost its pitched roof in an 1886 fire and has been remodeled several times, so even if Custer had been here he might not recognize it. Still, there's no harm in having a fine Kansas steak while imagining the general sitting at a table across the room.

Recommended Reading

Fort Riley and Its Neighbors: Military Money and Economic Growth by William A. Dobak (University of Oklahoma Press); *Fort Riley: Citadel of the Frontier West* by William McKale and William D. Young (Kansas State Historical Society); *Fort Riley* by William McKale and Robert Smith (Arcadia Publishing).

Fort Harker

Kanopolis, Kansas

The first fort at the Santa Fe Trail crossing of the Smoky Hill River was built in 1864. Known as Fort Ellsworth, the very crude affair had buildings of rough logs plastered with mud and topped by roofs of mud, straw, sticks, and boughs.

Troops built a more substantial fort a mile and a half to the north in 1866. Named Fort Harker after Brig. Gen. Charles Garrison Harker, killed in the Civil War battle of Kennesaw Mountain, the new post used native stone and framed lumber. Captain Barnitz wrote his wife after his arrival on March 22, 1867, reporting "I am much pleased with Fort Harker . . . The officers' quarters are progressing finely, and they will be indeed handsome—even more pleasant and cozy than those at Fort Riley."

Not impressed was newspaper correspondent Henry M. Stanley, the man who would become famous for finding Dr. David Livingstone in Africa in 1871. Upon his visit to the fort in 1867, Stanley wrote that "the fort in its

One side of a stereoview of army troops at Fort Harker in 1867. KANSAS HISTORICAL SOCIETY

present naked state appears like a great wart on the surface of the plain."

Fort Harker didn't need to be pretty; its importance came from its role in protecting the construction crews along the Union Pacific's Eastern Division line and travelers on the Smoky Hill Trail and other routes. General Hancock selected the fort as his base camp for the 1867 campaign, billeting eight companies of the Thirty-Eighth Infantry and four companies of the Seventh Cavalry there. Fort Harker became the headquarters of the Department of the Upper Arkansas, with Colonel Smith overseeing the Seventh Cavalry from the fort and George Custer leading the regiment in the field.

During Custer

Custer came to Fort Harker on April 1, 1867, while the Seventh Cavalry moved from Fort Riley to Fort Larned. He set up camp to the west of the post and broke camp on April 3. His second visit, on June 19, was unexpected. While on unauthorized leave from his command in western Kansas to see his wife at Fort Riley, he came to Fort Harker at about 2:30 in the morning and woke Colonel Smith to advise him of his plans to return to Fort Riley on the morning train.

When Smith found out Custer had made the trip without orders, he contacted Custer at Fort Riley and ordered his immediate return. Smith had Custer arrested when he and Libbie came to Fort Harker on June 21, but sent the both of them back to Riley out of fear that Libbie would contract the cholera that was sweeping the plains. Altogether, Custer spent barely a day at this important post of the Kansas Indian Wars.

After Custer

Troops from Fort Harker were assigned to special duties and escorts 195 times in 1867, a record for a military post after the Civil War. As a quartermaster depot during the Hancock campaign, the fort once inventoried 162 horses, 1,586 mules, 337 army wagons, and 31 ambulances.

After the railroad and the Indian problems moved farther and farther from Fort Harker, the army closed the post in April 1872, opening the military reservation to settlers and selling the buildings to speculators. Settlers established the town of Kanopolis in 1886, thinking that its central location might eventually lead to it becoming the capital of Kansas and (to some *truly* excited boosters) the capital of the United States.

The Site Today

Obviously, Kanopolis (pop. 543) didn't achieve its goal of becoming the state capital, but it did absorb the remains of Fort Harker. There are four original buildings, built in 1867 and all present at the time of Custer, that remain today. Three of the buildings—the commanding officer's quarters and two junior officers' quarters—went on to become private residences, which has helped keep them standing for nearly a century and a half.

Visiting Fort Harker

Fort Harker Museum
309 W. Ohio Street, Kanopolis, KS 67454
(785) 472-5733 • echs@eaglecom.net
myellsworth.com/echs/

How to Get There: Located in Kanopolis in Ellsworth County, central Kansas. From Ellsworth, take U.S. 40 six miles east to its intersection with State Highway 111. Turn south and continue for two miles. Fort Harker is two blocks west of the center of Kanopolis.

Hours: Summer (May through September): Tuesday through Saturday, 10 A.M. to 5 P.M.; Sunday, 1 P.M. to 5 P.M. Winter (November through March): Saturday, 10 A.M. to 5 P.M.; Sunday, 1 P.M. to 5 P.M. Spring and Fall (April and October): Tuesday through Friday, 1 P.M. to 5 P.M.; Saturday, 10 A.M. to 5 P.M.; Sunday, 1 P.M. to 5 P.M. Closed Mondays and major holidays.

Admission: $3 for adults, $1 for children 7 to 12, free for children 6 and under.

Amenities: Historic buildings, museum, restrooms.

Special Events: Fort Harker Days, held the second weekend in July, is a community-wide celebration featuring a few performances relating to fort history. Contact the Ellsworth/Kanopolis Chamber of Commerce (785-472-4071) for more information.

One of four surviving buildings from the post, the Fort Harker Guardhouse Museum now presents the history of the fort and surrounding community.

Two of those buildings, the commanding officer's quarters and one of the junior officers' quarters, are now owned and maintained by the Ellsworth County Historical Society and open to the public. The commanding officer's quarters are presumably where Custer woke Colonel Smith to inform him he was headed off to Fort Riley, and where Smith ordered his arrest. The other junior officers' quarters is a private residence.

The historical society also owns the fourth original building, the fort's guardhouse. The two-story red sandstone building houses the Fort Harker Museum, which includes a collection of artifacts from the fort and community. It's a little rough around the edges, but how many fort guardhouses from the 1860s are still standing? That alone makes it a must-see.

Related Attractions

The admission fee to the Fort Harker Museum also covers that of the Hodgden House Museum in nearby Ellsworth. Perry Hodgden and his wife Phebe were among the first arrivals in the town and used native stone to build their home in 1873. *Address:* 104 West South Main Street, Ellsworth, KS 67439. *Hours:* Tuesday through Saturday, 9 A.M. to 5 P.M.; Sunday, 1 P.M. to 5 P.M. *Phone:* (785) 472-3059.

Recommended Reading

Fort Harker: Defending the Journey West by Leo E. Oliva (Kansas State Historical Society); *Life in Custer's Cavalry: Diaries and Letters of Albert and Jennie Barnitz, 1867–1868,* edited by Robert M. Utley (University of Nebraska Press).

Fort Zarah

Great Bend, Kansas

The first Fort Zarah (named by Maj. Gen. Samuel R. Curtis for his dead son, Maj. Henry Zarah Curtis) was built in central Kansas in July 1864 to protect mail service along the Santa Fe Trail. It was three miles away from the Arkansas River near the crossing of Walnut Creek, a popular watering stop for the wagon trains. An 1867 drawing shows the first fort as a single pitched-roof building with a walkway across the top.

The order came in April 1865 to relocate Fort Zarah a half mile away from its original location. It's not known when the second fort was completed, because the 1867 drawing shows the first one still in use. It's also not readily known where the troops got their plans for this second post, because it was truly unique among Great Plains forts. Measuring 120 feet long and 52 feet wide, the new fort was constructed from reddish sandstone quarried three miles away. It had two-story towers built at its northwest and southeast corners with gun slits to fire from should the fort be attacked. A tin roof covered the post, enclosing its officers' quarters, barracks, commissary, kitchen, and mess hall, with the stables and corral attached to the structure.

An artist's conception of Fort Zarah as it would have appeared in Custer's time. BARTON COUNTY HISTORICAL MUSEUM

During Custer

The Hancock Campaign forces stopped at Fort Zarah on April 5, 1867, during the march from Fort Harker to Fort Dodge. Custer, along with the rest of the Seventh Cavalry, set up camp about two miles upstream from Fort Zarah along Walnut Creek, according to staff at the Burton County Museum. It's not known if he went to the fort during the stop.

After Custer

Fort Zarah continued to protect the most dangerous stretch of the Santa Fe Trail. Kiowa warriors attacked the fort itself in 1868 and were driven off after a brief fight. It may have been some nineteenth-century journalistic hyperbole when a newspaper account of the time said a thousand Kiowas attacked, as a contemporary state historical marker reports it as only one hundred. Besides Custer, other well-known names who visited the post were Wild Bill Hickok, Buffalo Bill Cody, Kit Carson, and the Kiowa chief Satank.

The drop-off in attacks and traffic on the Santa Fe Trail led to the fort's abandonment in December 1869. The valuable tin roofing material, the flooring, and all other materials of value that could be removed were taken to Fort Harker. Highway marauders and bats then took over the shell of Fort

Fort Zarah is commemorated in a roadside park east of Great Bend, Kansas.

Zarah, and its dilapidation increased at a much more rapid pace. The military transferred the reservation in 1871 to the Interior Department, which sold the land to settlers. The stonework of Fort Zarah disappeared soon after that.

Visiting Fort Zarah

How to Get There: Fort Zarah Park is located three miles east of Great Bend on U.S. 56 in Barton County, central Kansas.

The Site Today

The remnants of both Fort Zarahs are gone, but the post is memorialized in a spacious wayside area on U.S. 56 east of Great Bend, Kansas. The park includes two markers. The first is large and made of limestone and identifies the park as the site of the fort along the Santa Fe Trail; the second is a state historical marker telling the abbreviated history of Fort Zarah. The second fort site was about a half mile east of the park.

Related Attractions

For more information on Fort Zarah, the Santa Fe Trail, and the area's history before and since then, visit the Barton County Historical Museum and Village, just south of Great Bend across the Arkansas River Bridge on U.S. 281. The five-acre village boasts several authentically furnished period buildings and collections that tell the story of the area from prehistoric times through the Indian Wars to the present day. For fort fans, the museum has a diorama of Fort Zarah that probably offers the best, most accurate depiction of the post's appearance.

Address: 85 S. Highway 281, Great Bend, KS 67530-1091. *Hours:* Summer (April–October), Tuesday through Friday, 10 A.M. to 5 P.M.; Saturday and Sunday, 1 P.M. to 5 P.M. Winter (November–March), Tuesday through Friday, 10 A.M. to 5 P.M. *Admission:* $2 for non-members 16 and older. *Phone:* (620) 793-5125. *Website:* bartoncountymuseum.org

Fort Larned

Larned, Kansas

In its early days, the Santa Fe Trail was limited mostly to traders, and the local tribes were usually friendly. Traffic increased during the Mexican War of 1846–48 and traders now shared the road with stagecoaches, emigrants, and mail carriers. The U.S. Army was dispatched when the Kiowa and Comanche started to take advantage of the "pickings."

William Bent, founder of Bent's Fort on the trail (in present-day southeastern Colorado) and the appointed Indian agent for the Kiowa and Comanche, suggested a post on the Pawnee Fork of the Arkansas River. The army established "Camp on the Pawnee Fork" later that year, renamed it Camp Alert, and finally named it Fort Larned in 1860 after the army's paymaster general. Troops lived in tents and dugouts while adobe structures and a corral were built.

Volunteers filled in at the new post during the Civil War, and no serious incidents occurred until 1864 when the Kiowa attacked settlements and travelers, hoping to drive them from the area. Fort Larned itself was raided, with Kiowa warriors taking 172 animals.

After the war, more substantial red sandstone structures replaced the adobe, with master stonemasons and civilian crews building nine quality buildings over three years. Fort Larned was undoubtedly one of the most attractive and comfortable posts on the plains, as well as one of the most important. Its troops protected those on the trail and those laying track for the Atchison, Topeka and Santa Fe Railroad, and the fort distributed annuities to the local tribes.

During Custer

The next stop westward after Fort Zarah, Fort Larned was the April 7–12 campsite for the 1867 Hancock Campaign; the Seventh Cavalry set up camp to the east of the fort. Custer would have toured the construction of the new buildings joining the blockhouse and commissary building, visiting the newly completed commanding officer's quarters and walking the parade ground amid the construction of the other stone buildings.

Edward Wykoop, the Indian agent for the Cheyenne, Arapahos, and Apaches, invited his chiefs to meet at Fort Larned and asked Hancock to stay until April 10. While the troops waited for the council, a powerful

Fort Larned in 1867. Custer witnessed several of these buildings under construction during his visit. FORT LARNED NATIONAL HISTORIC SITE

spring snowstorm hit the fort on April 9. "It was our good fortune to be in camp rather than on the march," wrote Custer. "Had it been otherwise, we could not well have escaped without loss of life from the severe cold and blinding snow."

The weather delayed the council until the 12th, when two chiefs of tribes came to meet with Hancock, Custer, and other leaders. They promised to bring more chiefs with them the next day; when they didn't, Hancock marched his command from Fort Larned toward the Cheyenne and Sioux village on the Pawnee Fork.

After Custer

Additional talks at Fort Larned in 1867 resulted in the Medicine Lodge council and treaties later that year. Most of the tribes that signed that treaty were sent to Indian Territory (Oklahoma), and annuity distributions were moved to Fort Cobb there in 1868. Wagon train escorts from Fort Larned ended in 1871, and at that point the troops at Larned had little to do. The Kansas governor persuaded the army to keep Fort Larned open longer than it should have been, but decommissioning finally came in 1878. Its troops went to Fort Hays, its supplies to Fort Dodge, and its land was sold to settlers and granted to the railroad.

The land with the buildings changed hands several times before it ended up with the Edward Frizell family in 1902. The Frizells developed a successful farming and livestock operation there, preserving the buildings while using them and eventually opening part of the fort as a tourist attraction. The National Park Service developed an interest in the fort in the 1950s due to the buildings' excellent condition, and in 1966, the government purchased the land and buildings to create the Fort Larned National Historic Site.

The Site Today

Since taking over the site, the National Park Service has restored eight of the buildings and rebuilt the blockhouse, which had been dismantled around 1900. Once again, Fort Larned is one of the most attractive forts on the Plains.

After parking, you'll cross the Pawnee River and pass through cottonwoods to enter the grounds of Fort Larned. The first stop is the visitors center, formerly barracks for two companies of infantry, and Custer is remembered in some of the museum displays and its audio-video presentation.

Used as farm structures for many years after Fort Larned closed, the surviving buildings were restored to their original appearance by the National Park Service in the 1960s.

Arrayed around the grounds clockwise are the second barracks and post hospital, the shops building (containing the bakery and blacksmith shops), and the "new" commissary, which besides being used for storage also served as a hospital annex, schoolroom, and library. At the southeast corner is the blockhouse, the sole reconstruction at Fort Larned. It, like the blockhouses at nearby Forts Hays and Zarah, is hexagon-shaped.

Continuing around the grounds are the "old" commissary (the oldest building at the fort), quartermaster storehouse, company officers' quarters, commanding officer's quarters, and the second company officers' quarters. If you're feeling just a little more ambitious, take the mile-long history and nature trail hike—you'll pass the sites of the Seventh Cavalry's 1867 camp, the quartermaster stables, mail station, beef corral, and the Santa Fe Trail. You can easily spend a couple hours touring Fort Larned.

Visiting Fort Larned

Fort Larned National Historic Site
1767 KS Highway 156, Larned, KS 67550-9321
(620) 285-6911 • fols_superintendent@nps.gov
www.nps.gov/fols

How to Get There: Located on Kansas Highway 156, six miles west of Larned in Pawnee County, central Kansas.

Hours: Open daily from 8:30 A.M. to 4:30 P.M. Closed Thanksgiving, Christmas, and New Year's Day.

Admission: Free

Amenities: Historic buildings, visitors center/bookstore, museum, research library, slide presentation, living-history programs, restrooms.

Tours: Reservations can be made year-round for guided tours; advance notice required.

Special Events: Fort Larned has staff and volunteers dressed in period clothing manning the fort in the summer season and during special events. Major living-history events are scheduled for the Memorial Day and Labor Day weekends. A candlelight tour is scheduled for the evening of the second Saturday of October (two-week advance reservation required) and Christmas Past, a free old-fashioned Yuletide celebration, is held the second Saturday of December. Contact the fort for more information.

Related Attractions

The Santa Fe Trail Center, between the fort and the town of Larned on Kansas 156, is a regional museum and library certified by the NPS for the interpretation of the trail. Besides exhibits on the people who passed through the area, the center also tells the stories of those who settled here. The six historic buildings include a sod house, one-room schoolhouse, and railroad depot. *Address:* Route 3, Larned, KS 67550. *Hours:* Open daily from 9 A.M. to 5 P.M. Closed Mondays from Labor Day through Memorial Day; closed Thanksgiving, Christmas Eve, Christmas Day, New Year's Eve, and New Year's Day. *Admission:* Adults $4, students (12–18) $2.50, children (6–11) $1.50, 5 and under free. *Phone:* (620) 285-2054. *Website:* www.awav.net/trailctr/.

Recommended Reading

Fort Larned: Guardian of the Santa Fe Trail by Leo E. Oliva (Kansas State Historical Society); *On the Plains with Custer and Hancock: The Journal of Isaac Coates, Army Surgeon* by W. J. D. Kennedy (Johnson Books).

The Cheyenne–Sioux Village

Hanson, Kansas

In the spring of 1867, many thought the Cheyenne and Sioux of western Kansas were more likely to run from the United States than seek a fight. Even though their brethren in Wyoming had fought and defeated the army less than four months earlier in the Fetterman disaster, the Kansas tribes were still agitated after the Sand Creek massacre in 1864 in which a Cheyenne village was all but wiped out by Colorado volunteers.

Colonel Smith and Maj. Alfred Gibbs of the Seventh and Indian agent Wykoop believed the Indians were more frightened than combative. Generals Sherman and Hancock, however, wanted a show of force to provoke a fight and establish the military's might on the plains. When the chiefs refused to reassure their peaceful intent at the Fort Larned meeting on April 12, Hancock decided to march on the Cheyenne and Sioux village west of the fort on the Pawnee Fork of the Arkansas.

Custer and up to six hundred of his men were ordered to ride ahead and surround the village to prevent escape. They did so and on April 15

Personal Battle: Custer and the Buffalo

Figuring he had time to get in a little hunting while the troops were getting started, Custer went out on horseback accompanied by his greyhounds and the chief bugler. He soon outpaced the bugler and rode miles away, eventually spotting a lone bull buffalo. He chased the bull many more miles until somehow, while aiming at the bull, he shot his horse in the head. The horse fell dead to the ground, sending Custer tumbling to face the bull. The buffalo regarded him for a moment then trotted away, leaving Custer and the dogs to find their way back to the column in hostile territory.

The dogs seemed to want to go in a certain direction, so Custer followed them. After about three or four miles, he noticed a column of dust rising several miles away. "A hasty examination soon convinced me that the dust was produced by one of three causes: white men, Indians or buffaloes," he wrote. "Two to one in my favor at any rate." He closed in on the column until he was near enough to spot the guidons of the Seventh with his fieldglass.

"Never was the sight of the stars and stripes more welcome," Custer related. "My comrades were greatly surprised to find me seated on the ground alone and without my horse." A small detachment retrieved the saddle and other equipment, and Custer was soon mounted on another horse.

A Buffalo Undecided as to an Attack on General Custer. *Sketch by Frederick Remington from* Tenting on the Plains.

found the village already abandoned, with the exception of an old man and woman and a young mixed-breed girl who had been viciously raped.

Custer and others were impressed with the location. He wrote of the village being "situated in a beautiful grove on the banks of a stream up which we had been marching . . . Like all Indian encampments, the ground chosen was a romantic spot, and at the same time fulfills in every respect the requirements of a good camping ground; wood, water and grass were abundant."

He felt the Indians left out of fear, but his commander was sure they were hostile. Hancock sent Custer and the Seventh in pursuit and, at a frosty 5 A.M. on the morning of April 16, he and his troops headed north. Joining him were two detachments of scouts, including one of Delaware Indians and one of white scouts, the most prominent among them being Wild Bill Hickok.

They made camp that evening on Walnut Creek, and the next day continued the pursuit—during which Custer embarked on the strangest hunting adventure of his Great Plains career (see page 37).

They camped that night at the Smoky Hill River. Arriving at Downer's Station on the 17th, Custer learned that a band of Indians had attacked and killed three employees at Lookout Station, thirty-five miles to the east in Colorado Territory. He got to Lookout on the afternoon of April 18th and found the station burned to the ground and the bodies of the men mutilated, burned, and partially devoured by wolves.

Custer planned to continue the pursuit, but having run out of supplies and worn out his horses with a march of more than 150 miles in four days,

Visiting the Cheyenne-Sioux Village Site

How to Get There: Located approximately 32 miles west of Fort Larned, or ten miles north of Hanston in central Kansas, near the Hodgeman/Ness County border. Take the gravel N.E. 228 Road (Bazine Road) nine miles north of Hanston; turn right on N.E. Y Road and go .2 miles, and then north on S. CC Road for about a half mile; after crossing the bridge over the Pawnee Fork, watch the east side of the road for the historical marker. The path to the unmarked site is about .4 miles to the north of the marker; follow it for about .2 miles east to reach the village site.

Special Events: The Fort Larned Old Guard occasionally hosts events and tours for members and interested parties. Contact Fort Larned NHS for more information.

An illustration by Theodore Davis for **Harper's Weekly** *of the burning of the Cheyenne and Sioux village on Pawnee Fork by order of General Hancock.* KANSAS HISTORICAL SOCIETY

he moved on to Fort Hays to replenish. He sent a courier to Hancock, reporting of the Lookout Station attack "which clears those Indians which were on Pawnee Fork . . . from the charge of being present at the murder." He knew the Indians fleeing from the village on the 14th could not have traveled sixty miles in a day and carried out the attack.

After Custer

Despite Custer's report, Hancock still decided that the fleeing Indians must be guilty of the Lookout Station attacks and should be punished. He ordered the abandoned village, which included around three hundred tepees and other property, torched on April 19, 1867. The destruction only served to further enrage the tribes and would make for a very long summer.

After the Indian Wars, settlers moved into the area. The village location was generally known to a handful of historians, but not precisely identified until 1976 when local history enthusiasts confirmed the site. In 1999, the private, not-for-profit Fort Larned Old Guard group purchased a quarter section of land that included the village site.

The Site Today

Farmland and power lines cover the site of the village, but the terrain has otherwise changed little from Custer's time. The Fort Larned Old Guard hasn't made improvements to the site, since it's to be used for public education, historical interpretation, and as a sanctuary for Plains Indians to commemorate their history. They did add a historical marker to the

A marker commemorates the Cheyenne and Sioux village site, located on the Pawnee Fork among the trees in the background.

southwest corner of the property, and a number of artifacts found at the site are on display at Fort Larned National Historic Site.

Recommended Reading

My Life on the Plains by General George A. Custer (University of Nebraska Press); *Life in Custer's Cavalry: Diaries and Letters of Albert and Jennie Barnitz, 1867–1868*, edited by Robert M. Utley (University of Nebraska Press); *On the Plains with Custer and Hancock: The Journal of Isaac Coates, Army Surgeon* by W. J. D. Kennedy (Johnson Books).

Old Fort Hays

Walker, Kansas

In 1865, merchant David A. Butterfield began a stagecoach and freight service to run on the well-established Smoky Hill Trail. The new Butterfield Overland Despatch [*sic*], or BOD, built stations and stables along the route, and was almost immediately beset with Indian problems.

Fort Harker was already near enough the main trail to protect it, but posts were also needed along the more remote routes. In October of that year, troops were garrisoned at Monument Station, Camp Pond Creek, and Fort Fletcher in central Kansas. Named for Missouri governor Thomas Fletcher, Fort Fletcher was six miles downstream from the Big Creek Station, at the creek's confluence with its north fork. Three companies of "galvanized Yankees" (former Confederate soldiers) initially manned the post, along with two companies of Missouri cavalry.

The post suffered constantly from short supplies and repeated Indian attacks, and the army abandoned it in May 1866. It was reestablished in October of that year to again protect the Smoky Hill Trail but also to guard

Personal Battle: Castigated by the Commander

It could be said that when Custer met with General Hancock at Old Fort Hays it had implications for the campaign, Custer's career, and his eventual end.

During the Civil War, when Hancock helped lead the Union to victory at Gettysburg, he was referred to as "Hancock the Superb." On the Kansas plains however, he was the ineffective commander of a campaign without results. When he arrived at Fort Hays on May 3, 1867, Hancock's frustrations likely resulted in a chewing out of Custer for dallying at the fort instead of chasing Indians. It would have been the first time as an officer that Custer was so severely criticized and his ego must have been damaged.

Hancock had barely left the post on May 5 before a marked attitude change was seen in Custer. In a letter to his wife on May 6, Captain Barnitz wrote "He appears to be mad about something, and is very much on his dignity! . . . He has evidently incurred the censure of Genl. Hancock, or some one, in some way." Custer criticized the officers on a regular basis. After a time, the officers became less cooperative; Captain Benteen and others often reported sick rather than serve as Custer's officer of the day.

To punish those spreading rumors of Indian attacks, Custer forced his entire command to march fifty miles to check out one of those rumors. The exhausting march increased desertions, leading to Custer's harsh actions against deserters later that summer. It also increased divisions between Custer and some of his officers, which profoundly affected his remaining years on the plains and the Battle of the Little Bighorn.

When Custer faced court-martial at Fort Leavenworth that fall, he didn't blame himself—he blamed Hancock for using him as a scapegoat for a failed campaign.

Winfield Scott Hancock. LIBRARY OF CONGRESS

the new Union Pacific Railroad (Kansas Pacific) route. The second Fort Fletcher got a new name within a month of its founding; General Hancock changed it to Fort Hays to celebrate Gen. Alexander Hays, killed in the Battle of the Wilderness in 1864.

By spring of 1867, the troops began building log huts and low stone structures at the site to replace tents, so when Custer and his troops arrived on April 19, Fort Hays had a look of permanence.

During Custer

Custer and the Seventh came to Fort Hays to replenish their stores, but found only enough materials to supply his immediate command. He set up camp about three-fourths of a mile southwest of the post and waited more than a month for additional supplies to arrive from Fort Riley.

In an initial description, Captain Barnitz found the fort suited him. "This post is beautifully situated, in a pleasant valley on Big Creek, a well timbered stream of good water," he wrote, "but the post is not equal to Riley or Harker so far as the appearance goes."

The failure of the Hancock Campaign and a cold, rainy spell discouraged most of the troops. Desertions began to occur, at least seventeen within the first week according to Barnitz, who wrote that Custer himself was discouraged by the campaign.

The general's attitude changed when he learned that Hancock had given him command of the sub-district of the Smoky Hill. Custer immediately ordered armed guards for the protection of the route and supplies for the Seventh at Fort Hays. He also ordered a quick cleanup of the camp in anticipation of Hancock's May 1867 visit, along with the immediate end of swearing. The three-day visit of Hancock certainly brought changes (see sidebar).

After weeks of trying, Custer succeeded in getting Libbie to Fort Hays from Fort Riley on May 17, and she received all of the comforts he could give her. Barnitz wrote enviously to his wife of the many tents Custer put up, including a large hospital tent "nearly as large as the little chapel at Fort Riley" (see photo on page 23). The Custers' camp included screens and bowers of evergreen branches. Libbie also enjoyed the sizeable "zoo" her husband had collected, with wolves, coyotes, prairie dogs, jackrabbits, raccoons, porcupines, wildcats, badgers, rattlesnakes, owls, eagles, hawks, young antelope, and deer and buffalo calves, along with his usual dogs and horses.

The rainy season coincided with Libbie's arrival. One night, a huge wind and rainstorm hit the camp and the Custer tent, leaving Libbie soaked and having to wear the general's clothing the next day. Desertions became almost

The first Fort Hays, shortly after its abandonment following the June 1867 flood. KANSAS HISTORICAL SOCIETY

Visiting Old Fort Hays

How to Get There: Located in east Ellis County in central Kansas. Take the Walker exit (exit 172) from I-70 and travel south approximately four miles to the Fort Fletcher Bridge. The fort site is northwest of the bridge.

as regular as the rain—Libbie counted forty in one night and a passenger on the Smoky Hill Trail said three hundred left the Seventh within two weeks.

Nearly six weeks after his arrival at Fort Hays, Custer finally received orders to continue his pursuit of the Sioux and Cheyenne. Six troops of the Seventh left the fort on the morning of May 31, each man with fifteen days of rations; Custer, two escorts, and his scouts followed at midnight. Before leaving, he moved Libbie's tent to a small rise he felt was out of range of any floodwaters. He expected to see her there in two weeks, but he never returned to the post again.

After Custer

One week after Custer's departure, on the night of June 6, 1867, a heavy storm hit the area to the northwest of the fort. The resulting floodwaters reached Fort Hays around 3 A.M., raising Big Creek by more than thirty-five feet within three hours. It made an island out of Libbie's campsite and—with a moonless night, flashes of lightning and thunder, and the cries of men in distress—created a very terrifying night for her. She and other women saw six men drown and they saved another with Eliza's clothesline.

The flooding forced the end of Fort Hays at this location. The army selected a new site, much closer to the Kansas Pacific, fourteen miles to the west near Big Creek. With the move in June 1867, the new post took on the Fort Hays name and the original was called "Old Fort Hays" in dispatches. Eventually, settlers moved onto the original fort site. From the 1950s to the '80s, a portion of the land served as a farmstead and the privately owned Fort Fletcher Campgrounds.

The site of Libbie Custer's camp as seen looking northwest from the Fort Fletcher Bridge. Repeated flooding from Big Creek has removed all signs of the fort.

The Site Today

The site of Fort Fletcher/Old Fort Hays is now private farmland, with no signs remaining of the post.

Recommended Reading

Fort Hays: Keeping Peace on the Plains by Leo E. Oliva (Kansas State Historical Society) and *Custer, Come at Once!* by Blaine Burkey (Society of Friends of Historic Fort Hays).

Fort McPherson

Maxwell, Nebraska

To fight the hostile Indians and protect civilians along the Platte River route in Nebraska, the army built Fort McKean in 1863 to the east of the North and South Platte confluence, at the mouth of Cottonwood Canyon. It later became known as Post of Cottonwood Springs, then Fort Cottonwood, and was formally and finally named in 1866 for Gen. James B. McPherson, killed in action during the Battle of Atlanta in 1864.

Fort McPherson ultimately served as the base for five cavalry companies, and as the setting for a commission examining the 1866 Fetterman Massacre. This fact-finding commission, which included Gen. Alfred Sully, held hearings at McPherson from March through April of 1867 before moving west to continue gathering evidence.

Less than two months later, Custer marched from old Fort Hays to Fort McPherson to drive hostile Indians away from the plains between the Smoky Hill and the Platte. The trek was largely without incident except for on June 8 when one of Custer's officers, Maj. Wickliffe Cooper, fatally shot himself in a fit of drunkenness.

During Custer

After pausing for Cooper's burial, Custer and the Seventh arrived at the fort on June 10, 1867, without discovering any Indian camps. The cavalry camped twelve miles to the west of the fort while awaiting General Sherman, then commanding general of the western forces. He was coming to Fort McPherson to give Custer orders for the campaign and get a report on his progress.

Shortly after his arrival, Custer parleyed with the Sioux war chief Pawnee Killer. The chief assured the general that he and his band were peaceful and were going to remain to the north of the Platte River. Custer, not yet experienced in negotiations with the plains tribes and under orders to "avoid collisions" with friendly bands, believed the chief and even gave him and his people rations before parting. Custer didn't know Pawnee Killer was among those who fled from the Sioux and Cheyenne villages at Pawnee Fork, nor did he anticipate that the Sioux chief and his band would attack him and his troops a week later.

General Sherman arrived at the fort and was angered to hear that Custer gave Pawnee Killer and his men rations rather than taking some of

Fort McPherson as it appeared around the time of Custer and William Tecumseh Sherman's meeting in 1867. NATIONAL ARCHIVES

them hostage to ensure their good behavior. Sherman spent two days reviewing his plans with Custer, ordering him to scout the forks of the Republican, come up to Fort Sedgwick in Colorado for supplies and orders, follow the Republican east, and come out near the Platte and Fort McPherson again. If Indians were found, Custer had all the discretion he needed to drive them out—Sherman did *not* want them in the area. Custer left for the forks of the Republican on June 18.

Custer next passed by Fort McPherson in January 1872 while escorting Grand Duke Alexis of Russia on their celebrated buffalo hunt to the south of the fort (see page 132).

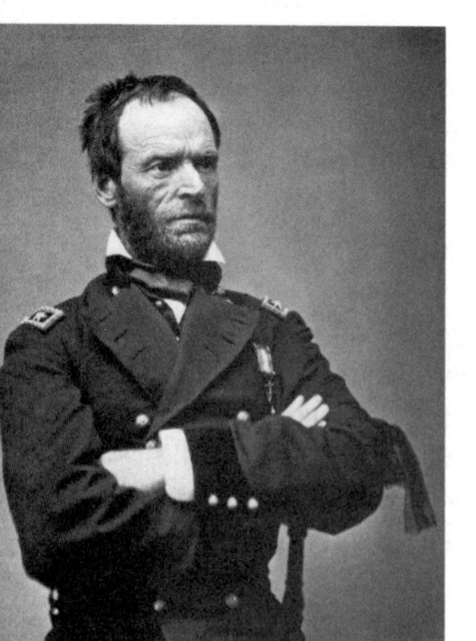

William Tecumseh Sherman. LIBRARY OF CONGRESS

After Custer

Fort McPherson protected Union Pacific work crews in the Platte River Valley in the late 1860s. Soldiers at the post continued to scout and patrol the area through the 1870s, and the fort went on full alert after the news of Little Bighorn arrived in 1876. Some of its troops were involved in the battles of the Cheyenne outbreak at Fort Robin-

son in 1879, but the increased quietness of the frontier led to the post's end. Fort McPherson was designated surplus property in 1880 and closed that year.

The Site Today

Fort McPherson is long gone, but its burial ground remains as Fort McPherson National Cemetery. Designated in 1873, the cemetery continued as such after the fort closed. As other forts in the region were shuttered, the soldiers of their cemeteries were disinterred and then reburied at Fort McPherson; in fact, the soldiers of twenty-three posts are buried here.

For those interested in all things Custer, the cemetery is the burial site of Moses Milner, better known as "California Joe." Joe was one of Custer's favorite scouts, serving as chief scout on the 1867 campaign until his alcoholism got him demoted.

A sandstone marker commemorating the Fort McPherson Trail and mentioning Custer, along with General Sheridan, Buffalo Bill Cody, and others, is located approximately seven miles south of the stone soldier marker on Cottonwood Canyon Road.

Visiting Fort McPherson

Fort McPherson National Cemetery
12004 State Spur 56A, Maxwell, NE 69151-1031
(308) 582-4433 or 4766
www.cem.va.gov/nchp/ftmcpherson.htm#hi

How to Get There: The cemetery is located on State Spur 56A, two miles south of the Maxwell exit (Exit 190) of I-80 in west central Nebraska.

Hours: Office hours are Monday through Friday, 8 A.M. to 4:30 P.M. Closed federal holidays except Memorial Day. The grounds are open daily from dawn until dusk.

He was back with Custer the following year for the Washita campaign, and rode one hundred miles in two days through hostile territory with another scout in order to report the results of the Washita battle to Sheridan at Camp Supply. Joe was scouting for General Crook at Fort Robinson in 1876 when he was murdered in a quarrel. He was originally buried at Fort Robinson but was reinterred at the McPherson cemetery when that post closed.

Also making a second home at the cemetery are the Grattan Massacre monument and the graves of the enlisted men killed in that incident near Fort Laramie (in present-day Wyoming) in 1854. This fight began the Great Sioux War, and the large white marble monument definitely stands out on the grounds. The body of Lieutenant Grattan was moved to Fort Leavenworth National Cemetery after Fort Laramie closed.

Fort McPherson is also the final resting place of army scout Baptistie "Little Bat" Garnier; Spotted Horse, a Pawnee who initially fought white settlement but later served as a military scout; and sixty-three Buffalo Soldiers of the Ninth and Tenth Cavalry who were stationed at Fort Robinson.

The monument commemorating Fort McPherson is at the fort's flagpole site, one mile south of the national cemetery.

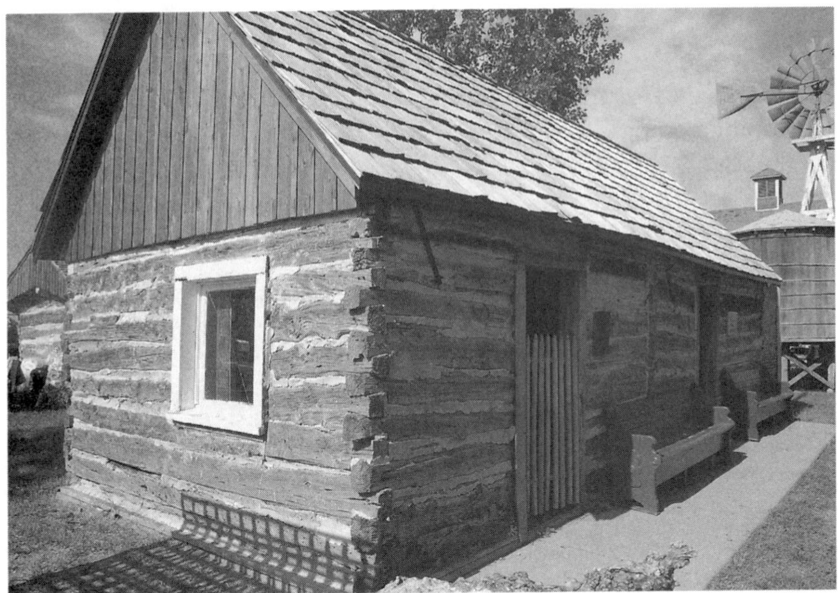

The only known remaining building from Fort McPherson is this log structure, now at the Lincoln County Historical Museum.

One mile southeast of the cemetery, at the site of the fort's flagstaff, is a 1928 stone monument commemorating Fort McPherson. A major supporter in the creation of the monument was Cyrus Fox, the last Civil War veteran of Lincoln County, who died in 1942 and is now buried at Fort McPherson. Coincidentally, Fox served under General McPherson during the Civil War.

Related Attractions

Several log structures in the North Platte vicinity have been reputed to be Fort McPherson buildings, but the only one assuredly from the fort is now located at the Lincoln County Historical Museum in North Platte. The two-room log building is identified as the fort's headquarters and a section of the fort's flagpole stands before the building; the museum itself contains numerous artifacts and displays from the county's rich history. *Address:* 2403 North Buffalo Bill Avenue, North Platte, NE 69101. *Hours:* Open daily Memorial Day weekend through the final Sunday in September, 9 A.M. to 8 P.M.; after Labor Day, 9 A.M. to 5 P.M. *Admission:* Adults age 16 and over, $3. *Phone:* (800) 955-4528 or (308) 534-5640. *Website:* npcanteen.net/lchm.html. *Note:* Near the museum is the home of the man who made the Great Buffalo Hunt possible, Buffalo Bill Cody. See page 125 for more information.

Recommended Reading

Fort McPherson, Nebraska, Fort Cottonwood, N.T. by Louis A. Holmes (Johnsen Publishing Company).

Custer's First Stand

Benkelman, Nebraska

Long the traditional hunting grounds of the plains tribes, the area that made up the southwest corner of the three-month-old state of Nebraska was still without white settlement in 1867 and would be for years. The Republican River—named for a branch of Pawnee Indians known as the Republicans—courses through the gently rolling hills of the region.

During Custer

Marching from Fort McPherson with about twenty wagons, Custer and six companies of the Seventh set up camp to the north of the Republican River on June 22, 1867. They were still in Nebraska, only three miles from the Kansas border.

Although he had orders from Sherman to put in at Fort Sedgwick in Colorado Territory for supplies, Custer instead sent twelve of his twenty wagons south to Fort Wallace to resupply; Maj. Joel Elliott and eleven others were dispatched to Fort Sedgwick for orders. It's conjectured that Custer sent the wagons to Fort Wallace to bring back Libbie if she was there.

Two days later, Indians attacked the camp at dawn in an attempt to drive off the cavalry horses. A sentry was wounded in the attack, but the troops were able to fight off the small force. Custer sent out an interpreter to signal to request a parley with the Indians, not only to find out who they were but also to tie up the attackers while the wagons and Major Elliott were still in the field. The Indians consented to talks, as long as there were an equal number of warriors to officers.

Custer found out his new adversary Pawnee Killer was among the Indians. Meeting a short distance from his camp, Custer let the chief know that his troops were prepared to escort Pawnee Killer's village north of the Platte River as per Sherman's orders. As they talked, more Indians joined the parley party. This continued until Custer warned them that a signal

Custer's meeting with Pawnee Killer, following the Sioux chief's attack on the Seventh Cavalry's camp. HARPER'S WEEKLY

from his bugler would bring up his entire command. The warriors stopped coming but the parley also ended.

Troopers pursued the Indians but lost them in the hills; when they got back, they found out the warriors had raided their camp while they were gone. A small group of them were spotted and pursued again by a detachment led by Capt. Louis Hamilton (the grandson of Alexander Hamilton), but this small group soon turned into a larger force that surrounded the detachment. The troops were able to fight off the braves in a two-hour skirmish, killing a few warriors while losing no soldiers themselves.

Although it was a small skirmish, June 24, 1867, would be marked as Custer's first battle with Plains Indians. The following day, nine years later, would be marked as his last.

The supply train returned on the 27th (after fighting a small battle itself) and Major Elliott on the 28th without new orders for Custer. The Seventh broke camp on June 29 to further scout the forks of the Republican.

The Site Today

Custer's camp on the Republican is today farmland. The camp and the attack by Pawnee Killer are commemorated by a state historical marker.

Related Attractions

The last great battle between tribes of the Great Plains took place about thirty miles to the northeast and six years after the Custer skirmish, at a site now known as Massacre Canyon. On August 5, 1873, a group of about seven hundred Pawnees from their reservation in Nebraska were hunting buffalo in the area; in a horrible bureaucratic mistake, more than a thousand Oglala and Brule Sioux—traditional enemies of the Pawnee—also had permission to be in the area and surprised the Pawnee. At least sixty-nine of them were killed by the Sioux, leading the Pawnee to leave Nebraska and relocate to a reservation in Indian Territory (now Oklahoma). The battle is commemorated as the Massacre Canyon Battlefield, three miles east of

The Nebraska historical marker noting Custer's time in the state is located outside of the town of Benkelman and a half mile southwest of the campsite.

Trenton, Nebraska, on Highway 34. The site includes an impressive thirty-five-foot pink granite monument featuring the likenesses of chiefs of both tribes along with a small visitors center and gift shop. *Hours:* Open Memorial Day through Labor Day, 9 A.M. to 5 P.M. *Phone:* (308) 334-5171.

Nine miles south of Benkelman on Highway 161 in Kansas is a well-marked and somewhat well-known U.S. Cavalry campsite known as Big Timbers. It was used by Custer and his troops on July 11, 1867, the night before they discovered the soldiers' bodies from the Kidder Massacre twenty-eight miles to the south (see page 56). Big Timbers, sometimes known as Thickwood, was also used by Col. Henry Bankhead and the Fifth Infantry in 1868 while on the way to assist Col. George Forsyth at the Battle of Beecher's Island in 1868. The contemporary marker—which includes plate-steel sculptures of a cavalryman and horse, a Gatling gun, and a flagpole—is located at the intersection of Highway 161 and Road Y; the campsite is one mile to the south and a half mile east.

Visiting Custer's First Stand

How to Get There: Located in Dundy County in southwest Nebraska. The historical marker is on U.S. Highway 34, southwest of the town of Benkelman. The campsite is about a half mile northwest of the marker.

Recommended Reading

Custer into the West by Jeff Broome (Upton & Sons).

Riverside Station

Iliff, Colorado

Custer and the Seventh moved into Kansas and then Colorado. He had learned that no orders were waiting at Fort Sedgwick. He and his troops instead went to Riverside Station on the South Platte River—about forty miles southwest of the fort and beyond the problem area with the Sioux and Cheyenne. The march put a tremendous strain on his men and horses as the heat, dust, and lack of water took their toll.

Custer and his men arrived just after midnight on July 5 and set up camp a mile west of Riverside Station. With the stress of the march, and the temptation of gold and coolness in the nearby Colorado Rockies, many men gave thought to giving themselves a discharge from the army.

Desertion plagued all regiments on the Plains, but none more than the Seventh and its demanding commander. During the Hancock Campaign of 1867, 52 percent of the regiment's soldiers deserted; during their July 6–7 encampment near Riverside Station, at least thirty-four soldiers took off in twos and threes, one group in plain view of the commander.

Outraged, Custer ordered Major Elliott with two officers and some soldiers to chase the men and "bring none in alive." Six were brought back;

Anton Schonborn's drawing of Fort Sedgwick, Custer's original destination in the Colorado Territory.

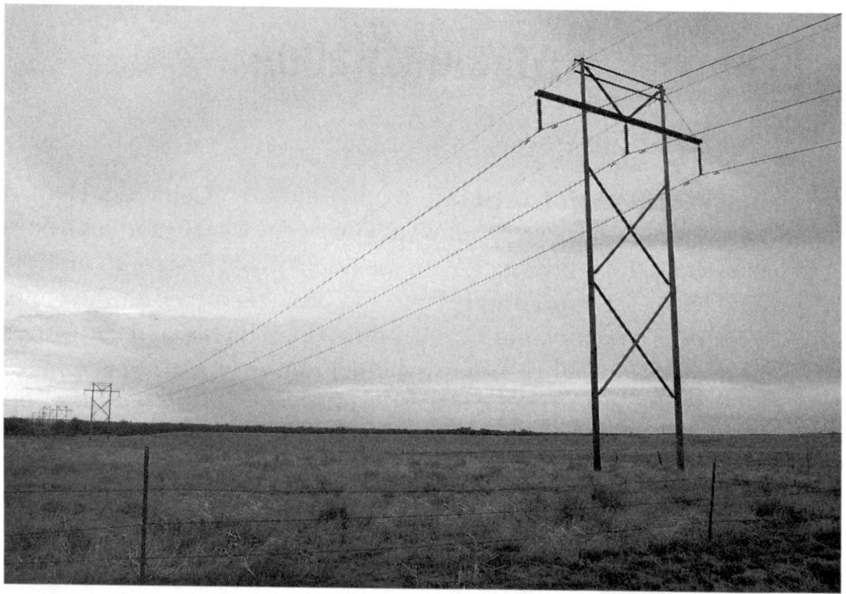

The site of Custer's "desertion camp" was to the right (east) of these power lines, with the South Platte River marked by the tree line in the background.

three were shot when they refused to halt, one of whom later died. In order to deter future desertions, Custer made sure the men heard when he ordered they were to be denied medical care, but then quietly okayed their treatment.

On July 6, the Seventh received word that a detachment of the Second Cavalry led by Lt. Lyman Kidder had departed from Fort Sedgwick after Major Elliott with orders for Custer. As the Seventh hadn't passed Kidder on the way, they broke camp the next day and began their pursuit of the lieutenant and his men.

After Custer

The railroad—and ultimately the frontier—moved farther west, and the need for stations such as Riverside waned. The station itself disappeared at an undetermined date as settlement took over.

The Site Today

Northeast Colorado is now ranch and farmland. There are no physical signs remaining or markers indicating the location of Riverside Station. The site of Custer's "desertion" camp, although on private land, is visible from the road. To see it, take the Iliff exit (Exit 134) from Interstate 76 and drive north for about a mile. Before reaching the South Platte River, turn right (east) on the unpaved 38.5 Road. About a mile to the east are large power lines crossing the road and running north toward the river; the camp was on the east side of these lines.

Riverside Station, where Custer and the officers camped, was about a mile northeast of this site. It is on private land and not visible from the road.

Related Attractions

Fort Sedgwick was the fort Custer *almost* visited and was about forty miles to the northeast of the Riverside Station on the South Platte River. The army decommissioned Fort Sedgwick in 1871; the buildings were dismantled and the soldiers in its cemetery reburied at Fort McPherson National Cemetery in Nebraska. The fort site is on private land, but information panels about Fort Sedgwick are located seven miles west of the Colorado Welcome Center at the Julesburg exit for I-76, following County Road 28.

If you want more on this historic and often beleaguered post, drive into Julesburg and visit the Fort Sedgwick Museum on the town's main street. This small museum contains many artifacts depicting the fort and the four Julesburgs, one of which was burned by Indians. *Address:* 114 East First Street, Julesburg, CO 80737. *Hours:* Open daily Memorial Day through Labor Day, 9 A.M. to 5 P.M. Winter hours are Tuesday through Friday, 9 A.M. to 1 P.M. *Phone:* (308) 334-5171.

There's also a Colorado state historical marker commemorating Fort Sedgwick in the town of Ovid. It's on the north edge of town on U.S. 138, right in front of the abandoned sugar beet factory.

Recommended Reading

Fort Sedgwick, C.T.: Hell Hole on the Platte by Dallas Williams (Fort Sedgwick Historical Society); *Custer into the West* by Jeff Broome (Upton & Sons).

The Kidder Massacre

Bird City, Kansas

Lyman Kidder was a first lieutenant with the Second U.S. Cavalry stationed at Fort Sedgwick in the Colorado Territory. On June 29, 1867, he received orders to immediately deliver dispatches to General Custer, believed to be still encamped on a fork of the Republican River.

Kidder, along with ten men from Company M of the Second and a friendly Sioux scout, left the fort on the day of his orders and headed southeast toward the Republican. They found the Custer camp in Nebraska on July 1, but unfortunately no Custer—after Pawnee Killer attacked the camp on June 24, the general and his troops had moved south toward Fort Wallace and then back to the northwest and to Riverside Station in Colorado. Kidder and his men followed the trail south but missed Custer's turnoff; they instead continued toward Fort Wallace and met with disaster.

They were spotted and attacked by a band of Sioux, likely Pawnee Killer's braves, on July 2. The resulting chase forced the soldiers off the trail and ultimately led them to set up a failed defense in a ravine north of Beaver Creek. It's not known how long the soldiers were able to hold out, but it wasn't long. All were killed, with at least one burned and tortured to death by fire.

While at Riverside Station, Custer received word that dispatches meant for him were sent with Kidder. He and the Seventh pursued the detachment back into Kansas.

During Custer

On July 12 Custer and his men found the body of a white horse branded "US." A second horse was found two miles away. Buzzards were observed floating above the valley of the stream known as Beaver Creek, and scouts fanned out to look for what likely were bodies.

"After riding in all directions through the rushes and willows," Custer later wrote, "one of the Delawares uttered a shout which attracted the attention of the entire command . . . Hastening, in common with many others of the party, to his side, a sight met our gaze which even at this remote day makes my very blood curdle. Lying in irregular order, and within a very limited circle, were the mangled bodies of poor Kidder and his party, yet so brutally hacked and disfigured as to be beyond recognition save as human beings."

Custer at the discovery of the Kidder Massacre, as depicted in Harper's Weekly.

Custer wrote that most of the bodies were found naked, with a couple still wearing a shirt or underclothes. Most were killed by numerous arrows, but many of those arrows had to be broken off for the clothing to be stripped. After they were scalped and mutilated, most of the bodies received another twenty to fifty arrows before the Indians left. Custer wrote that his men collected hundreds of arrows at the site.

They dug a trench near the site of the ravine and buried the twelve bodies of the Kidder Massacre. Officers killed in battle were usually recovered to bring home to their families, but Custer reported that Kidder's body was indistinguishable from the others. He and the Seventh continued down the trail to Fort Wallace.

After Custer

Kidder's father, Judge Jefferson Kidder of Vermillion, Dakota Territory (now South Dakota), very much wanted his son's body returned to his family. He wrote letters to those who were friends of his son or who knew of the fight, including Custer. The general wrote back to the judge and gave his accounting of what they found at the site, even mentioning that the only identifiable item of clothing at the massacre was a small piece of black-and-white checked flannel.

Judge Kidder sent Custer a sample of cloth that his wife had used to make a shirt for their son. From that piece, Custer (by this time in the midst of his court-martial at Fort Leavenworth) confirmed it matched that seen on one of the slain soldiers. He wrote instructions to the judge on the best means of reaching the massacre site if he wanted to collect his son's remains, and who to contact at Fort Leavenworth and Fort Wallace that would assist in the recovery. Custer also had a request of his own: If Judge Kidder retrieved his son's remains, might he not also bring back those of the others?

Judge Kidder went to Fort Wallace in late February of 1868. His escort was Lt. Frederick Beecher of the Third Infantry who, later that year, became the second lieutenant in the area to be killed in battle and have the fight named for him (Beecher's Island, Colorado, in September). Lieutenant

Visiting the Kidder Massacre Site

How to Get There: Located in Sherman County, northwest Kansas. Take the Edson exit (Exit 27) off Interstate 70 and drive north on State Highway 161 (County Road 28) for about twelve miles until you come to the intersection of County Roads 28 and 77. At the intersection is the 1969 historical marker with a recounting of the incident. The mailbox at the site allows you to log in your visit.

From the historical marker, drive about a mile east on CR 77. In the field to the north, at the foot of the hill, you'll notice the silhouetted figures of a soldier on foot and an Indian on horseback indicating the approximate site of the Kidder Massacre.

The more adventuresome can actually go to the site and visit the memorial stone and plaque. A very short distance north of the 28/77 intersection and across Beaver Creek is a dirt road that winds east in the general direction of the memorial. "Road" is used in a very loose sense here—this is more of a path than a road, with tall grass and weeds that all but make the road disappear, not to mention high centering, dips, and unmarked turns. Try always to keep Beaver Creek in sight and follow the road for about a mile. The memorial is on the side of the hill facing the creek.

This is privately owned land with minimal public access. The road is not maintained; you are responsible for maintaining the integrity of the site as well as for getting yourself out if you get stuck. Four-wheel drive is recommended. You can also make the walk to the site, but keep an eye out for rattlesnakes.

A stone marker bearing the names of those killed overlooks Beaver Creek and the site of the massacre.

Kidder's remains were recovered and placed in a coffin for forwarding to his family in St. Paul, Minnesota.

The recovery party, following Custer's request, also collected the remains of the others; they were interred in a common grave at Fort Wallace. A few years after that fort closed, the remains were transferred to Fort Leavenworth National Cemetery.

The Site Today

Like the surrounding country, the Kidder site became farm and grazing land after the Indian wars. In 1969, local citizens erected two commemorations of the incident: a large metal historical marker on the county road near the site, and a memorial stone and plaque at the massacre site.

Related Attractions

The High Plains Museum in Goodland, Kansas, features an HO-scale diorama that depicts the Kidder Massacre among many other displays, artifacts, and stories of Sherman County history. *Address:* 1717 Cherry Street,

At the intersection of County Roads 28 and 77 is a 1969 historical marker that recounts the incident.

Goodland, KS 67735. *Hours:* Monday through Friday , 9 P.M. to 5 P.M.; Saturday, 9 P.M. to 4 P.M.; Sunday, 1 P.M. to 4 P.M. *Admission:* Donation. *Phone:* (785) 899-4595. *Website:* www.goodlandnet.com/museum/.

Recommended Reading

A Dispatch to Custer: The Tragedy of Lieutenant Kidder by Randy Johnson and Nancy Allen (Mountain Press Publishing) and *Custer into the West* by Jeff Broome (Upton & Sons).

Fort Wallace

Wallace, Kansas

To protect the Smoky Hill Trail in western Kansas, the army built Camp Pond Creek in 1865 near Pond Creek Station, at the junction of Pond Creek and the south fork of the Smoky Hill. It was renamed Fort Wallace the following year after Brig. Gen. William H. L. Wallace, killed in 1862 at the Battle of Shiloh.

Fort Wallace was the last fort on the trail and probably the least comfortable, with troops spending their first winter in dugouts. The troops moved to better land two miles away in April 1866, and construction started on new stone buildings. They completed one barracks by December, while most of the troops remained in tents. Five new buildings were complete by the time of Custer's arrival in mid 1867.

During Custer

Custer and the Seventh arrived at Fort Wallace on July 13, 1867, just one day after the discovery of the remains of Lt. Lyman Kidder and his party. He made the first report of the massacre here. The Seventh was exhausted, having marched 181 miles in seven days. Custer had no orders beyond reporting to Fort Wallace, and it certainly made sense to make camp there for at least a few days to allow the men and horses to recover. But he expected Libbie to be there and she was not.

Drawing of Fort Wallace during Custer's campaign in 1867, by Theodore Davis. HARPER'S WEEKLY

Under the pretense of advancing down the trail to seek orders, Custer made the decision to return to Libbie at Fort Hays (she was actually at Fort Riley) and to do it immediately. It may have been out of fear for her after what he had just witnessed at the Kidder massacre site, or fear of losing her to the cholera epidemic that ravaged the plains that summer, or it may have been as simple as an intense longing that he had for her.

He left Major Elliott in command of the Seventh and initiated a forced march on the evening of July 15 with seventy-two troopers, three officers (Capt. Louis Hamilton, Lt. Tom Custer, and Lt. William W. Cooke), and Theodore Davis, an illustrator with *Harper's Weekly* who accompanied the entire summer campaign.

Custer left Fort Wallace after less than two days there—just enough time to make a rash decision that would blot an already less-than-stellar summer on the Plains.

After Custer

Fort Wallace was in the midst of some of the greatest hostilities during the Indian wars, as Cheyenne and Sioux constantly attacked stations and travelers in the region. Stagecoach travel was difficult with escort and impossible without it. A sizeable battle between around three hundred Cheyenne and about fifty soldiers led by Captain Barnitz took place on June 26 near Pond Creek Station.

Visiting Fort Wallace

Fort Wallace Museum
U.S. Highway 40, Wallace, KS 67761
(785) 891-3564 • www.ftwallace.com

How to Get There: Located in Wallace in Pawnee County, northwest Kansas. From Interstate 70, take the Oakley exit (exit 76), go west through town on U.S. 40, and continue on that highway for approximately forty-five miles until you reach Wallace. The museum is on the east end of town.

Hours: Open from the first Monday following the first Sunday in May through October 1. Monday through Saturday, 9 A.M. to 5 P.M.; Sunday, 1 P.M. to 5 P.M. For winter or after-hours visits, call (785) 891-3780.

Admission: Free.

Attacks picked up again in 1868, and Maj. George A. Forsyth marched from the fort on an expedition that led to the nearby Battle of Beecher's Island in September of that year. The Fifth Cavalry under Maj. Eugene Carr was also stationed at Fort Wallace, along with a couple of their yet-to-become-famous scouts, Buffalo Bill Cody and Wild Bill Hickok.

Construction continued on the post through the rest of the 1860s, as forty buildings—many of stone and others framed—ultimately made up the fort. They weren't built well; the men weren't trained in construction and it was always expected that Fort Wallace would be a temporary affair.

Indian attacks eventually dwindled and then disappeared along with the buffalo herds. The garrison strength of Fort Wallace was reduced from more than 540 in 1867 to about 135 in 1872. The fort remained open to help convince people the area was safe for settlement, but by 1882, with no threat from Indians and the buildings falling into disrepair, Fort Wallace was decommissioned. Settlers began removing buildings and materials from the site; by the time the army opened the military reservation for settlement, all buildings had been removed or destroyed.

The Site Today

The grounds of Fort Wallace are today privately owned farmland and not accessible. The sole physical remnant of the fort still on its grounds is the Fort Wallace Cemetery, east of the town of Wallace. Signs direct you to this still-active cemetery, which held the remains of Indian Wars soldiers until 1885–86, when those remains were disinterred and reburied at Fort Leavenworth.

Within the cemetery is an 1867 cenotaph erected by the men of the Seventh Cavalry and the Third Infantry to honor their comrades killed in that year. Unfortunately, the climate of western Kansas has done its damage to the memorial. The cemetery board has enclosed it in a wood and metal shed to protect it; the downside is the shed itself isn't that attractive.

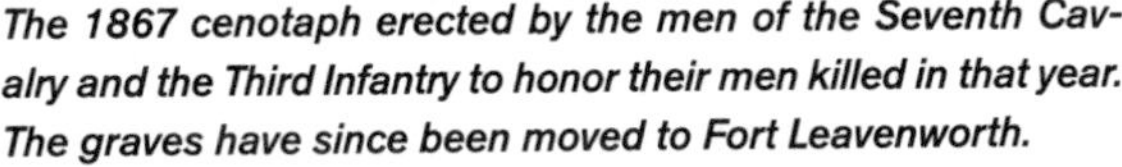

The 1867 cenotaph erected by the men of the Seventh Cavalry and the Third Infantry to honor their men killed in that year. The graves have since been moved to Fort Leavenworth.

The Fort Wallace Museum complex has the original Pond Creek Station (left), which includes bullet holes from potshots taken by area tribes in the 1860s.

There is an original building from the area of the first fort location. The Pond Creek Stagecoach Station, built in 1865, now stands at the Fort Wallace Memorial Museum on the eastern edge of the town of Wallace. The station gives testimony to the danger of that time, with numerous bullet holes in its sides from Cheyenne, Kiowa, and Sioux rifles.

Of course, the Fort Wallace Memorial Museum holds the most information about the post. The museum includes several displays on Fort Wallace, including a new wing containing a diorama of the post and many artifacts found on the fort site.

Recommended Reading

Fort Wallace: Sentinel on the Smoky Hill Trail (Kansas Fort Series) by Leo E. Oliva (Kansas State Historical Society).

The Kansas Dash

Western Kansas

The stations of the Butterfield Overland Despatch had operated on the Smoky Hill Trail for two years by the time of the 1867 Hancock Campaign. This was the primary coach route to Denver across Kansas and saw fairly active business—and frequent Indian attacks—during its period of activity.

Several of the stations, especially those in the remote parts of western Kansas, received military protection from small garrisons stationed nearby. Custer passed through these stations when he and his men left Fort Wallace on the evening of July 15, 1867.

During Custer

After thirty-two miles, Custer reached Smoky Hill Station at dawn of Tuesday, July 16, and took a two-hour rest. The troops then continued twenty miles down the trail toward Monument Station, named for the unusual rock formations to its north, and they arrived there later that morning.

While there, they met with four large supply trains being escorted to Fort Wallace by Capt. Frederick Benteen. They took on forage for their horses and without doubt exchanged information. Custer surely asked about Libbie and her location; they probably also talked about the cholera epidemic that had recently hit Fort Harker. Unknown to all, one of the trains carried the disease and would soon deliver it to Fort Wallace.

Smoky Hill Trail ruts, passing to the south of Monument Rocks in this undated photograph.

KANSAS HISTORICAL SOCIETY

Despite the dryness and the high temperatures, the Custer group moved on through the afternoon for another twenty miles before stopping near the Chalk Bluffs before sundown. Giving themselves less than an hour, they made coffee and rested; the march then continued into its second night, with the men moving for fifty minutes and resting for ten of each hour. Many of the men would fall asleep in these few, spare moments and sometimes the horses would leave them when the march picked up again. Horses gave out as well—five were left at Grinnell Springs Station during the night, some were shot on the trail rather than allow Indians to take them, and others were abandoned on the trail when they couldn't stand.

On Wednesday, July 17, the column met two mail stages two miles east of Castle Rock Station. Custer searched the stages' bags for mail from Libbie but found none. He did find that his mare, Fanchon, and the man who led her were missing, and he dispatched a sergeant and six men to find them. The horse and her leader were found at Castle Rock; when the group hurried back to the column, they were attacked by Indians. Several of the men were wounded and left behind in the attack. The surviving members caught up with the column, by this time stopped at Downer's Station.

News of the attack created a stir among the dozing men, yet Custer did not order a rescue party. The complaints grew to the point that Lieutenant Hamilton recommended Custer do so; he responded that they needed to continue to the east (Custer later claimed that the missing men were reported to him as dead). An infantry captain sent out a detail to find the missing men, one of whom was found dead and another wounded. They buried the first and retrieved the second for treatment.

The men and horses marched on into the afternoon and evening, now much slower. They finally reached the camp of the Seventh near Fort Hays on the early morning of Thursday, July 18. They had marched an incredible 150 miles in a little more than fifty-five hours of riding, only five to ten hours of which were spent at rest. About twenty of the men who had enough energy deserted that night.

Custer wasn't done, however. He, his brother Tom, Lieutenant Cooke, and the illustrator Davis boarded two ambulances and rode on. Two days later Custer would be arrested for abandoning his command and a court-martial would await him at Fort Leavenworth.

After Custer

After completion of the Kansas Pacific Railroad, the Smoky Hill route and its stations were abandoned and soon disappeared through vandalism and the elements. The land eventually became farm and ranchland for settlers in western Kansas.

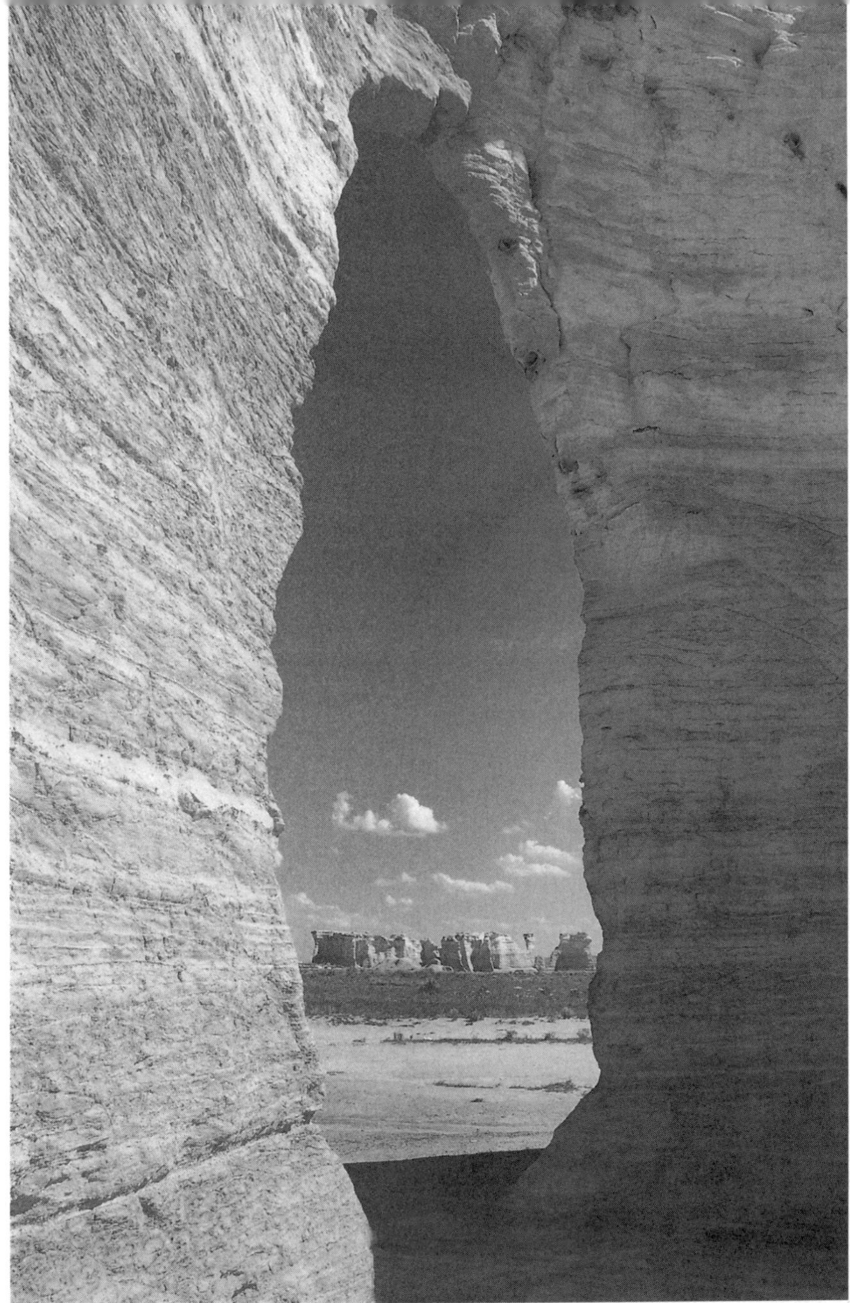

Monument Rocks impressed all those passing along the Smoky Hill Trail in the 1800s and continues to astound visitors today.

The Sites Today

The stations are long gone, but the natural landmarks that Custer and his men saw along the Smoky Hill Trail are still there . . . and in the course of visiting these landmarks, you'll definitely get a feel for the expanse and loneliness of the western Kansas plains.

Visiting Monument Rocks and Castle Rock

How to Get There: To visit Monument Rocks, drive south of Oakley on U.S. Highway 83 for twenty miles, turn east on Jayhawk Road and go four miles, and then go south on Gove 14 for about three miles, and finally south on Gove 16 for one mile. You'll see the rocks before you get there.

To get to Castle Rock from the west, take exit 107 off I-70 at Quinter, turn south on Castle Rock Road, go fifteen miles, turn east on County Road 466 (also known as Castle Rock Road), and follow the signs. From the east, take exit 115 at Collyer, turn south on Banner Road, go 12.5 miles, turn west on County Road 466, and watch for the sign on the right.

One of the sites is Castle Rock, the large limestone pillar near the station of the same name. It's disintegrating fairly quickly due to people repeatedly attempting to climb it. The much larger formation is Monument Rocks. It's hard to believe that, after miles upon miles of flat Kansas prairies and a two-hour stopover at nearby Monument Station, Custer wouldn't visit the rocks for closer examination.

These limestone spires were the first national natural monument in Kansas. Like Castle Rock, they are what remain from an ancient inland sea that once covered this land. When its waters receded, the sea's limestone bed went through an eighty-million-year process of wind and water erosion that created chalk buttes and spires rising up to seventy feet from the ground. They're worth the drive and you'll definitely want to park your car and walk among the spires and archways of these giants.

Related Attractions

The last Indian battle in Kansas, the Battle of Punished Woman's Fork, took place not far from Monument Rocks. This 1878 skirmish was part of the Cheyenne attempt to return to Montana from reservations in Oklahoma. The Cheyenne women, children, and elderly hid in a side canyon—now called Battle Canyon—while braves battled troops from Fort Dodge. The battle site is located about one mile southeast of Lake Scott State Park. Owned by the Scott County Historical Society, a marker designates the battle site and a monument has been placed over Battle Canyon.

To get there from Scott City, drive north on Highway 83, then west on Highway 95, for a total of about twelve miles. Watch for a sign on the left for the Griffith Ranch. An easement exists for the gravel road that crosses private land to reach the battle site—this is a very rough road, however, and you may want to hike the half mile instead.

Just north of Battle Canyon on Highway 95 is Lake Scott State Park, which hosts the ruins of El Quartelejo, the northernmost pueblo in the United States. Built by Taos Indians escaping Spanish rule in New Mexico in the 1600s, the seven-room pueblo is now marked by rebuilt stone foundations and a twelve-foot gray granite obelisk placed by the Daughters of the American Revolution.

For more on the history of Monument Rocks, the Indian tribes of the area, and the Battle of Punished Woman's Fork, visit the El Quartelejo Museum in Scott City. Operated by the Scott County Historical Society, this free museum focuses on local interests as well as the area's fossil history. There's also a replica of one room of the El Quartelejo pueblo. *Address:* 902 W. 5th Street, Scott City, KS 67871. *Hours:* Open daily from 1 P.M. to 5 P.M. (Closed weekends during winter). *Admission:* Free. *Phone:* (620) 872-5912. *E-mail:* scmuseum@sbcglobal.net.

Recommended Reading

"The West Breaks in General Custer" by Minnie Dubbs Millbrook in *The Custer Reader*, edited by Paul Andrew Hutton (University of Nebraska Press).

Fort Leavenworth

Leavenworth, Kansas

In 1827, the Sixth Infantry was called from Fort Atkinson in present-day Nebraska. The upper Missouri fur trade that Atkinson protected had collapsed, and the United States was now more interested in protecting the lucrative Santa Fe Trail to New Mexico.

Following the decommissioning of Fort Atkinson, the Sixth built Cantonment Leavenworth near the head of the Santa Fe Trail on a bluff over-

Fort Leavenworth in 1867.
KANSAS HISTORICAL SOCIETY

looking the Missouri River in the unorganized territory. It was named in 1832 for its commander, Col. Henry Leavenworth.

With the westward expansion of the United States, Fort Leavenworth became the chief unit in the nation's frontier defense. The First U.S. Dragoons—predecessor of the cavalry—came to the fort in 1834, and in 1846–48 the facility served as an outfitting post for the Mexican War. Troops from Fort Leavenworth were heavily involved in the border conflict between Missouri and Kansas during the Civil War; Confederate general Sterling Price made it one of his objectives in an 1864 raid.

Leavenworth became the headquarters for the Department of Missouri, which included Kansas, Colorado, New Mexico, much of Indian Territory, and parts of Texas and Wyoming. It would oversee some of the largest campaigns of the Indian Wars.

During Custer

Custer passed through Fort Leavenworth several times on his travels and also wintered at the post, but the fort figures largest in one of the darker chapters of his career, the 1867 court-martial (see Personal Battle). General Sheridan, named commander of the Department of the Missouri prior to Custer's trial, couldn't be at Fort Leavenworth until a later date. The Custers needed a home, so he invited them to stay in his quarters at the former post sutler's house, known as "the big house."

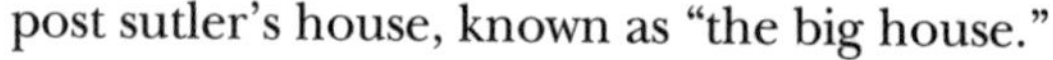

Sheridan would take command of the department at Fort Leavenworth in December, after the court-martial was concluded, but said he had no plans to live in the "big house" and offered it to the Custers for as long as needed. They stayed at the fort and enjoyed the social life of the town of Leavenworth until June 1868, when they returned to Monroe, Michigan. Custer returned to Fort Leavenworth during the winters of 1869–70, when he worked on his Civil War memoirs, and 1870–71.

After Custer

Fort Leavenworth continued as the headquarters of the Department of the Missouri through the Indian wars. When the Nez Perce under Chief

Philip Sheridan. LIBRARY OF CONGRESS

The Post Sutler's house (left of center) at Fort Leavenworth, traditionally occupied by the post commander and turned over by Sheridan for the Custers' use during the court-martial. FRONTIER ARMY MUSEUM

Joseph were defeated in Montana in 1877, he and his people were relocated to a temporary village at Fort Leavenworth while the army determined their disposition. They were eventually removed to Washington State.

In 1881, General Sherman directed the establishment of a "school of application for infantry and cavalry" at Fort Leavenworth that eventually became today's U.S. Army Command and General Staff College.

The Site Today

Fort Leavenworth is the oldest continuously active fort west of the Appalachians, and arguably one of the most important and historic forts in the United States. Names like Fremont, Kearny, Lee, Grant, Sherman, Sheridan, MacArthur, Eisenhower, Patton, Bradley, and Schwarzkopf all passed through these gates.

The Fort Leavenworth National Historic Landmark District comprises 217 buildings, including sixty-four still standing from the Plains Indian Wars period. This is one of the nation's most active military posts, home to the U.S. Army Combined Arms Center and the Command and General Staff College.

Visiting Fort Leavenworth

Frontier Army Museum
100 Reynolds Avenue, Fort Leavenworth, KS 66027
(913) 684-3767
usacac.army.mil/cac2/csi/FrontierArmyMuseum.asp

How to Get There: Located in Leavenworth County, northeast Kansas. If you do not have a military/civilian ID for accessing Fort Leavenworth, you must have a photo ID (driver's license), proof of vehicle insurance, and vehicle registration available.

From Interstate 70 (East or West): Take Exit 224 towards US-73/KS-7/ Bonner Springs/Leavenworth. Turn right (north) onto US-73/KS-7. Drive through Lansing (Main Street) and Leavenworth (4th Street). Turn left onto Metropolitan Avenue (KS-92/7) and proceed to North 7th Street. Turn right to enter the main gate of Fort Leavenworth.

From Kansas City International Airport (KCI), Missouri: Take Interstate 29 North to Platte City, Missouri. Exit on Highway 92 West and follow to Leavenworth, Kansas. Turn right at the second stoplight after the bridge to enter the main gate on Metropolitan Avenue and North 7th Street. Total distance is just less than 17 miles.

Hours: Monday through Friday, 9 A.M. to 4 P.M.; Saturdays, 10 A.M. to 4 P.M. The museum is closed Sundays and all federal holidays.

Admission: Free

Those visiting the fort should enter at the Grant Avenue gate at the southeast corner of the post. The first stop for the Indian Wars aficionado would be the Buffalo Soldier statue at the intersection of Grant and Stimson. Gen. Colin Powell dedicated this magnificent monument in 1992 to honor the African American soldiers who served in the Ninth and Tenth Cavalry regiments (the Tenth was organized at Fort Leavenworth in 1866).

Continue north and then turn east on Reynolds Avenue to visit the Frontier Army Museum. This inauspicious building hosts an amazing collection of artifacts that tell the stories of the nineteenth-century frontier army and Fort Leavenworth. The museum has an amazing collection of restored wagons used over a century by the U.S. Army, and for the Custer fan, a sleigh built for the Custers in 1872 to the general's specifications. Remember to get a copy of the self-guided tour of the fort when at the gift shop.

From the museum, drive east until you reach Scott Avenue, on which you turn north. The Victorian home at No. 1 Scott Avenue, built in 1861 as the residence of the arsenal commander, is now the residence of the commanding officer of the Combined Arms Center and Fort Leavenworth.

Continue north on Scott Avenue (and take in its magnificent view of the Missouri) until its intersection with Kearny and Grant Avenues, the original site of Cantonment Leavenworth. You'll immediately notice the prominent Ulysses S. Grant statue, dedicated in 1889; a large wooden archway once stood here as the entrance to Fort Leavenworth. Find a place to park and take a walk around this historic neighborhood.

The large white house to the south of the statue at 611 Scott Avenue is the Post Sutler's Home. Built in 1841, this was "the big house" to which Sheridan referred and where Custer and Libbie stayed during the general's court-martial. This was the home of General Powell during the time in which he established the Buffalo Soldier memorial, and is now a private residence.

An ongoing and erroneous story has the Custers staying in one of the duplex 1855 Syracuse Houses (located on the east side of the main parade ground north of Kearny Avenue) during the general's court-martial. Because they were built for junior officers, it's doubtful that the Custers ever stayed in these homes; according to museum staff, it's more likely the Custers stayed at what is now the Artillery Barracks (at the northwest corner of Kearney and Warehouse Avenues) during their later stays.

On Scott Avenue is Memorial Chapel, built in 1878 after Little Bighorn to recognize the Seventh Cavalry. The walls of the chapel are adorned with numerous plaques and memorials commemorating the officers of the Seventh and of other regiments who died in the service of their country. You are welcome to visit the chapel during its public hours.

At the north end of Grant Avenue is the site of the 1875 U.S. Disciplinary Barracks, which for 125 years was the nation's only maximum-security military prison. The current facility is about a mile to the north, so there's no one splitting rocks here today—you're more likely to find someone splitting hoagie buns. The 12th Brick Grille serves up sandwiches, salads, and soups inside the walls of the old prison. The name refers to the bricks made by inmates to build the prison—every twelfth one was stamped "USMP" for United States Military Prison. *Phone:* (913) 684-2293.

The Post Sutler's house today.

Personal Battle: The Court-Martial of George A. Custer

Ulysses S. Grant, commanding General of the Army, ordered the formal court-martial for Fort Leavenworth because it was the best post at which to convene a panel with enough officers senior to Custer; the colonel still complained that only four of the nine panelists outranked him and several had no field experience.

The court-martial convened on September 15, charging Custer with leaving his command without permission, specifically for leaving Fort Wallace for Fort Harker while on campaign against hostile Indians. The charges also covered his forcing already exhausted men and horses to march on from Wallace to Hays, his using ambulances for personal transport from Fort Hays to Harker, and his not taking action against the hostiles at Downer's Station. The *Leavenworth Daily Conservative*, wrote "We presume he will not be dealt with very severely if this is all the Government has against him."

Both Hancock and Smith were surprised by additional charges attached by Capt. Robert West of the Seventh, whom Custer had reprimanded at Fort Wallace for drunkenness. West, perhaps in retribution, charged Custer with ordering deserters shot at Riverside Station without a trial and with denying them treatment when they were shot and wounded, which resulted in the death of one of the soldiers.

Custer pled not guilty to the charges. He was found guilty on all counts and sentenced on November 11 to a suspension in rank and command, and to forfeit his pay for one year. Grant felt the sentence was lenient and that Custer's previous service kept it from being harsher, but Libbie wrote to friends that "the sentence is as unjust as possible."

This building was used for Custer's court-martial at Fort Leavenworth in 1867. It previously housed offices for the first territorial governor of Kansas, leading to some debate as to whether this or the building at Fort Riley (page 20) was the first territorial capitol. The brick structure—which also had use as a post school, assembly hall, and chapel—no longer stands. KANSAS STATE HISTORICAL SOCIETY

Fort Leavenworth National Cemetery. In the foreground are the graves of Algernon Smith, George Yates, Tom Custer, and James Calhoun, all killed in the Battle of Little Bighorn.

The parking lot south of the disciplinary barracks was the site of the territorial capitol of Kansas and the headquarters building used for George Custer's court-martial. A kiosk at the east end of the parking lot has an illustration that depicts the buildings.

Finally, no visit to the fort is complete without paying your respects at Fort Leavenworth National Cemetery at 395 Biddle Boulevard. President Abraham Lincoln designated this as one of the first twelve national cemeteries in 1863, although the military graves here go back to 1846 with the burial of Dragoon Captain James Allen. More than 22,500 graves are here, representing every war since the War of 1812. More than a thousand Union and seven Confederate soldiers are buried here. The tallest monument in the cemetery is that of Gen. Henry Leavenworth, originally buried in New York but later reinterred in his namesake fort.

Those with an interest in the Indian Wars won't have a shortage of gravesites to visit. You might start with the man many suggest started the Great Sioux War: Lt. John Grattan of the so-called Grattan Massacre in 1854. Near the Leavenworth monument is the grave of Col. Edward Hatch, who commanded the Ninth Cavalry for more than twenty years. And four officers of the Seventh Cavalry killed at the Battle of the Little Bighorn are buried here—Algernon Smith, George Yates, James Calhoun, and Custer's brother Tom, whose name is inscribed in gold for winning two Medals of Honor. *Office Hours:* Monday through Friday, 8 A.M. to 4:30 P.M. Closed federal holidays except Memorial Day. *Visitation Hours:* Open daily from dawn to dusk. *Phone:* (913) 758-4105 or 4106.

Recommended Reading

Sentinel of the Plains: Fort Leavenworth and the American West by George Walton (Prentice Hall); *Fort Leavenworth: Gateway to the West* by J. Patrick Hughes (Kansas State Historical Society); *The Court-Martial of General George Armstrong Custer* by Lawrence A. Frost (University of Oklahoma Press).

Custer sported a buckskin jacket and full beard for the winter campaign of 1868–69. WASHITA BATTLEFIELD NATIONAL HISTORIC SITE

1868–69

Into the Indian Territory

Fighting Indians proved as difficult for Phil Sheridan in 1868 as it had for Winfield Hancock in 1867. The natives' ability to attack swiftly and fade immediately into their surroundings made them hard to find; the expanse of the plains and lack of soldiers and supplies made them impossible to fight. Cheyenne and Kiowa in Indian Territory exploited this by launching continued raids and committing depredations in Kansas.

Sheridan requested a winter campaign against the tribes. During the winter, the tribes went into camps along the rivers and lived off of their food stores, waiting for the return of spring and fresh grass for their ponies and the buffalo herds. Although hard on the troops, a winter war allowed them to surprise and attack concentrated numbers of Indians, to destroy their food and property, and force their surrender in order to survive. This policy of "total war" was used effectively by the army against the South in the Civil War and Sheridan was ready to use it against the tribes.

Captain Benteen wrote in 1896 that Sheridan offered him field command of the Seventh since the more senior officers would be on leave, but he passed on the honor and instead recommended (so he claimed) that Sheridan try to get Custer back early from his suspension.

From the new Fort Hays, Sheridan wrote to Custer in Monroe that his commanding officers and nearly all of the officers of the Seventh asked for him, and that Sheridan applied to waive the last two months of the suspension. "Can you come at once?" he asked in the telegram. Custer was already crossing the plains before the official orders reached him.

Fort Dodge

Fort Dodge, Kansas

Custer didn't make it to Fort Dodge in 1867 during the Hancock Campaign, having left for Fort Hays before the burning of the Cheyenne and Sioux villages. Hancock marched his troops into Fort Dodge on April 22, 1868, three days after the burning; he met with Kiowa chiefs Kicking Bird and Stumbling Bear the next day.

Hancock also met with Kiowa chief Satanta a week later at Fort Larned. There, the chief so strongly avowed his intentions of goodwill that an impressed Hancock gave him a general's uniform. Soldiers saw Satanta proudly wearing the uniform a few weeks later at Fort Dodge as his band stampeded the fort's horse herd.

Fort Dodge was at the halfway point on the trail between Fort Leavenworth and Santa Fe. Maj. Gen. Grenville Dodge ordered the construction in 1865 of a fort on the Arkansas River near a previous post called Fort Atkinson. Lacking wood and other building materials, soldiers used sod to construct around seventy dugouts, each ten by twelve feet and about seven feet deep. What the crude fort lacked in accommodations it made up for in dysentery, pneumonia, diarrhea, and malaria.

Scouts found a stone quarry twelve miles to the north of the fort and permanent facilities were built between 1867 and 1869, including the headquarters and commanding officer's quarters, two barracks, a hospi-

Officers' quarters at Fort Dodge in 1867. The commanding officer's quarters, known as the Custer House, is the second from the right.

tal, and quartermaster buildings. In 1868, Sheridan began his fall and winter offensives against the Cheyenne from Fort Dodge. Gen. Alfred Sully, who successfully fought the Sioux in the Dakotas in 1863, was also there; he had made a halfhearted effort against the tribes from the fort during September.

During Custer

Custer arrived at Fort Dodge on October 9, 1868, and the Seventh bivouacked at Camp Sandy Forsyth south of the fort. Custer left shortly afterward to lead troops in search of hostiles in south central Kansas. They left in November for Camp Supply in Indian Territory.

After the successful campaign, which included the Battle of the Washita, Custer spent most of the winter in the Indian Territory. He last came to Fort Dodge on April 2, 1869, on his way to summer camp at Fort Hays.

After Custer

Custer's campaign reduced Indian attacks in western Kansas, but it was the extermination of the buffalo herds that had once blanketed the Great Plains that had greatest effect on the Indian threat.

Dodge City—originally named Buffalo City—was established five miles from Fort Dodge in 1872 to process the hides of slaughtered buffalo by the hundreds of thousands. When the buffalo-hide business moved on and the cattle shippers moved in, Dodge City became a trailhead and one of the wildest towns of the West. Gunfights, gambling, prostitution, and heavy drinking became the norm. The soldiers from Fort Dodge didn't fare well, as they were frequently the butts of jokes and unprovoked attacks, and were often cheated out of their pay at the bars and gambling tables.

Fort Dodge provided cemetery space for the upper class of Dodge City (those families preferring not to have deceased loved ones buried at the town's Boot Hill). There was also a column in the local newspaper about military and social goings-on at the fort. The army opened some of the fort's reservation to homesteading in 1880, with many of Dodge City's gamblers, saloon keepers, and prostitutes buying up the land.

Fort Dodge was closed in 1882, with the last of the troops assigned to Fort Supply in Indian Territory. The Interior Department administered the post for eight years, and then deeded it to the state of Kansas for use as a soldiers' home. Veterans from the Mexican War, Civil War, and Indian Wars made their homes there, although records show many were kicked out for drunkenness and for quarreling. Veterans at the home were later

Visiting Fort Dodge

Fort Dodge Museum
218 Pershing Street, E. Highway 154/400, Fort Dodge, KS 67843
(620) 227-2121 • www.kcva.org/sh/

How to Get There: Located on Kansas Highway 400, five miles east of Dodge City, Ford County, in southwest Kansas.
Hours: Monday through Friday, 10 A.M. to 4 P.M.
Admission: Free

joined by Confederate and black veterans, followed by soldiers from the Spanish-American War, Boxer Rebellion, both world wars, and the Korean and Vietnam wars.

The Site Today

For more than 120 years—about six times as long as it was a military post—Fort Dodge has served as a home to veterans. It's no longer the Santa Fe Trail but rather a quiet highway that passes by the entrance to the Kansas Soldiers' Home and its peaceful campus of tree-lined streets. The home

The Custer House, which today serves as the residence of the Kansas Soldiers' Home superintendent.

features a modern long-term nursing facility, recreation center, three residence halls, and sixty-five cottages.

The self-guided tour points out a surprising number of buildings that were there in the time of Custer, including the one popularly known as the Custer House, 228 Custer Street. This building originally quartered the fort's commanding officer, with the first floor used as headquarters and the second as his residence; today it's the private residence of the superintendent of the veterans' home. Not only Custer visited the building; generals Sherman, Sheridan, and Sully were guests as well.

Among the other Custer-era buildings are the 1865 sutler's store and café at the fort's entrance; an officers' quarters duplex at 226 Custer; the Nimitz Building on Sheridan Street (originally the two enlisted men's barracks but united as one building in 1931); the Pershing Barracks at 300 Custer, once the hospital and now the clinic for Fort Dodge; and an original stone cottage on East MacArthur Street.

The one building from Custer's time that you *can* visit is the former granary and dispensary of the post, today the Fort Dodge Library and Museum. The small museum gives the history of the fort through artifacts and displays and there's also a corner dedicated to Custer.

Related Attractions

Fort Dodge protected not only the trail but also the rip-roaring town of Dodge City, one of the meanest and wildest of the Old West. Much of the Old West legend was born here—names like Wyatt Earp, Bat Masterson, and Doc Holliday were here, and terms like "red light district" (a brothel area), "joint" (a saloon), "stiff" (a rigid dead body), and "Boot Hill" (a cemetery) came into use here.

The former jail of Fort Dodge is now appropriately located at the Boot Hill Museum on Front Street. A recreation of 1870s Dodge City, this attraction features a number of historic buildings from the town and, during the summer, Front Street gunfights and can-can dancing at the saloon. History buffs can make an appointment for the research library at the museum to examine old photos, maps, and other documents from the period. *Address:* 500 Wyatt Earp Boulevard, Dodge City, KS 67801. *Hours:* Open daily from Memorial Day to Labor Day, 8 A.M. to 8 P.M.; in the off-season, open Monday to Saturday, 9 A.M. to 5 P.M.; and Sunday, 1 P.M. to 5 P.M. Closed New Year's Day, Thanksgiving, and Christmas. *Admission:* Adults $10, children ages five through ten $8, four and under free, and family (two adults and their children seventeen and under) $35. *Phone:* (620) 227-8188. *E-mail:* info@boothill.org. *Website:* www.boothill.org.

The strategic importance of this area on the trail is evident by two other forts that protected it before Fort Dodge. The earliest of these was Fort Mann, established in 1845 near the Cimarron Crossing and abandoned in 1850; Fort Atkinson followed later that year and was abandoned in 1854. The sites of both of these small sod forts are commemorated with stone markers. To visit them, drive west of Dodge City on Highway 50/400 for one mile; turn south on 108 Road and drive .2 miles; turn right (west) onto Kettle Way Street. The Fort Mann marker is .4 miles west on the south side of the road and the Fort Atkinson marker is .4 miles farther at the end of the road.

Recommended Reading

Fort Dodge: Sentry of the Western Plain by Leo E. Oliva (Kansas State Historical Society); *Dodge City: The Most Western Town of All* by Odie B. Faulk (Oxford University Press).

Camp Supply

Fort Supply, Oklahoma

The army had Fort Dodge in Kansas and Fort Cobb in the Indian Territory, but both were too far away from major Indian activity to be effective in any winter campaign against the tribes. While waiting for approval of his winter campaign, Sheridan ordered Gen. Alfred Sully out of Fort Dodge to hunt down raiding Cheyenne. Sully made a weeklong, 255-mile scout through southwest Kansas and northwest Indian Territory in early September. He had little success in making attacks himself but his troops were attacked several times by the Indians.

One of Sully's campsites among the low sand hills of the territory was in a wide, flat valley near the confluence of the Beaver River and Wolf Creek. After approval of the winter campaign, Sully selected the confluence site as a supply base.

Large stockpiles of supplies began to accumulate at Fort Lyon in southeast Colorado and Fort Dodge in anticipation of the winter campaign. Custer and the Seventh Cavalry led troops and supply wagons out of Fort Dodge to begin the offensive. After marching south for about one hundred miles, they hit the confluence site on November 18, 1868.

During Custer

The men immediately began construction of quarters, storehouses, and wells; a stockade went up to prevent surprise attack. It got the name "Camp of Supply" or "Camp Supply," which one soldier wrote was not quite true, "for while there was a partial supply of everything, there was not an adequate supply of anything."

Sheridan arrived on November 21. He liked the site, finding it had adequate wood, water, and grass in the heart of the Indian country. The weather did not please him, however, and when the Nineteenth Kansas Volunteers didn't arrive on the 22nd as anticipated, Sheridan ordered Custer to begin the campaign before the weather worsened.

Custer and the Seventh Cavalry left the next day in a blizzard and headed south toward the Washita River with a foot of snow already on the ground. The snowstorm brought an end to work on the camp, but the storm's clearing on the 25th allowed the men to resume construction, hauling in cottonwood logs from as far as a mile away while under protection from armed troops. They celebrated Thanksgiving on the 26th, enjoying wild turkey, roast buffalo, broiled quail, rabbit pies, canned vegetables, and rice pudding.

Custer's chief scout, California Joe, rode into Camp Supply three days later, reporting that the Seventh Cavalry had destroyed Black Kettle's Cheyenne camp on the Washita. Sheridan readied the camp for Custer's arrival two days later on December 1—his staff and officers and the camp's garrison formed up in the snow outside to review the returning heroes.

The Osage scouts marched in first, shouting war songs and firing their weapons. Behind them were California Joe, who had ridden back to rejoin the Seventh; the sharpshooters; and the Seventh Cavalry's band playing "Garryowen." The widows and orphans of Black Kettle's camp were next, many of whom rode their own ponies. One of the wagons carried the body of Capt. Louis M. Hamilton, killed in the battle.

Custer marched at the head of his troops in his fringed buck-

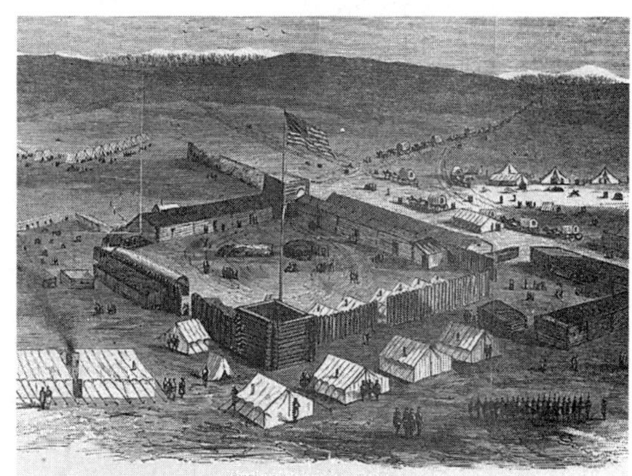

The original "Camp of Supply," located near the confluence of the Beaver River and Wolf Creek. HARPER'S WEEKLY

Personal Battle: A Question of Command

When General Sheridan arrived at Camp Supply with the Nineteenth Kansas Volunteers, most assumed Col. Samuel J. Crawford of the regiment (and former governor of Kansas) would lead the winter campaign. According to the reminiscences of Gen. Edward S. Godfrey of the Seventh, however, Alfred Sully issued an order asserting his command of the troops. Custer almost immediately responded with the same.

"At that time, the Rules and Articles of War provided that when troops of the regular army and volunteers came together, brevet rank took effect," wrote Godfrey. "Both Sully and Custer were lieutenant colonels. Colonel Crawford of the 19th Kansas was the senior in rank. General Sully issued an order assuming command of the troops by virtue of his brevet rank of brigadier general, U.S.A. When this order reached General Custer, he issued an order assuming command by virtue of his brevet rank of major general, U.S.A."

Sheridan—already disappointed with Sully's passivity on the campaign—ruled in favor of Custer. Sully was relieved from duty and ordered to Fort Harker to command the District of the Upper Arkansas. "I heard General Custer say that had the question not been raised he would not have taken his stand and would have been perfectly satisfied to have served under Colonel Crawford," wrote Godfrey.

Neither Sheridan nor Custer wrote of this incident at Camp Supply in their memoirs, said Godfrey, but it becomes one of the intriguing "what-ifs": What if Sully or Crawford had commanded at Washita instead of Custer?

Alfred Sully. LIBRARY OF CONGRESS

skin shirt and leggings. The Seventh followed him in precision march, with the train and the guard bringing up the rear. The march continued across the parade grounds and then up the Beaver Creek for about a half mile to where the Seventh went into camp. The captive women erected a white Indian lodge that Custer had brought from Washita as a trophy.

The Osage held a scalp dance at Camp Supply that night in honor of the victory, displaying the scalps of Black Kettle and other Cheyenne. On

December 3 the post held the funeral of Captain Hamilton, with Custer acting as one of the pallbearers (Hamilton's family later reinterred him in their plot in Poughkeepsie, New York).

Accompanied by around three hundred wagons and sixteen hundred men, Custer and Sheridan left the camp on December 7, hoping to strike the Indian camps again but to also attempt to find a party under the command of Major Elliott that had become separated from the main force at the Washita battle. After visiting the battlefield and encampments at Fort Cobb (see page 94) and the soon-to-be Fort Sill site (see page 101), Custer returned to Camp Supply on March 28, 1869, departing two days later for Fort Hays in Kansas.

After Custer

Camp Supply continued an uneasy existence amid the tribes in that part of the Indian Territory, at least through the early 1870s. Mail service was fairly regular, wrote the post surgeon in 1870, "but liable to interruptions from snow, floods, thieves, and Indians." Soldiers from the camp protected railroad survey crews and also pursued whiskey traders and horse thieves in the region. After ten years of operation, including the construction of more substantial wood-frame buildings, Camp Supply finally received the more permanent designation of "Fort Supply."

Fort Supply protected Cheyenne and Arapaho reservations to the south from white intrusion, or tried to. Those reservations included some of the

A reconstruction of the stockade now occupies part of the Fort Supply Historic Site, although about a half mile or three quarters of a mile southwest of the original.

The 1892 Guardhouse serves as the museum for today's historic site.

great cattle trails leading north and plenty of grazing land, and soldiers from the fort were responsible for keeping the herds moving through.

A particular problem was the unoccupied Cherokee Outlet. Cattlemen coveted this 60-by-225-mile strip of land owned by the Cherokees for its pastures, and many of them organized an association to lease the land from tribal leaders. They then asked the soldiers at Fort Supply (located within the outlet) to patrol the area and remove those not in the association. When the Cherokee Outlet was opened to settlement in 1893, the soldiers ejected "sooners" who attempted to grab land before the opening and guarded land offices and registration booths.

Fort Supply wasn't needed once the territory was opened; the army abandoned it in 1894, turning the grounds and buildings over to the Interior Department. Oklahoma established its first insane asylum on the old fort grounds in 1908, which held up to fifteen hundred patients by 1940. Most of the fort's original buildings were occupied by the hospital until a fire destroyed many of them. In 1988 the state legislature designated the remaining buildings at the old fort as the Fort Supply Historic District and shortly afterwards, a minimum-security prison opened at the site.

The Site Today

The Fort Supply Historic Site is operated by the Oklahoma Historical Society and includes five original structures of the fort that are being preserved and restored to their original appearances. The buildings include the 1874 Ordnance Sergeant's Quarters and 1882 Civilian Employee Quarters, both picket-style log buildings; the frame-style 1878 Commanding Officer's Quarters and duplex 1882 Officers' Quarters; and the brick 1892 Guard House. The Guard House features exhibits of artifacts and photographs.

The site also includes a reconstruction of the 1869 stockade built by Custer's troops. This was not reconstructed on the original site—that was actually about a half to three-quarters of a mile to the west—but it still gives a fair idea of what it looked like.

Note: If you visit the site on a Sunday or Monday and find the gate to the historic site closed, the temptation might be to circle the gate to enter the grounds. Don't follow that temptation! On those days the grounds are taken over by the William S. Keys Correctional Center, the state minimum-security facility that occupies part of the former post site; inmates are on work duty and the guards don't take kindly to those entering the site. The author speaks from experience!

Recommended Reading

Fort Supply: Indian Territory by Robert Carriker (University of Oklahoma Press); *Kansas in the Sixties* by Samuel J. Crawford (Kansas Heritage Press).

Visiting Fort Supply

Fort Supply Historic Site
P.O. Box 247, Fort Supply, OK 73841
(580) 766-3767 • fortsupply@okhistory.org
www.okhistory.org/outreach/military/fortsupply.html

How to Get There: Located in Woodward County in northwest Oklahoma, Fort Supply is thirteen miles north of Woodward on Highway 183, on the east edge of the town of Fort Supply.

Hours: Tuesday through Saturday, 9 A.M. to 4 P.M The site is closed Sunday and Monday (see above "Note").

Admission: Free

Special Events: Each September, Fort Supply hosts Cavalry Day, with costumed interpreters portraying military life on the frontier. Call for information.

Related Attractions

For interpretation of the history of northwest Oklahoma, visit the Plains Indians and Pioneers Museum & Gift Shop in Woodward. This museum has undergone a recent renovation and includes exhibits on the Cheyenne and Arapaho, as well as a log structure that likely served as the blacksmith shop of Fort Supply. *Address:* 2009 Williams Avenue, Woodward, OK 73801. *Hours:* Tuesday through Saturday, 10 A.M. to 5 P.M.; closed Sunday and Monday. *Admission:* Free. *Phone:* (580) 256-6136. *E-mail:* contact@pipm1.org. *Website:* wwww.pipm1.org.

The Battle of the Washita

Cheyenne, Oklahoma

Generations of Cheyenne, Kiowa, and Arapaho made their winter camps in the valley of the Washita River in the western Indian Territory. The river provided the water needed for the tribes as they lived off of the buffalo meat harvested during the warm months, and for many years the valley offered a safe haven for winter villages.

One of those villages on the Washita was that of the Cheyenne chief Black Kettle. He and his people had already had their fill of warfare, having been the victims of a devastating attack by the Third Colorado (a volunteer regiment led by Col. John Chivington) at Sand Creek, Colorado Territory, in 1864. Black Kettle pursued a policy of peace and worked to discourage his young braves from raiding white property. On November 20, 1868, he traveled to Fort Cobb to convince its commander, Col. William B. Hazen, he wanted peace. Hazen believed him, but said Black Kettle would have to persuade General Sheridan. The chief returned to the Washita, where he and the elders decided November 26 that they would move their camp the next day and then seek peace with Sheridan.

To the north, Custer and the Seventh struggled on toward the Washita through the snow by using his compass. They lost their trail under the whiteness, but Maj. Joel Elliott found another over which at least a hundred and fifty Indians had crossed after the snowfall. The men and horses were forced on, despite their exhaustion and the bitter cold. Plans were made for an attack the next day, when they were expected to reach the villages. One officer worried that there might be too many Indians, to which

Custer and the Seventh made their way toward the Washita in a four-day march, which included a snowstorm. LIBRARY OF CONGRESS

Custer replied, "All I am afraid of is we won't find half enough. There are not Indians enough in the country to whip the Seventh Cavalry."

During Custer

They discovered Black Kettle's village in the predawn hours of November 27th. The troops were split into four groups to attack the camp from the northeast, north, west, and south. At dawn a shot was heard from the village. The Seventh's buglers blew the charge and the band played "Garryowen."

Custer led the charge across the Washita, crossing the stream in one bound and plunging into the village. He fired his pistol at one Indian and then took a position on a small knoll overlooking the camp. Most of the village was still sleeping as the Seventh began its attack. Tepees were slashed by sabers as running Indians were killed or captured. Those who escaped ran to the east into the freezing river; others made for ditches and trees to defend themselves. Black Kettle and his wife were able to get to a pony and run, but were shot and killed at the river.

The attack ended in ten minutes. Between forty and sixty Cheyenne were killed and fifty-three Cheyenne women and children were taken as captives. There were few casualties among the Seventh—four killed and a dozen wounded—but the greatest immediate loss was that of Capt. Louis Hamilton, shot and killed at the beginning of the fight. Capt. Albert Barnitz was also shot and feared to be mortally wounded, but recovered and eventually retired from the army. Missing were Custer's second in command, Maj. Elliott, and seventeen soldiers who had left the field in pursuit of fleeing Indians.

Custer's attack on Black Kettle's village began at dawn, catching many members of the village asleep. LIBRARY OF CONGRESS

Custer then began to destroy the resources of the tribe, following the conditions of "total war." Tepees, food, and other belongings were torched and a herd of more than 625 ponies was slaughtered. Evidence of raids on white settlements was found among the tepee contents. The destruction and slaughter continued into the afternoon.

Visiting Washita Battlefield

Washita Battlefield National Historic Site
P.O. Box 890, Cheyenne, OK 73628
(580) 497-2742 • www.nps.gov/waba

How to Get There: Located in western Oklahoma in Roger Mills County, the Washita Battlefield National Historic Site Visitor Center is one half mile west of Cheyenne, Oklahoma, on Highway 47A. The visitors center is home to both the park's administrative offices and the U. S. Forest Service's Black Kettle National Grasslands headquarters.

Hours: Visitors center open daily from 8 A.M. to 5 P.M. except Thanksgiving Day, Christmas, and New Year's Day. Overlook and trail open daily from dawn to dusk.

Admission: Free

Amenities: Visitors center, bookstore, restrooms, trails, historical markers, tours, picnic area.

A scouting party was sent to find Elliott, but returned without locating him or his soldiers. It was soon evident that Indians from other villages were now closing in on the Seventh as the sun sank in the sky. Custer ordered a march toward the other villages, causing the Indians to retreat; he then turned and made a march away from the river and back toward Camp Supply. The Seventh marched through the night and the next day, not stopping to camp until the afternoon of the 28th. Custer sent California Joe and other couriers back to the post with reports of the successful attack.

Custer returned to the battlefield on December 11 with Sheridan and a small detachment to search for Elliott and his men. They found their butchered bodies within a couple miles of the battlefield. Farther down the river, at the site of an abandoned Indian village, they found the bodies of two white hostages, a mother and her child.

After Custer

The Cheyenne never thought the soldiers would attack in winter, but the Sheridan Campaign completely changed that thinking for them and other southern Plains Indians. They gradually and grudgingly came to accept the

The south bank of the Washita River, near the site of Black Kettle's village.

reservation system, ceding their lands. Settlement by whites came with the 1892 Oklahoma land rush.

Farming, flooding, and even railroad tracks changed the battlefield's appearance, but the event was not forgotten. The site became a national historic landmark in 1965, and on November 12, 1996, Congress established Washita Battlefield National Historic Site as a unit of the National Park Service.

The Site Today

Since the installation of a permanent marker in 1965, the NPS has built an overlook, an interpretive trail, and now an impressive visitors center. Stop at the center to begin the tour. There's an exhibit depicting the clash of cultures leading to the attack and a great little movie on the battle, *Destiny at Dawn: Loss & Victory on the Washita.* There are few artifacts, but the displays aptly tell the story of this significant battle.

A short distance east on Spur 47A is the overlook of the battlefield and the trailhead. The overlook's platform helps identify important landmarks on the battlefield if you're not inclined to take one of the two trails.

The NPS land includes 315 acres, covering an area between the row of trees on the east, a second row on the north, a third row to the west, and the road (Spur 47A) on the south. If you take the trails, stay on them—not only is this a sacred site to the Cheyenne, but ticks and rattlesnakes are common. The 1.5-mile walking trail consists of two loops, with guide booklets available at the trailhead; you can also use your cell phone for commen-

The new National Park Service visitors center for the Washita Battlefield National Historic Site.

An observation platform gives a panoramic view of the battlefield and hosts ranger talks.

tary along the trail. The Upper Trail (closest to the parking lot) covers the initial attack, the escape routes of the Cheyenne, the site of the pony kill, and the knoll from which Custer viewed the battle. The Lower Trail takes you to the Black Kettle village site, the Washita River, and the historic channel of the river. There are ranger-led tours on weekends, Memorial Day to Labor Day, at 9, 10, and 11 A.M. and 2, 3, and 4 P.M.

Recommended Reading

Washita: The U.S. Army and the Southern Cheyennes, 1867–1869 by Jerome A. Greene (University of Oklahoma Press); *Black Kettle: The Cheyenne Chief Who Sought Peace but Found War* by Thom Hatch (Wiley); *Custer, Black Kettle, and the Fight on the Washita* by Charles J. Brill (University of Oklahoma Press); *The Battle of the Washita* by Stan Hoig (University of Nebraska Press); *Washita Battlefield* by Mark L. Gardner (WNPA); *Washita Memories* by Richard G. Hardoff (University of Oklahoma Press); *My Life on the Plains* by George Armstrong Custer (University of Oklahoma Press); *Custer and the Cheyenne* by Louis Kraft (Upton & Sons); *A Hoosier Quaker Goes to War: The Life & Death of Major Joel H. Elliott, 7th Cavalry* by Sandy Barnard (AST Press)

Fort Cobb

Fort Cobb, Oklahoma

Even though it was the Comanche from Indian Territory raiding white settlements in Texas in the 1850s, the Wacoe, Caddoe, Tonkawa, and Penateka Comanche from Texas got the blame. The tribes were driven out of their homeland and into the Indian Territory, requiring a new agency and fort to protect them.

Most expected the agency to go up at the old Wichita village site at Medicine Bluff, but tribal leaders and the agency superintendent preferred the Pond Creek site about thirty miles to the north. The tribes were moved there in 1859, without consulting the Kiowa and Comanche who already lived there.

The army picked a fort site on the high ground northeast of the creek's confluence with the Washita River. Fort Cobb was named for U.S. Treasury Secretary Howell Cobb (who, two years later, became one of the founders of the Confederate States of America), and Pond Creek became Cobb Creek as well. It was simple, with a small parade ground and picket-and-adobe buildings with sod roofs and sand floors; stone buildings were built for the post commander and officers.

The army abandoned Fort Cobb to the Confederate government during the Civil War. The Confederates operated the agency as well, failing in an attempt at a treaty with the Kiowa and Comanche and harming relationships between whites and the tribes. There was even bad blood between the tribes—the Tonkawas' reputation for cannibalism didn't sit well with the Caddoe, Kiowa, or Comanche, and those tribes conspired to wipe out the Tonkawas.

The combined tribes burned down the abandoned fort on October 22, 1862, and hit the agency the next day. The Indians killed many whites, throwing their bodies into the buildings as they burned to the ground. The Tonkawa were pursued from their village along the Washita River to a site now known as Tonkawa Valley, south of present-day Anadarko, Oklahoma. Nearly all were exterminated.

Federal troops returned to Fort Cobb in the fall of 1865, and Colonel Hazen used the site in October 1868 as a relocation and supply base for the scattered, peaceful tribes in the Indian Territory. Black Kettle and Arapaho chief Big Mouth met Hazen here to ask for peace and safety from the army before Hazen referred them to Sheridan. A week later, at the Battle of the Washita, Black Kettle was killed along with many other members of his village (see previous chapter).

During Custer

After examining the Washita battle site, Sheridan and his command reached Fort Cobb on December 17, 1868, with Custer's cavalry troops establishing camp to the west of the fort's stockade. The last of Sheridan's column arrived the following day, bringing the encampment to a total of two thousand troops, four thousand horses and mules, and three hundred wagons.

Hazen told Sheridan and Custer that the Kiowa near the fort were friendly and should not be attacked. In spite of that, Kiowa leaders Lone Wolf and Satanta were arrested and brought to the fort. Custer, issuing an ultimatum ordered by Sheridan, demanded that all Kiowa surrender. Both chiefs would be hanged if the tribe did not report. The Kiowa were camped around Fort Cobb by the next morning.

The winter weather probably contributed to flash points between Custer and other officers (see page 96). While at Fort Cobb, the column seemed subject daily to either rain or cold. Heavy showers hit during Christmas week, turning the soldiers' snug dugouts into deep pits of water. They were permitted to quit shaving and they quickly gave up bathing too. Misery came the horses' way as well when feed and grazing ran out. Cottonwood trees were cut down to allow the animals to graze on their leaves, but hundreds of horses were ultimately shot due to starvation.

Custer's Demand ***by Charles Shreyvogel (1903), depicting the general's 1868 meeting with the Kiowa at Fort Cobb.***

Personal Battle: A Former Ally Is Turned . . .

So great was Custer's anger toward the Kiowa at Fort Cobb that he urged an attack on their camps, claiming they were with the Cheyenne at the Battle of the Washita. Blocking that action was Col. William Hazen, who in heated arguments with Custer told him it would be foolish and unfair since the fort was protecting the Kiowa. The colonel said he also knew that at least nine-tenths of the Kiowa were at Fort Cobb the day before the battle and incapable of traveling more than one hundred miles to Black Kettle's village. He won out in the battle with Custer, but the two didn't keep any kind of a friendship.

Fort Cobb was not Hazen's first personal battle involving Custer. Their initial conflict took place at West Point seven years earlier in 1861 when Custer was a cadet and Hazen (then a first lieutenant and assistant instructor) his immediate commander. Hazen arrested Custer for allowing a fight between two other cadets, but then gave a character reference for him during the court-martial. This likely helped keep Custer at West Point and in the military.

Fort Cobb wouldn't be their last run-in, either. While both were stationed in the Dakota Territory, Custer and Hazen had a profound and very public difference of opinion (see page 181).

William Hazen. LIBRARY OF CONGRESS

. . . And an Enemy Is Confirmed

Most military regiments develop factions, and the Seventh definitely had its own "camps." There were those who respected and revered their commander, and those who despised him. Capt. Frederick Benteen met Custer for the first time at Fort Riley and took an immediate dislike to the brash new colonel five years his junior.

Custer knew Benteen didn't like him, but must have felt the bad relations with Captain Benteen in Kansas were over and behind them before they arrived in the Indian Territory. In a letter to Libbie before the Washita battle, Custer said he had a higher opinion of Benteen than he had previously expressed. "(H)e is one of the superior officers of the regiment and one that I can rely upon," he wrote. "(H)e has become one of the most frequent visitors of mine."

Benteen either fooled Custer or the Elliott incident at the Battle of the Washita had completely soured the captain on his commander. While at Fort Cobb, he wrote a highly inflammatory letter to a friend in St. Louis, accusing Custer of abandoning Elliott at the battlefield and giving a slanderous review of the colonel's conduct. Unknown to Benteen—or perhaps not—the friend forwarded the letter to the *Missouri Democrat*, which published it without attribution.

A copy of the newspaper found its way to Custer at Fort Cobb and he naturally became enraged. He called the officers of the Seventh to his tent and threatened to horsewhip the letter's author if he found out who'd written it. Surprisingly, Benteen was happy to admit to it, no doubt stunning and confusing Custer and the assembled officers. The general reportedly dismissed them all without a word.

Benteen told a more colorful version of the story in a letter to a friend in 1896. He said he arrived late to the officers' call and heard Custer's rant while standing outside the tent. He readied his revolver, walked in, and said, "General Custer, while I cannot father all the blame you have asserted, I guess I am the man you are after, and I am ready for the whipping promised." He said Custer stammered and said, "Col. Benteen, I'll see you again, sir!" and walked out. Benteen wrote that he returned to the tent a short while later with a newspaperman as witness to any confrontation and that Custer "wilted like a whipped cur."

Many said Custer backed off of his horsewhipping threat for the good of the outfit, while others say he lacked the courage to address Benteen. Perhaps the threat was a scare tactic to ensure a letter like that was never written again and Benteen called his bluff. Perhaps Benteen, already known to revise accounts to increase his importance, built up the incident nearly thirty years after the fact.

Whatever happened that December day at Fort Cobb, for the next seven-and-a-half years Benteen continued to ignore army protocol in order to confront and humiliate Custer.

Frederick Benteen. NATIONAL ARCHIVES

Sheridan had had enough. "This is a hell of a place," he stated with disgust. He knew of the Medicine Bluff site two hours away, the spot that was originally considered for the post. A reconnaissance party spent the day examining the site; they came back with a glowing report of the grazing, water, and limestone there and recommended a move. Sheridan agreed, ordering the transfer as soon as the rains stopped.

The weather turned clear and cold on January 6, 1869, and the column—including Custer's Seventh Cavalry—immediately moved to the south and the Wichita Mountains. Two days later, they drove a stake to begin the layout of Camp Wichita, soon to be known as Fort Sill.

After Custer

On March 12, 1869, Fort Cobb was abandoned with the transfer of the Kiowa and Comanche Agency to Fort Sill. A peace commission of delegates from the Five Civilized Tribes and Indians of the Wichita Agency met at Fort Cobb in 1872 to head off talk of an Indian war in the region. By that time, nature had taken its course on the old fort, which soon disintegrated into the Oklahoma soil.

The Site Today

The site of the military post of Fort Cobb is approximately three-fourths of a mile east of the town on private land along Washita Road. There is nothing left of the fort.

To walk in Custer's footsteps, stay in town—his tent camp covered most of what is now Fort Cobb. There are two historical markers in town commemorating the post; both are located on Hazlett Street (Oklahoma State Highway 9), the town's main north-south route. The newer and grander of the two is at the south entrance to the town at a pull-off on the east side of the road; the Oklahoma Historical Society erected this large granite marker in 1960. The second marker—also erected by the historical society but in 1949—is about two blocks north of the first marker and has a more abbreviated history of the post.

Visiting Custer's Camp at Fort Cobb

How to Get There: Located in the town of Fort Cobb, Caddo County, in southwest Oklahoma. From Interstate 40, exit 101, take US 281/OK 8 south twelve miles to Binger. Turn right onto OK 152 and go 4.3 miles to the junction with OK 146; follow OK 146 for about thirteen miles to OK 9 and Fort Cobb.

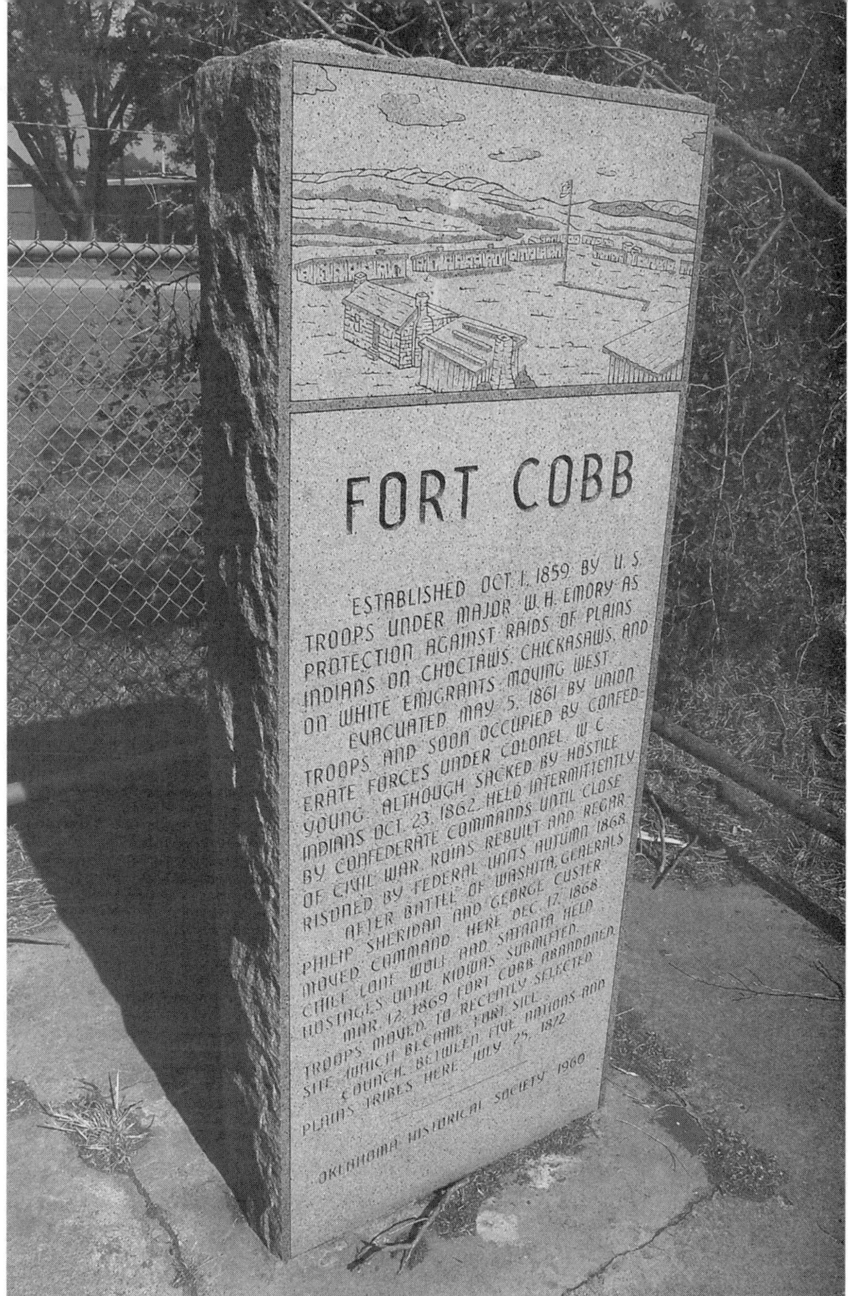

A marker at the south entrance to the town of Fort Cobb includes an image of the fort.

Related Attractions

As mentioned, many Indian tribes made their homes in this area of Oklahoma. The best source of information about the arts and crafts of the tribes is the Southern Plains Indian Museum in Anadarko, fifteen miles east of Fort Cobb. The museum displays the richly varied arts of the Kiowa,

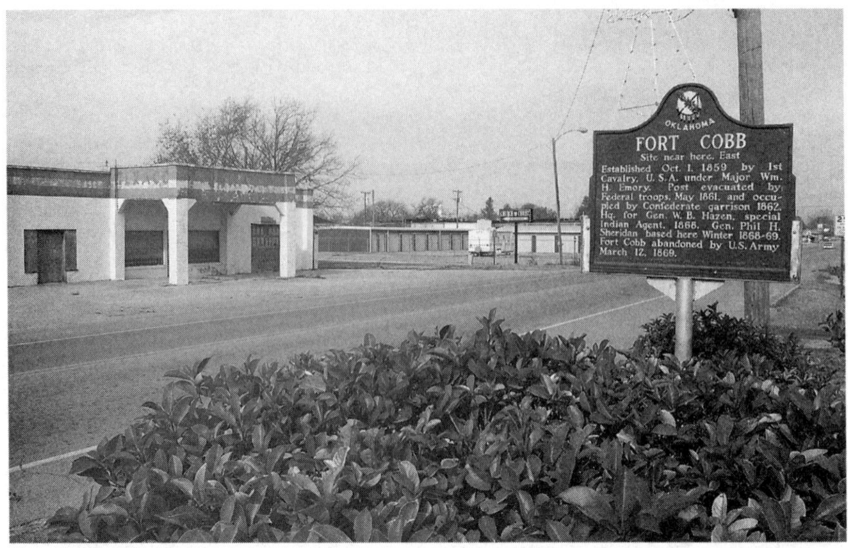

The present-day town of Fort Cobb is built on the site of Custer's camp; the fort itself stood three-quarters of a mile east.

Comanche, Kiowa-Apache, Southern Cheyenne, Southern Arapaho, Wichita, Caddo, Delaware, and Fort Sill Apache. Their historic clothing, shields, weapons, baby carriers, and toys highlight the exhibits, and if you're looking for contemporary American Indian arts, check out their sales exhibitions for emerging artists and crafters. *Address:* 715 East Central Boulevard, Anadarko, OK 73005. *Hours:* Tuesday through Saturday, 9 A.M. to 5 P.M.; closed Sunday and Monday. *Admission:* Free. *Phone:* (405) 247-6221. *E-mail:* spim@netride.net. *Website:* http://www.doi.gov/iacb/museums/museum_s_plains.html.

Eleven miles to the west of Fort Cobb is the Kiowa Tribal Museum, located within the Kiowa Tribal Complex. The museum includes artifacts and other items from the tribe, as well as ten large mural panels depicting the tribe and its heritage. *Address:* West Highway 9, Carnegie, OK 73015. *Hours:* Monday through Friday, 10 A.M. to 6:30 P.M. Appointments needed for weekends and special tours. *Admission:* Free. *Phone:* (580) 654-2300. *E-mail:* webmaster@kiowatribe.net. *Website:* kiowatribe.net.

Recommended Reading

Carbine and Lance: The Story of Old Fort Sill by Col. W. S. Nye (University of Oklahoma Press).

Fort Sill

Lawton, Oklahoma

This area north of the Red River—highlighted by the Wichita Mountains and Medicine Bluffs—first hosted a military camp in 1834 with Camp Comanche. This was the site of the first official contact between the American military and the Plains Indians, where the First U.S. Dragoons came to meet with the Comanche, as well as the Kiowa and Wichita tribes. Gen. Henry Leavenworth died on this expedition; 150 out of 500 soldiers perished on the march.

Capt. Randolph Marcy passed through the area in 1852 to explore the Red River and recommended a permanent fort for the area. Col. Douglas Cooper made a similar recommendation in 1858 from his scouting of the area with the Chickasaw Indians.

During Custer

General Sheridan, disgusted with conditions at Fort Cobb, finally acted on the recommendations by moving his column, which included Custer and the Seventh Cavalry, to the Medicine Bluffs in January 1869.

The new site, which replaced Fort Cobb, was first called "Camp on Medicine Bluffs Creek" and "Camp Wichita." Soldiers of the Seventh wanted to call it Fort Elliott after their battle-slain major, but Sheridan decided to name it after his West Point classmate, Brig. Gen. Joshua Sill, killed in battle during the Civil War.

Once the army established the site, the Indian tribes were compelled to come in. Kiowa and Comanche arrived and set up camp nearby, but Cheyenne and Arapaho stayed out despite warnings of military action against them. Custer took a small escort of soldiers and some hostages—including chiefs Little Robe of the Cheyenne and Yellow Robe of the Arapaho—to negotiate with the tribes to come in. They traveled about 180 miles but found no villages. Little Robe offered to go on his own to find his people; Custer trusted him and granted the request. Little Robe didn't come back and Custer returned to Camp Wichita.

Custer left Camp Wichita on March 2, 1869, with about fifteen hundred members of the Seventh Cavalry and the Nineteenth Kansas Volunteers. They headed west to locate Cheyenne and bring them in to Camp Supply. Finally, Custer returned to Fort Sill as part of the 1870 investigation and hearings into the Indian trade scandals.

Circa 1870 view of officers' row looking east. FORT SILL NATIONAL HISTORIC LANDMARK MUSEUM

After Custer

Col. Benjamin H. Grierson and Buffalo Soldiers of the Tenth Cavalry continued construction of the new fort after Sheridan and Custer left. Dugouts and canvas-covered wooden frames were replaced by log buildings and then by structures of local stone.

General Sherman came to Fort Sill in 1871 to check on the fort's progress, but also to find the Indians responsible for the massacre of a wagon train in Texas. Kiowa chiefs Satanta, Satank, Eagle Heart, and Big Bow were identified in the raid and summoned to the fort and the quarters of Col. Benjamin Grierson. Soldiers were hidden in the quarters and surrounding residences. The talks started peacefully on the Grierson porch, but when Satanta confessed and Sherman ordered him arrested, the chief moved for a revolver in his robe; the shutters of the home opened to reveal the soldiers and rifles. Chiefs Stumbling Bear and Lone Wolf also produced weapons but were stopped. Satanta, Satank, and Big Tree were all manacled and taken to the guardhouse for their transfer to Texas, but Satank attempted to escape and was killed just outside the fort. The commanding officer's quarters were known as the "Sherman House" after the incident.

The yearlong Red River War of 1874–75 involved Fort Sill. Quanah Parker, the last chief of the Comanches, and his tribe surrendered here in 1875 and thus ended warfare on the southern plains. Fort Sill is also where Geronimo and other Chiricahua Apache prisoners of war were brought in 1894. They had free rein of the fort, and Geronimo even rode in the inaugural parade of Theodore Roosevelt and met the president in Washington. He died of pneumonia at Fort Sill in 1909.

Custer enthusiasts may know that Troop L of the Seventh Cavalry was wiped out at the Battle of Little Bighorn in 1876. In 1890, the unit was reactivated at Fort Sill with all Native American soldiers from the Kiowa, Comanche, and Apache tribes.

After the Oklahoma Territory opened for settlement in 1901, Fort Sill's emphasis changed from cavalry to field artillery. The School of Fire for the Field Artillery was founded here in 1911, eventually evolving into today's U.S. Army Field Artillery School. Fort Sill became the permanent home of the Field Artillery in 1930 and in 1934–35 of the Field Artillery and Fort Sill Museum.

Visiting Fort Sill

Fort Sill National Historic Landmark Museum
437 Quanah Road, Fort Sill, OK 73503
(580) 442-5123 • sill-www.army.mil/Museum/

How to Get There: Located in Comanche County in southwest Oklahoma, three miles north of Lawton on U.S. Highway 44. Take Exit 41 off of Interstate 44 and go west on Sheridan Road to enter Fort Sill. After passing through the checkpoint, make an immediate right on Randolph Road and follow it to its intersection with Chickasha Road. Turn right onto Chickasha Road and go one block before turning left onto Quanah Road. The museum is on the corner of Chickasha and Quanah Roads.

Hours: Tuesday through Sunday, 8:30 A.M. to 5 P.M.; closed December 25 and 26 and January 1 and 2.

Admission: Free.

Amenities: Museums, gift and book shop, tours, historic structures, historical markers, restrooms.

Special Events: Soldiers of the Seventh Cavalry and the Nineteenth Kansas Volunteers played the very first organized baseball game in what is now Oklahoma in 1869. Today, a vintage baseball game is played on the second Saturday of July, using authentic equipment on the original baseball diamond, with descendants of Native American soldiers playing active-duty soldiers.

The Site Today

Fort Sill is not just a very active military post—it is an incredibly rich historic site. The installation includes 145 square miles of mountains, rolling hills, and prairie, most of which is used for field artillery training. It is home to the Field Artillery School, the Field Artillery Training Center, the Non-Commissioned Officers Academy, and the Air Defense Artillery School. About sixteen thousand military personnel make their home here, supplemented by a civilian workforce of around six thousand.

Fort Sill National Historic Landmark Museum Interpretive Center is located at the southeast corner of the parade ground. The museum tells the early military, Native American, and settlement history of this area through displays, artifacts, and a twenty-minute film. The Post Trader's Store within the museum contains an excellent bookstore and gift shop as well.

To the immediate west of the museum is the first post headquarters of Fort Sill, built in 1870, and Custer undoubtedly spent some time in this building during his last visit to the post. At the north end of the parade ground is the Sherman House, where General Sherman narrowly escaped death. The house is today the private residence of Fort Sill's commanding officer.

Be sure to visit the new U.S. Army Artillery Museum, south of the historic fort on Corral Drive. Astounding in its scope and presentation, the museum covers the history of army artillery from 1775 to the present with more than seventy guns and artillery pieces. Among the more curious

The Sherman House, where the general narrowly escaped death, is the residence of the current commanding officer at Fort Sill.

The marker for Custer's bivouac is adjacent to the post's golf course.

exhibits is an experimental gun that strapped to the back of a mule (that experiment failed). Adjacent to the museum is Artillery Park, with pieces from both world wars. *Hours:* Tuesday through Saturday, 8:30 A.M. to 5 P.M.; Sunday, 1 P.M. to 5 P.M. *Admission:* Free. *Phone:* (580) 442-1819. *Website:* sill-www.army.mil/famuseum/.

West of the national historic landmark, the Seventh Cavalry's camp or "Custer's Bivouac" is noted with a stone marker adjacent to the post's golf course. This marker at Lee and King Roads tells of the open dugouts that made up that first camp of the site—in fact, some of the sand bunkers you see on the golf course were once those dugouts. Although the ten-foot chain-link fence offers some protection against errant golf balls, it's still a good idea to keep an eye out.

Driving northwest on King Road, you'll eventually reach Apache Gate Road; turn right, cross Medicine Bluffs Creek, and then turn left onto Punch Bowl Road. On your left are the four bluffs of the Medicine Bluffs Historic Site, long visited by the tribes of the area and certainly explored by the soldiers of the Seventh. The road to Fort Elliott, Texas, runs parallel with Medicine Bluffs and was the road that Custer took when leaving Fort Sill.

The campsite of the Seventh extends farther to the southeast from the Custer's Bivouac marker. Follow King Road southeast to Quinette Road; make a left and continue to drive around the golf course. You'll soon come to a concrete bridge at the site of the Quinette Crossing (named for post trader William Quinette). On the south side of the road is a monument for the location of "Sheridan's Camp" during the fort's founding.

Follow Quinette Road to the northeast, under Interstate 44, and you'll reach the Comanche and Apache P.O.W. cemeteries. Within the Apache Cemetery you'll find the pyramidal gravesite of Geronimo and those of fellow chiefs Loco and Nana.

Returning to the post, no site visit is complete without a stop at the Post Cemetery at Donnelly and Macomb Roads. Within the cemetery is Chief's Knoll, considered the "Indian Arlington" of the southern Plains Indian Wars. The most prominent marker is the red granite monument to Quanah

Two of the four Medicine Bluffs. Bluff No. 3, at right, abruptly rises 310 feet above Medicine Bluffs Creek.

Parker, the last chief of the Comanche (the graves of his mother, Cynthia Ann Parker, and sister, Prairie Flower, are adjacent). Walking east, you'll see the graves of Satanta, Satank, Ten Bears, Big Bow, Kicking Bird, and other prominent signers of the 1867 Medicine Lodge Treaty. Of course, Satanta was one of two chiefs Custer threatened to hang at Fort Cobb; he ultimately died jumping from a prison window in Texas in 1878. Lone Wolf died in 1879 from natural causes and was buried in an unmarked grave on the north slope of Mount Scott to the west of the fort.

Related Sites

The Indian tribes associated with Fort Sill are spotlighted at the Museum of the Great Plains in adjacent Lawton. One exhibit features the Tingley Collection, with its more than thirty-two hundred Native American artifacts. *Address:* 601 NW Ferris Avenue, Lawton, OK 73507. *Hours:* Monday through Friday, 10 A.M. to 5 P.M.; Saturday, 10 A.M. to 5 P.M.; Sunday, 1 to 5 P.M. *Admission:* Adults $6, Seniors $5, ages seven through eleven $2.50, Young children and museum members free. *Phone:* (580) 581-3460. *Website:* museumgreatplains.org.

If you're interested in seeing the buffalo that once dominated the plains in this part of the country, be sure to drive through the Wichita Mountains

Custer's adversary Satanta is among those buried on Chief's Knoll at the Fort Sill Cemetery. The obelisk to the right is the grave of Quanah Parker.

Wildlife Refuge to the immediate west of the Fort Sill Military Reservation. Rocky Mountain elk, white-tailed deer, and Texas longhorn cattle also roam the range here, sharing 59,000 acres with 50 other species of mammals, 240 species of birds, 64 species of reptiles and amphibians, 36 species of fish, and 806 plant species. This was one of the first national wildlife refuges in the country, and the original grasslands, granite outcroppings, and hardwood trees make it easy to see why. A modern visitors center and headquarters building gives the complete story of the refuge, but take time to enjoy a trail or two as well. *Address:* Wichita Mountains Wildlife Refuge, 32 Refuge Headquarters, Indiahoma, OK 73552. *Hours:* Daily from 8 A.M. to 4:30 P.M. Visitors center closed on major holidays. *Admission:* Free. *Email:* wichita mountains@fws.gov. *Website:* www.fws.gov/southwest/refuges/oklahoma/ wichitamountains/.

Not part of the Custer Trail, but nonetheless a very interesting remnant from one of the Indian Wars' major participants, is in the nearby town of Cache: Quanah Parker's "Star House." Half-white himself, Quanah adapted to the white man's ways after the wars and became a very wealthy rancher and possibly the richest Indian in America. He retained his long hair and practice of polygamy, however, taking eight wives (including five at one time), and fathering a total of twenty-five children. Quanah built a large two-story house for his family; he had stars painted on the roof after being inspired by the stars on the uniforms of army generals.

Years after Quanah's 1911 death, Fort Sill grew to cover the grounds on which the house stood. The structure was moved and eventually came to the Eagle Park historic village and amusement park. The park closed in 1984 and—sadly—the Star House is deteriorating rapidly along with the other buildings.

You can't see the house from the road and it is secluded among trees behind a locked gate. However, the Quanah Parker Society (he has many descendants) frequently hosts powwows and other public events at the Star House. For information on dates, visit quanahparker.org or email quanah parker@gmail.com.

Quanah Parker Star House

Recommended Reading

Carbine and Lance: The Story of Old Fort Sill by Col. W. S. Nye (University of Oklahoma Press); *Silent Witness: The Diary of a Historic Tree at Fort Sill* by Towana Spivey (Donning Publishing).

Quartz Mountain

Lone Wolf, Oklahoma

The western end of the Wichita Mountains chain, known as the Quartz Mountains, was a favorite camping site for the tribes of the southern plains. Kiowa, Kiowa-Apache, Comanche, Cheyenne-Arapaho, and the Wichita-Caddo all frequented the mountains on the north fork of the Red River. The Spanish claimed the land in the 1500s and even mined for gold in Devil's Canyon. Next, the French took over, and then sold the land to the United States as part of the Louisiana Purchase; Mexico later claimed it along with the Republic of Texas.

The U.S. Dragoons under Gen. Henry Leavenworth and Col. Henry Dodge visited a Wichita village at Devil's Canyon in 1834 for the purpose of establishing peace with the tribes. They were the first white explorers to the area, and were accompanied by the artist George Catlin and future Confederate president Jefferson Davis (then a first lieutenant). In 1852, Capt. Randolph Marcy explored the area and mistakenly determined that the north fork of the Red River was the main stem; Texans began settling the area south of the fork, calling the area Greer County.

As part of the winter campaign of 1868–69 and less than a month after the Seventh Cavalry's attack on Black Kettle's village at the Washita, companies of the Sixth Cavalry and Thirty-Seventh Infantry attacked and defeated Comanche and Kiowa at their Devil's Canyon village. The Christmas Day 1868 engagement was known as the Battle of Soldier Spring.

During Custer

In pursuit of Cheyenne, Custer and the Seventh and the Nineteenth Kansas Volunteers camped at Quartz Mountain on March 5, 1869, where the force met a large supply train from Camp Supply. While encamped, the chief bugler of the Nineteenth, a Pvt. William Gruber, was killed in a hunting accident and buried near Quartz Mountain. Following his burial, the contingent continued their pursuit into the Texas Panhandle.

After Custer

Indians continued to come to Quartz Mountain, and Satanta resigned his chieftainship here in 1874 before surrendering to U.S. authorities for his presence at the Second Battle of Adobe Walls in the Texas Panhandle.

The U.S. Supreme Court ruled in 1896 that Greer County, Texas, actually belonged to the United States; the federal government transferred the land to the Oklahoma Territory, which in 1897 opened the land to homesteaders.

Visiting Quartz Mountain

22469 Lodge Road, Lone Wolf, OK 73655
(888) 401-2715 • www.quartzmountainresort.com

How to Get There: From the Clinton exit (exit 66) on Interstate 40, take U.S. 183 south thirty-five miles toward Cordell/Hobart. Turn right onto OK 9 west and go nine miles to Lone Wolf. At Lone Wolf turn left onto OK 44 south and go eight miles. Turn right onto junction 44A, go one mile, and follow the signs to the lodge.

Amenities: Boating, golf, camping, canoeing, swimming, RV hookups, cabins, playgrounds, conference and performing arts center, hiking, rock climbing, dining.

In 1935, Quartz Mountain became one of the seven original Oklahoma state parks, with the land acquired through local donations and the assistance of the National Park Service. The Civilian Conservation Corps constructed roads, trails, and structures in the park. The U.S. Bureau of Reclamation dammed the North Fork in 1946 to provide water and flood control for the city of Altus and irrigation for the surrounding land.

The Site Today

Quartz Mountain State Park is truly one of the state's beautiful sites. Lake Altus, created by the dam, provides boating, fishing, swimming, and other water activities, but you'll also find plenty to do in the mountains surrounding the lake. As Custer often took the high ground to get the lay of the land, it's entirely possible he climbed the 520 vertical feet to reach the summit of Quartz Mountain.

To the north of the park is the Quartz Mountain Resort Arts and Conference Center and Nature Park. The centerpiece of the park is the Quartz Mountain Lodge, a resort center rebuilt after an electrical fire leveled it in 1995. The lodge features an amphitheater, performance hall, café, library,

View from the summit of Quartz Mountain, overlooking Lake Altus.

and art galleries containing the work of more than fifty artists, commissioned specifically for the resort. The soldiers of the Seventh, camping at the mountain in the winter of 1869, would scarcely believe what they'd find there today.

Two historical markers relating to the Custer Trail once stood on the resort grounds but are now gone, removed after the lodge fire. One titled "Custer's Rendezvous" involved his meeting with the supply wagons at the site. The second, "Chief Bugler's Grave," referred to Private Gruber's burial near what's now the lakeshore.

The interesting aspect of Gruber's burial is that historians didn't know about it. An artifact collector accidentally discovered the grave alongside Lake Altus in 1957, and an excavation by the University of Oklahoma revealed that it was a soldier's. Months of research led to a diary of one of Custer's troopers, who reported Gruber's accidental death by a fellow soldier shooting at a prairie dog. His entry for March 6, 1869, read: "Reveille at 4 o'clock and breakfast before daylight. Our chief bugler was buried, with honors of war, before the sun came up." Buried and forgotten for almost one hundred years.

Related Sites and Attractions

Between Fort Sill and Quartz Mountain is another campsite with a connection to the Indian Wars: the site of Camp Radziminski. This temporary camp, active from September 1858 to December 1859, never had permanent buildings and was long gone by the time Custer and his troops made camp near its grounds. A state historical marker stands near the site on U.S. Highway 183, one mile north of Mountain Park in Kiowa County, Oklahoma.

The Museum of the Western Prairie in Altus examines the development of southwest Oklahoma, the geographic area making up the former Greer County. Exhibits depict the lives of Native Americans, frontier soldiers, cowboys, homesteaders and farmers, merchants, and lawmen. Topics include the prairie, the frontier, the Great Western Cattle Trail, the coming of barbed wire and plows, the quest for land and water, farm mechanization, railroads, the Depression and the Dust Bowl, and war. *Address:* 1100 Memorial Drive, Altus, OK 73521. *Hours:* Tuesday through Friday, 9 A.M. to 5 P.M.; Saturday and Sunday, 2 P.M. to 5 P.M. Closed Monday and state holidays. *Admission:* Donation. *Phone:* (580) 482-1044. *E-mail:* muswestpr@ok-history.mus.ok.us.

On the Sweetwater Creek

Wheeler County, Texas

The Cheyenne continued to evade Custer and his troops out of the Wichita Mountains, escaping to the Staked Plains of the eastern Texas Panhandle. Slowed by the cold and mud, Custer sent half of his 1,500 troops north to the Wichita River while he took the remainder west. Here in Texas, on March 15, 1869, he found the villages of Medicine Arrows and Little Robe on the Sweetwater Creek.

During Custer

Only Custer and Lt. William W. Cooke made contact with the Indians. Escorted into village, which totaled more than 250 lodges, Custer met with Medicine Arrows in his lodge. As a medicine man performed ceremonies and incantations around the general, the Indians told Custer that if he ever betrayed their trust, he and all his command would be wiped out.

The cavalry soon arrived at the camp. The Nineteenth Kansas Volunteers wanted to attack, believing the Indians were holding two white women abducted in Kansas. Custer didn't want to repeat the mistake of the Washita in which hostages were killed during the attack, so when Little Robe (who escaped Custer more than a month earlier) and a Cheyenne delegation later came to his camp, he detained them, demanding the release of the Kansas women. After Custer later threatened to hang the chief and his men, the women were freed and the Cheyenne promised to come in to Camp Supply.

After Custer

Custer and his troops returned to Camp Supply on March 28, 1869, completely spent from their participation in the campaign. The Cheyenne failed to come in to the post, but the war against the tribe ended later that year with their defeat at the battle of Summit Springs in Colorado on July 11. Custer and the Seventh then spent the summers of '69 and '70 at Fort Hays (see page 117).

Little Robe. SMITHSONIAN INSTITUTION

Sweetwater Creek got a military post six years after Custer's meeting with the Cheyenne. In 1869, men of the Seventh had wanted to see Fort Sill named after their fallen major, Joel Elliott; instead, Fort Elliott became the name of the new post built on the Sweetwater Creek in 1875. This was perhaps more fitting since it was considerably closer to the site of his death (Washita Battlefield is about an hour from here). The Tenth Cavalry "Buffalo Soldiers" were posted at Fort Elliott. Among them was Lt. Henry O. Flipper, the first black graduate of West Point.

Visiting Sweetwater Creek

How to Get There: Located in eastern Wheeler County in the Texas Panhandle. Take exit 163 off of Interstate 40, and travel on U.S. 83 north for sixteen miles to Wheeler. The Cheyenne village was approximately a mile north of town along the creek. There is no marker at the site.

Buffalo hunters started moving into the area after the Indians left and a small village named "Hidetown" sprung up in 1876 to market the hides. It was later called Sweetwater City and finally named Mobeetie (the Indian word for "sweet water") and became the seat of the new Wheeler County.

As civilian government took hold, the need for Fort Elliott disappeared and the army closed it in 1890. Mobeetie itself took a hit when the railroad came through to the north and the town was moved to be closer to it. County officials transferred the seat of government to the new town of Wheeler in 1908.

The Site Today

Sweetwater Creek begins here and meanders through the county, looking much as it did during Custer's time. The surrounding prairieland, however, is now hay, cotton, and oil fields, and cattle have replaced the buffalo.

Related Sites

Bounded on three sides by Sweetwater Creek is the town of Mobeetie. The second one, that is—Old Mobeetie is about a mile to the south and it is there you'll find the Mobeetie Jail Museum. Finished in 1886 of local limestone, the jail served its original purpose until its closure with county government moving out of town. Today it is an excellent museum featuring the history of the first organized county in the Texas Panhandle, with artifacts, photos, and stories of Fort Elliott and the Indian tribes that once occupied the area. The original flagpole of the fort graces the front lawn, and one of its iron jail cells is also on the grounds. The fort is further commemorated

Cavalry display at the Old Mobeetsie Jail Museum.

by a stone Texas historical marker west of town on Highway 152. *Address:* FM 48 and 5th Street, Mobeetie, TX 79061-0066. *Hours:* Open daily, 1 P.M. to 5 P.M.; closed Wednesdays. *Admission:* Free (donations accepted). *Phone:* (806) 845-2028. *Website:* www.mobeetie.com. *Special Events:* The best times to visit are during the Mobeetie Music Festival on the fourth weekend in July, when bluegrass, country, and western swing bands from around the country are here; or on Labor Day, when the Old Settlers' Reunion treats all visitors to a free pit barbecue lunch. An Old Town Hoedown has recently been added for the last Saturday in June.

Recommended Reading

My Life on the Plains by George A. Custer (University of Nebraska Press); *The Texas Panhandle Frontier* by Frederick W. Rathjen (University of Texas Press); *Sheridan's Troopers on the Borders: A Winter Campaign on the Plains* by De Benneville Randolph Keim (University of Nebraska Press).

Custer posed for this photo while in Omaha, wearing the sealskin hat that he'd also wear during the hunt with Grand Duke Alexis. KANSAS HISTORICAL SOCIETY

1869–73

Custer Between Campaigns

Custer emerged from the Winter Campaign of 1868–69 as one of the nation's premier Indian fighters—the only sticking point was that there weren't any Indians to fight. Those of the southern plains were now on reservations and those of the northern plains were more or less under the peace provisions of the Fort Laramie Treaty of 1868.

Reductions in the size of the army limited Custer's chances for promotion. Sheridan promised to help him, but it didn't happen. When Andrew Smith retired in 1869, Samuel D. Sturgis became colonel of the Seventh Cavalry by way of seniority. Knowing that the regiment didn't need two commanders, Custer wrote to General Sherman—now Commanding General of the Army—and asked to be named commandant of cadets at West Point. Sherman appointed another man to that post, however.

Custer and the Seventh were assigned to Fort Hays for the summers of 1869 and 1870. With no campaigns, Custer used the ample free time to hunt buffalo, antelope, and other game of the Great Plains. As those high in politics, industry, and society took the new rails to Denver, they would visit Custer in his buckskin at Hays; the lucky ones got to hunt with him.

Custer took leaves to look for other opportunities to find wealth in the civilian world. He got involved in a mining scheme and promoted it to New York investors before it failed. He associated with higher-ups in the

Democratic Party and considered going into politics, in spite of the Republican administration of Ulysses Grant no doubt frowning upon it.

He came back to active duty with the army in 1871. The Seventh was split up around the South for Reconstruction duty and Custer was sent to Kentucky to repress the Ku Klux Klan and inspect horses. He began writing letters about his life on the frontier, which were turned into a successful series of articles for *Galaxy* magazine that gained him new fame as a writer.

Fort Hays

Hays, Kansas

The distance of the original Fort Hays from the construction on the Union Pacific Railroad's Eastern Division (later the Kansas Pacific) lines told the army that it needed a new fort. They selected a site fourteen miles upstream Big Creek from the first Fort Hays; just before the move in June 1867, a major flood destroyed the original fort and killed eight soldiers and very nearly Libbie Custer (see page 43).

The move finished with the first flag raised at the new Fort Hays on the Fourth of July. Two weeks later, on July 18, 1867, Custer arrived in his hurried dash across Kansas.

1869 view of officers' row at Fort Hays, including the Fifth Infantry Band. KANSAS HISTORICAL SOCIETY

During Custer

Custer's first visit to Fort Hays was short. After giving Capt. Louis Hamilton of the Seventh instructions to rest the men for a day at the fort on July 18, he immediately left for Fort Harker in pursuit of Libbie. He didn't return to the post for more than a year because of his court-martial and suspension.

General Sheridan took over command of the Department of the Missouri in 1868 and made Fort Hays his field headquarters. One of his first acts was to bring Custer back to the fort in September to lead the winter campaign against the Cheyenne. Most of the fort's buildings were built by this time, including its unique hexagonal limestone blockhouse, later used as the post headquarters. Fort Hays became a major supply depot to forts off the rail line; in fact, the largest military freight wagon train ever seen on the plains originated there in support of Custer's winter campaign. Custer departed Fort Hays on the morning of October 5, 1868, bound for Fort Dodge and escorted by two non-commissioned officers and eighteen enlisted men of the fort's garrison.

Custer arrived at Fort Hays for the third time on April 7, 1869, but for the first time as a hero. In the five months since his departure, his winter campaign had almost completely wiped out Black Kettle's village on the Washita, he had driven most of the southern Plains Indians onto reservations, and the Seventh had even rescued two Kansas women held by the Indians. Brev. Maj. Gen. Nelson Miles, colonel of the Fifth Infantry at Fort Hays, welcomed Custer and the Seventh with his regimental band playing "Garryowen."

The Seventh settled in at Camp Sturgis (named for regimental commander Samuel D. Sturgis) one mile east of the fort on Big Creek, because the regiment's size completely overwhelmed the fort's capacity. Custer and some of the officers then went east by rail to Fort Leavenworth. He returned to Hays City with Libbie on April 28 and she stayed at the fort for the summer of 1869.

The Custers and the Seventh made Fort Hays their home for 1870, too. While there, Custer continued a series of letters to the magazine *Turf, Field and Farm* under the pen name "Nomad," describing a thrilling hunting life on the plains. So popular was the series that an extraordinary amount of dignitaries and well-connected strangers hit up Custer to take them on buffalo hunts. Libbie wrote to a friend that they had more than two hundred such visitors in the summer of 1870. "It is such a bore to us," she wrote a friend. "We tremble at every dispatch for fear it announced buffalo hunters."

The Custers got away in early September for a train trip to Denver and Cheyenne after completion of the Kansas Pacific. When they returned,

The Custers take a meal at their hospital tent on Big Creek, a mile east of Fort Hays. This was the tent described by Captain Barnitz as "nearly as large as the little chapel at Fort Riley." KANSAS HISTORICAL SOCIETY

George immediately took several senators on a big hunt, and when that trip was over, he took out one of his more interesting guests, the famed American showman P. T. Barnum. The Custers made an October trip to Topeka and St. Louis to visit friends and relatives, and then returned to Fort Hays and made plans for winter quarters at Fort Leavenworth.

Custer's last visit to Fort Hays came on January 21, 1872, as he, the Grand Duke Alexis of Russia, and their party headed east by rail from their great buffalo hunt. The limited accounts of their Fort Hays stop report that they were received enthusiastically.

An agitated buffalo readies for one of Custer's hunting parties out of Fort Hays. The photo was taken south of the fort, near Big Timber Creek; Custer is directly above the buffalo's head, facing left. KANSAS HISTORICAL SOCIETY

After Custer

Decimation of the buffalo herds and forced relocation of the tribes brought an end to the Indian Wars around Fort Hays. It stayed active longer than most military posts, but the army finally abandoned it in 1889. The Interior Department administered the site for eleven years, and then turned it over to the State of Kansas in 1900. The state used the land for branches of the state agriculture college and normal school and as a public park.

The Site Today

More than one hundred years later, the state's division of Fort Hays's military reservation remains. The Kansas State University Agricultural Research Center is the largest dryland experiment station in the world; Fort Hays State University is the only state university in western Kansas; and Fort Hays State Historic Site, its museum, and its historic structures are there to tell the story of one of the Great Plains' great forts.

Operated by the Kansas Historical Society, the site and its spacious grounds contain four original buildings that have been restored or rehabilitated (foundation markers show the locations of several other buildings). The most recognizable is the 1867 limestone blockhouse and its two-story hexagonal center structure. When originally built, it had no roof or windows and the plans were for mountain howitzers to be installed on the second level to protect the fort; instead, rifle slots were built into the structure. Quickly realizing that a blockhouse wasn't needed, fort occupants converted it into a headquarters building within a year. Today it contains the interesting story of the history and design of the building, which

The unique hexagonal blockhouse and former post headquarters was once the clubhouse of the nearby golf course.

Visiting Fort Hays

Fort Hays State Historic Site
1472 Highway 183 Alternate, Hays, KS 67601-9212
(785) 625-6812 • thefort@kshs.org
www.kshs.org/places/forthays/

How to Get There: Located on the south side of Hays in Ellis County, central Kansas. Take Exit 157 from I-70 and drive four miles south on Highway 183 Alternate.

Hours: Tuesday through Saturday, 9 A.M. to 5 P.M.; Sunday, 1 P.M.to 5 P.M.; closed Monday.

Admission: $3 adults; $2 seniors and students. KSHS members, current military, and children five and under admitted free.

Amenities: Historic buildings, museum, historical markers, visitors center with gift shop, tours.

Special Events: Annual Independence Day Picnic and Band Concert; Historic Fort Hays Days, fourth weekend in September; Fort Hays Cemetery Graveside Conversations, fourth weekend in October; Christmas Past, first Friday and Saturday in December. Call or write for more information.

also once served as the clubhouse of an adjacent golf course; new exhibits cover the officers of the fort, including Custer.

The 1872 guardhouse is also built of limestone mined three miles away. The stone blocks contain original and sometimes ornate carvings made by the soldiers of Fort Hays, as well as the crude scratchings of present-day vandals. New exhibits and displays inside tell the story of the enlisted men, including the Buffalo Soldiers of the Ninth and Tenth Cavalries; several lifelike mannequins even "speak" to visitors. There's also a simulation of the Post Trader's Store, a number of artifacts found at the fort, a uniform station where kids can dress like a soldier for photo opportunities, and a touch-screen monitor with examples of period literature and music.

Two furnished officers' quarters remain out of the ten that originally occupied officers' row. A vegetable garden is nearby, planted with seeds of the nineteenth century. To fill out the visit (or if you don't want to take the tour), there are twenty-one interpretive markers.

A newly refurbished visitors center and museum covers the role of Fort Hays in the Indian Wars, and displays a number of period firearms and Indian weapons. A touch screen explores the various fort buildings, a short video covers the Indian tribes in the area at the time of the fort, and there are now lifelike mannequins of Custer and Black Kettle. If walking in Custer's footsteps isn't enough, you can see something the general himself stepped into—one of his cavalry boots.

Not visible is the site of the Seventh Cavalry camp, east of the fort and on the south bank of Big Creek. The site is now administered by the KSU Agricultural Research Center and is used as cropland with no public access.

Related Attractions

The Ellis County Historical Society Museum in Hays tells the history of one of the wildest towns of the west; it also includes a small display on Custer and the founding of Fort Hays. *Address:* 100 West 7th Street, Hays, KS 67601. *Hours:* Tuesday through Friday, 10 A.M. to 5 P.M. Also open Saturdays from June through August, 1 P.M. to 5 P.M. Closed on major holidays. *Admission:* $4 adults; $1 children ages three to twelve; free to members and children under three years. *Phone:* (785) 628-2624. *Website:* www.elliscountyhistoricalmuseum.org.

Recommended Reading

Fort Hays: Keeping Peace on the Plains by Leo E. Oliva (Kansas State Historical Society); *Custer, Come at Once!* by Blaine Burkey (Society of Friends of Historic Fort Hays); *Nomad: George A. Custer in Turf, Field and Farm* edited by Brian W. Dippie (University of Texas Press).

Porch of one of two restored 1867 officers' quarters at Fort Hays.

Custer posed in his hunting gear for this photo taken in St. Louis following the hunt.

NATIONAL ARCHIVES

1872

The Great Buffalo Hunt

The American bison once spanned the North American continent like a great black blanket. In 1800, it's estimated that thirty million covered the Great Plains, providing an endless source of food and shelter for the Indian tribes of the region.

The railroad drastically changed that, as the "iron horse" and its track split the massive herd in two. William Cody hunted for the Kansas Pacific as it crossed that state in 1867. Within a seventeen-month period, he reportedly killed more than four thousand buffalo, earning the nickname "Buffalo Bill." Meanwhile, George Custer was doing his share of buffalo hunting in Kansas, too. During his summer encampments near Fort Hays, Custer took scores of dignitaries out to hunt these "monarchs of the plains."

Both of these young men (Cody was twenty-five and Custer thirty-two at the beginning of 1872) would prove perfect hosts for Grand Duke Alexei Alexandrovich of Russia. Better known as Alexis during his 1871–72 visit to the United States, the grand duke was the fourth child of Czar Alexander II and handsome, young (twenty-one), and with a lust for life. He spoke English, French, German, and other languages and was highly experienced in diplomatic affairs.

Grand Duke Alexis

The germ of the hunt began with artist Albert Bierstadt, who met the grand duke in Russia. Bierstadt passed along the idea to General Sheridan for Alexis's tour of the United States. An experienced hunter himself, Sheridan began organizing an expedition, adding Cody and Custer.

Cody, living in North Platte, Nebraska, located a herd near Red Willow Creek in southwest Nebraska. He may also have carried a message to the Brule Sioux agent, forwarded to Chief Spotted Tail, asking him to bring about one hundred of his leading warriors and chiefs to the encampment.

Meanwhile, Alexis was traveling across the country. He visited the devastation of the recent Chicago fire (donating today's equivalent of $250,000 for its relief) and spent about a week in St. Louis before heading to Omaha. He arrived there on Friday, January 12, 1872, with about a dozen diplomats, staff, and servants on a specially appointed Pennsylvania Railroad train.

Omaha

Nebraska

Less than twenty years old in 1872, Omaha was already one of the one hundred largest cities in the United States and among the fastest growing on the frontier with a population of sixteen thousand. Several major building projects were underway at the time of Custer's visit, including a long-awaited railroad bridge over the Missouri River that would permanently link the Union Pacific Railroad to the rest of the country.

The railroad established Omaha as a major shipping point on the plains, but it was also a significant military town. Omaha was the headquarters of the Department of the Platte, the military district covering Iowa, Nebraska, Wyoming, and Utah. During the era of the Indian Wars, the department was said to have put more generals, colonels, majors, and captains on the streets of Omaha than there were city police officers.

The day before Grand Duke Alexis's arrival, Custer and Sheridan made the four-mile ride north of Omaha to visit Omaha Barracks, depicted in this sketch by Anton Schonborn.

The first stop on Alexis's tour of Omaha was the new Missouri River Bridge, built by the Union Pacific Railroad; it opened two months after the grand duke's visit. The view is looking east toward Council Bluffs, Iowa. The river today is much narrower and deeper after channelization by the U.S. Army Corps of Engineers.

The city was also the location of the Omaha Quartermaster Depot, or Government Corral. This facility—consisting of a dozen buildings surrounding a corral—provided the horses, mules, uniforms, weapons, ammunition, foodstuffs, and other goods needed by the western army, all of it shipped on the U.P. line.

Finally, four miles north of the city were the Omaha Barracks. This small, forty-acre post of cheaply built wooden quarters was established in 1868 to guard against a supposed Indian threat to Omaha, but instead took on an expanded role in providing reserve troops to the western posts.

During Custer

Custer had been in Louisville, Kentucky, on Reconstruction duty and he met Sheridan and his brother, Col. Mike Sheridan, in Chicago. They rode in Sheridan's private railcar to Omaha, crossing the temporary ice bridge over the Missouri River. They arrived on January 11, 1872, the day before the duke's scheduled arrival.

The officers were welcomed by Gen. E. O. C. Ord, commander of the Department of the Platte, which was headquartered in Omaha. Ord escorted them to the Omaha Barracks north of the frontier city, undoubtedly passing by if not stopping at the Government Corral along the way.

While in the city, Custer made time to visit the photography studios of Edric Eaton for a shot of him in his new sealskin cap. It's not known if plans had already been made or were made at this time, but Eaton would join Custer and the hunting party to photograph the big event.

Custer and the other army officers slept on Sheridan's railcar and were at the depot the next morning—along with former Nebraska Territorial Gov. Alvin Saunders and other local officials—to welcome Alexis to Omaha. The next few hours were reserved for a chamber-of-commerce-style tour of the city, including the nearly completed Missouri River Bridge, the soon-to-open Grand Central Hotel, and the monumental, one-hundred-fifty-foot-spired Omaha High School, itself less than two years old.

Alvin Saunders. LIBRARY OF CONGRESS

The group then went to the home of Governor Saunders for lunch. Saunders was one of the commissioners appointed by Congress to create the Union Pacific Railroad; he was also the last territorial governor of Nebraska, and would later be elected U.S. Senator from the state. It was at his home "where he [the grand duke] received about 50 of the crème de la crème of Douglas County," reported the *Omaha Herald*. After the lunch, Saunders opened his doors to the people of Omaha to allow them to meet the grand duke and Sheridan, still very much the Civil War hero.

Custer arrived late, reported the *Herald*. No reason was given—perhaps he left the party at the Grand Central Hotel to walk across the street to the Eaton studio to make final travel arrangements for the photographer. But Custer arrived to the Saunders home, reported the *Herald*, "escorting the beautiful and fascinating Miss Bates. Many ladies and gentlemen sought and obtained an introduction to the General." Apparently well-known in Omaha then, further information on Miss Bates is not easily found today.

The party returned to the depot, where Sheridan's car had been coupled to the five cars of Alexis's train. They left the city at 3 P.M. for the overnight trip to North Platte, with all other traffic having been cleared from the line by the Union Pacific.

After Custer

Like most cities on the plains, Omaha went through booms and busts in the economy and saw some wide population swings as a result. It has gone on to have one of the more stable economies in the country, with a steadily growing population of more than four hundred thousand.

The Sites Today

None of the structures visited by Custer, Sheridan, and Alexis survive today, although several have been replaced by very visible landmarks.

The Department of the Platte headquarters building was located at the southeast corner of 15th and Harney Streets, now the back of the city's Orpheum Theatre. The site of the Government Corral is today's TD Ameritrade Park, the new home of the College World Series. Omaha Barracks became Fort Omaha when the Department of the Platte was relocated to the site in 1878; all of the buildings seen by Custer and Sheridan were torn down at the end of the century and replaced by redbrick quarters.

An 1872 view of Omaha. The high school is at the upper right and Governor Saunders' home at the upper left.

The 1872 Missouri River Bridge lasted only until 1877, when it was hit by a tornado. Two spans were destroyed, and the rest of the bridge was demolished soon thereafter. The Grand Central Hotel, which opened shortly after the visit, was destroyed by fire in 1878. The site (14th and Farnam) is now home to the second edition of the Paxton Hotel; the first Paxton hosted presidents William McKinley, Theodore Roosevelt, and Woodrow Wilson.

The first Omaha High School was dismantled in the 1890s and 1900s as a new school—today's Central High School—was built around it at 20th and Capitol. The location of Governor Saunders' home at 18th and Farnam is now the site of Omaha's second-tallest skyscraper, Woodmen Tower.

Related Attractions

Adjacent to the site where Custer and Sheridan first met Alexis is the city's largest and grandest rail depot, the art deco Omaha Union Station. The depot was closed when the passenger trains stopped coming; today the building is the Durham Museum, featuring the history of the city, along with an outstanding presentation of rail engines and cars. Just walking through the front door and seeing the cavernous waiting area will give you an idea of the importance the Union Pacific put on its hometown. *Address:* 801 South Tenth Street, Omaha, NE 68108. *Hours:* Tuesday, 10 A.M. to 8 P.M.; Wednesday through Saturday, 10 A.M. to 5 P.M.; Sunday, 1 P.M. to 5 P.M. Closed Mondays and major holidays. *Admission:* Adults $8, seniors (62+) $6, children (ages 3 to 12) $5, children 2 and under free. *Phone:* (402) 444-5071. *Website:* www.durhammuseum.org

If you need more railroad history, be sure to take a trip across the Missouri to Council Bluffs, Iowa, for the Union Pacific Railroad Museum. Housed in a former Carnegie Library, the museum contains artifacts, exhibits, photographs, and documents tracing the development of the railroad and the American West. *Address:* 200 Pearl Street, Council Bluffs, IA 51503. *Hours:* Tuesday through Saturday, 10 A.M. to 4 P.M. Closed Sunday and Monday. *Admission:* Free. *Phone:* (712) 329-8307. *Website:* www.uprr.com/aboutup/history/museum/index.shtml

As mentioned, Omaha Barracks became Fort Omaha, which in 1975 became a campus of Metropolitan Community College. You can still walk the same grounds Custer and Sheridan did in 1872, and visit the historic home of Gen. George Crook, now operated as a museum by the Douglas County Historical Society. *Address:* 30th and Fort Streets #11B, Omaha, NE 68111-1657. *Hours:* Monday through Friday, 10 A.M. to 4 P.M.; Saturday and Sunday, 1 P.M. to 4 P.M. *Admission (museum):* Adults $5, students $4, children (6 to 12) $3. *Phone:* (402) 455-9990. *Website:* www.omahahistory.org.

North Platte

Nebraska

Situated near the confluence of the South Platte and North Platte Rivers, the town of North Platte was born as a Union Pacific work camp in 1866 during the railroad's construction across Nebraska. The boomtown had up to five thousand residents—not just rail workers but also gamblers, saloonkeepers, and other unsavory types. Most tore down their buildings and moved them to Julesburg, Colorado, as the railroad continued west, but the U.P. established machine shops, a roundhouse, and a hotel in North

Special Train of the Union Pacific Rail Road, conveying the Grand Duke Alexis of Russia, And Suite. Will leave Omaha, 8 p.m. FRIDAY, JANUARY 12th, 1872.

This Train will have the Right of Road over all other Trains.

T. E. SICKELS, Chief Engineer and General Superintendent.

His Imperial Highness and Party, Will leave the Union Pacific Railroad at McPherson Station, Saturday morning, Jan. 13th, 1872, for a Grand Buffalo Hunt, under direction of Lieutenant General P. H. Sheridan, U. S. Army.

Elm Creek
Overton
Plum Creek
Cayote
Willow Island
Warren
Brady Island
McPherson

S. H. H. CLARK, Assistant General Superintendent.

Complimentary to His Imperial Highness the Grand Duke Alexis of Russia, and Suite. Union Pacific Railroad Company, Omaha, Jan. 12th, 1872.

Omaha Herald Print.

The special commemorative schedule printed by the Union Pacific. DREXEL UNIVERSITY ARCHIVES

Platte in 1867. The new town survived and among those who made North Platte their home was Buffalo Bill Cody, who moved there with his family in 1870.

During Custer

To speed the overnight trip to North Platte, the Union Pacific restricted westbound traffic on its line to the Grand Duke's train alone. The steam locomotive was pulling only six cars and could reach speeds up to thirty-five miles per hour with occasional stops for water and fuel.

The Union Pacific published a special gold-leafed schedule to commemorate the run, listing all of the Nebraska towns and stations along the route. Listing a station didn't mean it was a stop, however. The people of Fremont took the schedule at its face: A huge crowd, including elected officials and other dignitaries, amassed at the station. Excitement was dashed, wrote the *Fremont Tribune*, when "the Imperial [train] passed through the city at such a fearful rate of speed it was almost impossible to discover the color of the cars."

The hunters slept through the night as their train rushed across the wintry Nebraska landscape. The special schedule had the train stopping at McPherson Station, across the Platte River from Fort McPherson. Sheridan had gone buffalo hunting the previous fall on the famous "Millionaires'

The Union Pacific Hotel and Depot in North Platte, where the hunting party was greeted by Buffalo Bill Cody. Photo is from 1906; the structure was destroyed by a fire in 1915.

Hunt," when Cody scouted for the general and wealthy businessmen and journalists, following the trail between that fort and Fort Hays. Perhaps the plan was to follow that trail again when the schedule was printed, but in any event, the last stop was now North Platte.

They arrived at 7 A.M. on Saturday, January 13, having just taken breakfast on the cars, and pulled into a siding next to the Union Pacific Hotel and Depot. Cody was there to welcome the ducal party to his hometown along with numerous other officers and dignitaries.

The stay in town was very short, however; they almost immediately left for the hunting site with five ambulances (one loaded with champagne), a light wagon for baggage, and a carriage for the duke. They would return on Tuesday the 16th, arriving at 5 P.M. They had dinner on the train, with Cody and Custer no doubt entertaining the party until 10 P.M., when Cody left for home and the train left for Denver by way of Cheyenne.

After Custer

Now a small city of just under twenty-five thousand people, North Platte has grown in large part because of its Union Pacific association. The railroad's north-south and east-west routes all come through the U.P.'s Bailey Yard, the largest railroad classification yard in the world. About fourteen thousand railcars are handled daily and eighty-five hundred locomotives are serviced and fueled here monthly.

The Union Pacific Hotel and Depot burned to the ground and was replaced by a new depot; that station gained fame during World War II as the North Platte Canteen, where local citizens fed more than six million servicemen and women being transferred between the coasts.

The Site Today

That second station was torn down in the early 1970s and there is now a plaza that commemorates the historic depot (where Custer, Buffalo Bill, the Grand Duke, and Sheridan also happened to have walked).

The plaza is on Front Street, two blocks east of the U.S. 83 viaduct across the U.P. tracks from the very large grain elevator reading NORTH PLATTE.

Related Attractions

You can't visit North Platte without knowing you're in Buffalo Bill and Union Pacific territory, from the large "Fort Cody" gift shop at the town's interstate entrance to the 150-plus trains passing through daily.

Buffalo Bill added to his legend with his participation in the Great Buffalo Hunt, a story told at his Scouts Rest Ranch home in North Platte.

The Bailey Yard is really something to see and the only way to see it is from the top of the eight-story Golden Spike Tower and Visitor Center. Shaped like a giant railroad spike, the platform gives a 360-degree view of the yards and city, and U.P. retirees and other rail enthusiasts are there to answer any questions. A museum and gift shop are on the ground floor. *Address:* 1249 North Homestead Road, North Platte, NE 69101. *Hours:* May 1 to September 30: Monday through Saturday, 9 A.M. to 7 P.M.; Sunday, 1 P.M. to 7 P.M. October 1 to April 30: Monday through Saturday, 10 A.M. to 5 P.M.; Sunday, 1 P.M. to 5 P.M. *Admission:* Adults $7, seniors (55 and older) $6, youth (6 to 16) $5, under 6 free. *Phone:* (308) 532-9920 *Website:* www.goldenspike tower.com.

Buffalo Bill made North Platte his home for more than thirty years. When he arrived, he was nationally known as a scout, guide, and buffalo hunter; when he moved on, he was arguably the most famous man in the world. It was in North Platte, ten years after the hunt, that Cody held a big Fourth of July celebration and rodeo that evolved into the "Buffalo Bill's Wild West" show that toured throughout the United States and Europe.

Using some of the fortune earned from the show, Cody in 1886 built a beautiful Victorian mansion on a four thousand-acre spread just outside of North Platte that he called the Scout's Rest Ranch. It's down to twenty-five acres now as the Buffalo Bill Ranch State Historical Park. The restored house and barn display a wealth of Cody memorabilia acquired over the years.

Amenities include camping, trails, picnicking, and fishing. *Address:* 2921 Scouts Rest Ranch Road, North Platte, NE 69101-8444. *Hours:* March 24 to Memorial Day: Monday through Friday, 10 A.M. to 4 P.M.; Memorial Day to Labor Day, daily, 9 A.M. to 5 P.M.; Labor Day to October 24, Monday through Friday, 10 A.M. to 4 P.M. *Admission:* State park permit required for all vehicles (daily permits available at house and barn). *Phone:* (308) 535-8035. *E-mail:* ngpc.Buffalo.Bill@nebraska.gov. *Website:* outdoornebraska.ne.gov/parks/guide/parksearch/showpark.asp?Area_No=38

Camp Alexis

Hayes County, Nebraska

The rapidly diminishing buffalo were becoming scarce in Nebraska, but Buffalo Bill Cody was able to find a herd large enough for the grand duke's party about a day's ride south of North Platte. This area was not unknown to Custer, who had passed through here in 1867 during the Seventh Cavalry's march from Fort McPherson to the Republican River.

Detail from the Eaton stereograph of the start of the hunt. Custer is second from the right on horseback; Alexis is fourth from the right and Sheridan is at the far left. NEW YORK PUBLIC LIBRARY

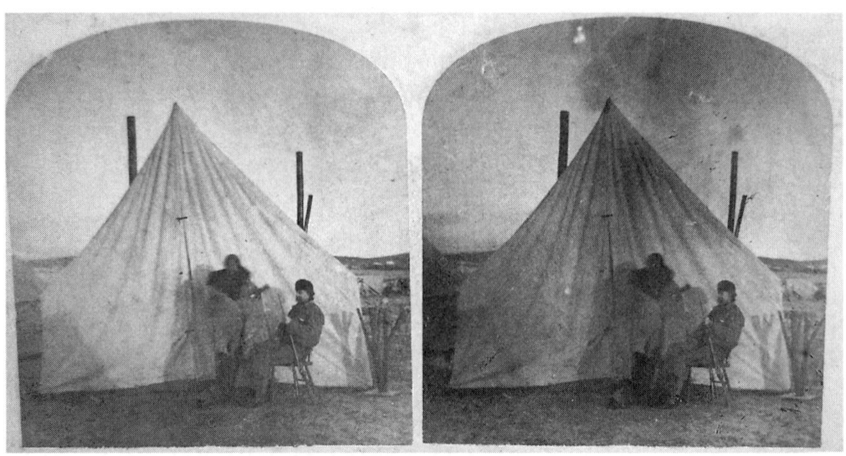

A stereoscope image of Custer with Spotted Tail in Camp Alexis. LARRY NESS

About twenty-five miles south of North Platte, they arrived at Medicine Creek, where the Second Cavalry from Fort McPherson waited with lunch and fresh horses. After an hour for rest, they resumed the trail and arrived at "Camp Alexis" on Red Willow Creek at 4:30 P.M., about fifty miles south of the Platte River. There were two large hospital tents for taking meals, ten wall tents (three with wood floors and the duke's carpeted) and numerous "A" tents for the soldiers and servants. All retired early in anticipation of the next day.

Sunday, January 14, was the day of the hunt and also the duke's twenty-second birthday. The hunting party left at 8 A.M. and traveled about fourteen miles before finding the main herd. With considerable help from Custer and Cody (the latter loaned him his horse and rifle), Alexis caught up with a young bull and dropped it with two shots. He quickly leapt from his saddle and cut off the buffalo's tail, waving it and howling over his trophy animal. After a celebration with champagne, the rest of the hunting party was then free to join in and within two hours had killed between twenty and thirty buffalo.

Champagne flowed freely back at Camp Alexis and bottles covered the campground. The hunters went out again on the 15th, a day described as more like September than January, and killed around fifteen buffalo during their last hunt in Nebraska. Finding the buffalo required more strategy and harder riding that day, and the horse ridden by Custer died shortly after they returned to camp after more than fifty miles of chase.

The day closed with a grand powwow and war dance for the duke's entertainment. Thoroughly thrilled with the spectacle, he gave the warriors fifty dollars in half-dollar silver pieces, twenty blankets, and hunting knives with ivory handles. Sheridan also gave the Indians ten thousand rations each of flour, sugar, and coffee along with a thousand pounds of tobacco. They broke camp at nine the next morning and were back in North Platte by 5 P.M.

After Custer

The area of the hunt was opened to settlement the year after the expedition, and several ranches were established in the Red Willow Creek area by the end of the 1870s. This was one of the last parts of Nebraska to be settled and organized; it was established as Hayes County in 1884, seventeen years after statehood.

The Site Today

Camp Alexis was about ten miles to the northeast of present-day Hayes Center in southwest Nebraska. There is a state marker near the site at the intersection of Avenue 370 and Road 740-A (five miles east and two miles north

The Nebraska historical marker commemorating Grand Duke Alexis's visit is a few miles south of the Camp Alexis site.

of Hayes Center) that tells the story of the duke and the great hunt. This is *not* an all-weather road—avoid it after a rain!

There is also a stone marker at the Camp Alexis site, although it is on private ground. If you want to see it and walk where scores of champagne bottles once were scattered, come during the last week of September for the Grand Duke Alexis Rendezvous. The three-day event, which is not held every year, takes place at the actual campground and features nationally known storytellers portraying Custer, the Grand Duke, and Buffalo Bill. Other activities include black-powder shoots and tomahawk and knife throws, a ladies' tea, a trail ride, children's games, and frontier-era craft demonstrations; buffalo burgers, buffalo stew, and roast buffalo are served. For more information, visit www.granddukealexis.com or call (308) 286-3463.

Denver, Golden, and Kit Carson

Colorado

The capital of the Colorado Territory, Denver was one of the great boomtowns of the West. The gold and silver mining out of the Front Range of the Rockies, coupled with the town's connection to the world with the railroad, put Denver on the verge of a population explosion.

The 1870 Census had the town's population at 4,759, but it would zoom to 35,629 in just ten years. The hunting party came to Denver as the explosion was just starting to sizzle.

During Custer

The party was met in Cheyenne by Colorado governor Edward McCook, former governor John Evans, and other members of the territorial government. As at the other planned stops, they were met at Denver on the evening of the 17th by hundreds of enthusiastic citizens wanting to catch a glimpse of Alexis, Sheridan, and Custer.

Coaches took the party from the depot to the American House, the city's most upscale hotel; it was also the governor's mansion, since McCook and his wife lived there. After a restful night, Alexis and the group were given a tour of the town, visiting the Denver Ale Company, the U.S. Mint,

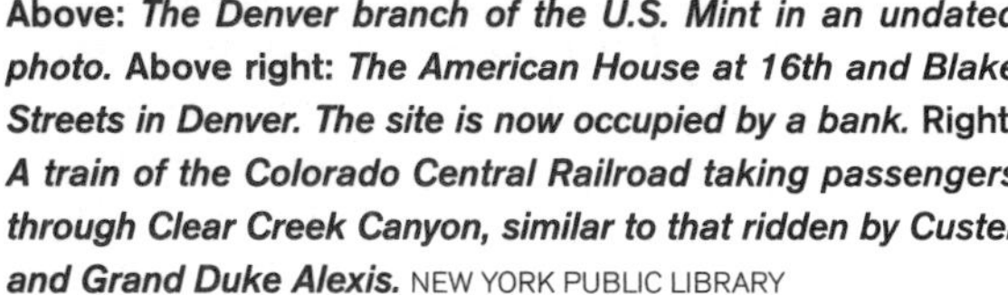

Above: ***The Denver branch of the U.S. Mint in an undated photo.*** **Above right:** ***The American House at 16th and Blake Streets in Denver. The site is now occupied by a bank.*** **Right:** ***A train of the Colorado Central Railroad taking passengers through Clear Creek Canyon, similar to that ridden by Custer and Grand Duke Alexis.*** NEW YORK PUBLIC LIBRARY

the city's waterworks, and the territorial legislature, then in session. The grand duke was feted with a grand ball that night at the hotel.

On Friday, January 19, the party took the Colorado Central Railroad through Clear Creek Canyon to Golden to see the gold- and silver-mining operations, followed by a reception at the Golden House. They returned to Denver and departed for the east on the Kansas Pacific.

Sheridan had found out about another buffalo herd to the south of Kit Carson, Colorado, near the Kansas border and Fort Wallace. Alexis wanted to hunt on the morning of the 20th, so horses provided by the fort were waiting for the group at Kit Carson. This time Custer and the grand duke rode out ahead while the rest of the party watched and waited. The cavalry horses were unfamiliar with and frightened by the buffalo, however, and it took considerable maneuvering by Custer to get the two of them in range to fire. Once Alexis took his first buffalo, it was again a free-for-all by the rest of the party. This was the last of their hunting on horseback and it was now on to Kansas for the final leg of the Great Plains adventure.

After Custer

Denver continued its spectacular growth, and by 1890 was the second-largest U.S. city west of Omaha; it dropped to third behind San Francisco and Los Angeles in 1900. After a century of booms and busts, Denver is close to among the twenty-five largest cities in the country.

The Sites Today

None of the buildings visited by Custer and the hunting party remain today. Although it's not in the same building, you can visit the U.S. Mint in Denver as Custer did. The present mint offers tours to learn about the minting process, from the original designs and sculptures to the actual striking of the coins. Reservations are required. *Address:* 320 West Colfax Avenue, Denver, CO 80204-2693. *Hours:* Monday through Friday, 8 A.M. to 2 P.M. Closed federal holidays. Tours are subject to cancellation without prior notice. *Admission:* Free. *Phone:* (303) 405-4761. *Website:* www.usmint.gov/mint_tours.

The Colorado hunting site, about five miles south of Kit Carson, has no historical marker. Further south in the town of Eads, there's an interpretive marker relating to the event on the east side of town on Colorado State Highway 96, although it erroneously reports that Wild Bill Hickok was part of the hunting party and that Cody was still with them in Denver.

Related Sites and Events

Buffalo Bill wasn't on this leg of the trip, but this is where his life's journey ended. Cody died in 1917 while visiting his sister in Denver. Per his request, he was buried on Lookout Mountain, looking east over the Great Plains. An adjacent museum started up soon afterwards. Today the city and county of Denver operate the Buffalo Bill Museum and Grave. Besides the fine exhibits and Cody's final resting spot, you'll see the fantastic views of both the plains and the mountains. *Address:* 987 1/2 Lookout Mountain Road, Golden, CO 80401. *Hours:* May 1 to October 31: daily, 9 A.M. to 5 P.M. November 1 to April 30: Tuesday through Sunday, 9 A.M. to 4 P.M. Closed Christmas Day. *Admission:* Adults $5, seniors (65+) $4, children (6 to 15) $1, 5 and under free. *Phone:* (303) 526-0744. *E-mail:* buffalobill.museum@denvergov.org. *Website:* www.buffalobill.org.

A highlight of the trip to the mountains for Custer had to be riding the rails from Clear Creek to Golden. That was formerly the only way to reach

Buffalo Bill's grave atop Lookout Mountain and overlooking the Great Plains.

the town of Golden, but now you can drive only twelve miles west of downtown Denver to Golden to visit the Colorado Railroad Museum. The museum features railroad equipment, artifacts, paper records, and artwork and photographs of Rocky Mountain–area railroads from the 1860s to the present. *Address:* 17155 W. 44th Avenue, Golden, CO 80403. *Hours:* Open daily from 9 A.M. to 5 P.M. and to 6 P.M. in June, July, and August; closed Thanksgiving, Christmas, and New Year's Day with special hours of operation on Easter Sunday, Christmas Eve, and New Year's Eve. *Admission:* Adults $8, seniors (over 60) $7, family (two adults and children under 16) $18, children (2 to 16) $5, under 2 free. *Phone:* (303) 279-4591 or 800-365-6263. *Website:* www.coloradorailroadmuseum.org.

Like Custer and the grand duke, you can also learn more about mining while in Golden. The Colorado School of Mines Geology Museum was founded just two years after the visit and has since told the story of Colorado's mineral heritage through minerals, fossils, gemstones, meteorites, and mining artifacts. Located on the school's campus, it's there for both the scientific and public communities. *Address:* Research Laboratory (GRL) building, 1310 Maple Street, Golden, CO 80401. *Hours:* Monday through Saturday, 9 A.M. to 4 P.M.; Sunday, 1 P.M. to 4 P.M. Closed certain legal and school holidays. *Admission:* Free. *Phone:* (303) 279-4591 or 800-365-6263. *Website:* www.mines.edu/Geology_Museum.

The Denver Ale Company is long closed, but if you want to continue your "Custer tour experience" in Golden, you could tour the Coors Brewery, which opened the year after the 1872 visit. The thirty-minute self-guided tour highlights the malting, brewing, and packaging processes, and you can cool off in the "fresh beer room," where of-age visitors can sip a cold sample and rest on ice-cube benches in a refrigerated room. Guests under 18 years old must be accompanied by an adult. *Address:* 13th and Ford, Golden, CO 80401. *Hours:* June 1 to Labor Day: Monday through Saturday, 10 A.M. to 4 P.M.; Sunday, noon to 4 P.M. Labor Day to May 31: Thursday through Monday, 10 A.M. to 4 P.M.; Sunday, noon to 4 P.M. Closed major holidays. *Admission:* Free. *Phone:* (800) 642-6116 or (303) 277-2337. *Website:* www.millercoors.com/golden-brewery-tour.

From Eads, Colorado, you are only a short distance from Sand Creek Massacre National Historic Site, where Col. John Chivington and about seven hundred volunteer troops attacked a peaceful camp of Cheyenne and Arapaho in 1864. The attack enflamed the tribes for years to come and helped lead to the arrival of George Custer on the plains. To visit the site, follow Highway 96 east of Eads past the village of Chivington. Turn north onto County Road 54. Follow the road to its intersections with County Road W, and then turn right to reach the site entrance. Mailing *Address:* PO Box 249, Eads, CO 81036. *Hours:* Visitors center open daily from 9 A.M. to 4 P.M.; check with park for winter schedule (December–March). *Admission:* Free. *Phone:* (719) 729-3003 or (719) 438-5916. *Website:* www.nps.gov/sand.

Topeka

Kansas

The party's final stop on the Great Plains was to be Topeka, the state capital of Kansas. Founded in 1854, Topeka survived the pre-Civil War "Bleeding Kansas" period and was enjoying postwar growth, with a population nearing six thousand. Many of the new residents of the city were "Exodusters"—former slaves who came to Kansas to begin new lives.

On the route from Colorado, the royal train stopped briefly at Fort Hays on January 21. The members of the hunting party were greeted enthusias-

The hunting party as photographed in Topeka. Standing, from left: Frank Thompson, Dr. Condrin, Col. George Forsythe, Count Olsonfieff, Maj. M. V. Asche, Col. Nelson Bowman Sweitzer, and Lt. Tudor. Seated, from left: Consul Bodisco, Chancellor Machin, Lt. Gen. Philip H. Sheridan, the Grand Duke Alexis, Admiral Possiet, and Lt. Col. George A. Custer. On floor, from left: Lt. Col. James William Forsythe, Lt. Sterlegoff, and Lt. Col. Michael Vincent Sheridan. KANSAS HISTORICAL SOCIETY

tically—it was always rare to have a visit from the division commander (Sheridan) and exciting to have European nobility, and, of course, Custer was already well known at the fort. Several of Fort Hays' officers were presented by Sheridan to the grand duke before his departure.

Buffalo were spotted from the train while crossing Kansas; rather than disembark, the hunting party fired on the animals from the comfort of the cars.

During Custer

The royal train arrived in Topeka at 11 A.M. on the morning of the 22nd. Waiting at the depot were the state's lieutenant governor and speaker of the house and other Kansas officials; after introductions, the party was taken to the Fifth Avenue Hotel, the city's finest, and given time to rest and freshen up.

While the party was at the hotel, Sheridan's car was uncoupled from the royal train for his separate return east. Before he left the city, however, he sat for two photographs in Topeka—one with the grand duke and members of the hunting party and another with the officers of his staff; Custer was included in both photos.

The east wing of the Kansas State Capitol in 1873. NEW YORK PUBLIC LIBRARY

Sheridan's train left town at 1 P.M. Alexis, Custer, and the rest were taken to the state capitol, then under construction with the east wing nearly complete. Ladies waved handkerchiefs out the building's windows as the party approached. Alexis was welcomed by Gov. James Harvey and presented to a joint session of the house and senate.

They returned to the hotel for an eleven-course dinner with the Kansas officials; reportedly more than one hundred meat dishes were served, including leg of mutton, buffalo, rabbit, venison, moose, squirrel, elk, bear, quail, antelope, and prairie chicken. The train left Topeka at 5 P.M. and Custer continued on with Alexis.

After Custer

Besides growing as a center of government and transportation, Topeka's expansion was also fueled by its status as an agricultural center. Today, the state capital is the fourth-largest city in Kansas with a population of more than 127,000.

The Sites Today

There are a few buildings still standing in Topeka from the time of the hunting party's 1873 visit, although only one from an official stop. The original Kansas Pacific depot at Kansas Avenue and Railroad Street is gone; the Fifth Avenue Hotel was damaged by fire in 1951, reopened as a residence hotel, and was torn down in 1960. The site (SE Fifth and SE Quincy Streets) is now the location of a parking garage.

Still standing—and much larger than it was in 1873—is the Kansas State Capitol. The building was completed in 1903, more than thirty years after the visit of Custer and the grand duke. It is currently undergoing a large-scale renovation, scheduled for completion in June 2012. Regular tours are offered Monday through Friday and self-guided tours can be done throughout the week. Take special note when visiting the Senate Chamber in the east wing—the Kansas legislature recognized the grand duke here, with Custer in attendance. *Address:* 10th Avenue and Jackson Street, Topeka, KS 66612. *Phone:* (785) 296-3966. *Website:* www.kshs.org/portal_capitol

Related Sites

Those looking for more Custer while in Topeka should visit the Kansas Museum of History. Besides telling the history of Custer's most-visited Great Plains state, there is a display that includes one of the general's boots (the other is at Fort Hays), donated by Libbie Custer, as well as a dumbbell used by him to stay fit while at Fort Hays and made by the fort's blacksmith. *Address:* 6425 SW 6th Avenue, Topeka, KS 66615. *Hours:* Tuesday through Saturday, 9 A.M. to 5 P.M.; Sunday, 1 to 5 P.M. Closed Mondays and state holidays, including New Year's Day, Thanksgiving, and Christmas. *Admission:* Adult $6, student with ID $4, children (5 and under) free with family. *Website:* www.kshs.org.

Custer and Alexis returned to their hunting gear for this photo taken in St. Louis. KANSAS HISTORICAL SOCIETY

Epilogue

Custer continued on with Alexis after the "official" part of the buffalo hunt concluded. On January 24 in St. Louis, they posed together for several photos in their hunting outfits. The train then rolled on to Louisville, where Custer retrieved Libbie from Elizabethtown, Kentucky, to join them for the tour's final leg through the southern states.

The Custers and the grand duke parted in New Orleans, where Alexis was made the honorary grand marshal of Mardi Gras during the city's celebration on February 13. It's said that the grand duke suggested the official colors of purple, gold, and green for the annual event.

The most famous of all buffalo hunts on the Great Plains, Grand Duke Alexis's hunt also was among the last. The buffalo herds disappeared at an even more rapid pace as their extermination became the primary tool for forcing Indian tribes onto reservations. The bison were almost driven to extinction, and only because a few cattlemen saved some for their ranches did the species survive.

Custer and Alexis developed a strong friendship from their great adventure and wrote to each other regularly after the grand duke's return to Russia. Custer's death at Little Bighorn saddened Alexis greatly. When he was in New York in late 1876, he sent $500 to Libbie through the United States Port Military Library Association, requesting that it be transmitted to her "in his name and without publicity, as a slight token of his remembrance and sympathy."

Recommended Reading

The Buffalo Book: The Full Saga of the American Animal by David A. Dary (Swallow Press).

Custer in Memphis, March 1873. LIBRARY OF CONGRESS

1873
Through the Dakotas

After a year and a half in Kentucky, Custer and Libbie were ready for a return to the Great Plains. He enjoyed the horse culture of the Bluegrass State with its breeding and racing, but most of his time was spent in reading and writing. The slower lifestyle was not agreeing with him and he was ready for action. "It seemed an unsoldierly life, and it was certainly uncongenial," wrote Libbie, "for a true cavalryman feels that a life in the saddle on the free open plain is his legitimate existence."

The Northern Pacific made it possible to return to that existence. The new railroad would extend from the Great Lakes to the Pacific Northwest, crossing the northern plains and the land of the Teton Sioux, Northern Cheyenne, and Northern Arapaho. "That Northern Pacific is going to give you a great deal of trouble," General Sherman wrote to Sheridan in 1872. "The Indians will be hostile to an extreme degree." The Indians had already attacked railroad surveyors and their escorts in the early 1870s. General Hancock, now heading the Department of Dakota, warned that more troops, especially cavalry, would be needed. Sheridan wanted the Seventh, and he sent a telegram to Custer in February 1873 advising him that his regiment would reassemble in Memphis and then move to Cairo, Illinois, for transfer to and service in the Dakotas.

Camp Sturgis

Yankton, South Dakota

Yankton was founded in 1857 on a bend of the Missouri River once occupied by the Yankton Sioux Indians. Its location in southeast Dakota Territory made it a gateway to the northwest and town founders successfully pushed for it to become the territorial capital in 1861. Scores of riverboats stopped here, Yankton had regular stage service, and local businesses and investors even financed their own railroad—the Dakota Southern—to link the town with the east.

Yankton immediately submitted itself to host the Seventh when the army announced the regiment needed a launching point in the territory. A heated campaign erupted between the town and Sioux City, Iowa, downstream, but Yankton received the nod and readied itself for the Seventh's arrival in the spring of 1873.

The contingents of the Seventh—about eight hundred or nine hundred men and an equal number of horses—met at Cairo, Illinois, and departed for Yankton on four different trains of the Illinois Central. Many

Yankton in 1874, a year after Custer and the Seventh camped in the town. STATE ARCHIVES OF THE SOUTH DAKOTA STATE HISTORICAL SOCIETY

of the officers also brought along their wives. It took nearly a week for the trains to reach the city as they passed through Illinois and the Iowa towns of Dubuque, Waterloo, Fort Dodge, and Sioux City, stopping daily for the watering and feeding of the animals.

During Custer

The first train, carrying one company, arrived at Yankton late in the evening of April 9, 1873. Five companies arrived the following day and began building camp a mile east of town. Two more arrived on the 11th and the final two came later in the day with Custer. He didn't like the site and moved it a half mile closer to Yankton, naming the post Camp Sturgis after Colonel Sturgis, who remained back at department headquarters (see page 152).

Tents went up to the north of the Missouri River and next to the Dakota Southern tracks. Around forty laundresses—many married to enlisted men and with children in tow—set up their tents next to Rhine Creek between the camp and town. Although it was spring, the weather was cold and clouded with spotty rain and snow showers.

The Blizzard of 1873 hit Yankton on Sunday, April 13. Warm, humid winds gave way to a bitter northwest gale and the rain turned to heavy snow. As the snowstorm pounded the tents the next day, Custer ordered the troops and animals into town for cover while he and Libbie stayed in a small log cabin at the camp. Word didn't get to the laundresses in the confusion of the storm, however, and Yankton citizens helped in a rescue effort on the 15th to bring them and the children into town.

Custer, meanwhile, was bedridden with a tremendous cold, probably caused by exhaustion and the rapid change in weather. He and Libbie eventually took lodging in town themselves. As the storm subsided on the 18th, pioneer crews went to work on digging out and repairing Camp Sturgis. The blizzard hospitalized many soldiers; there were no fatalities but there were some amputations from frostbite.

Both Yankton and the Seventh showed their gratitude for each other. "We were called upon, asked to dine, and finally tendered a ball," wrote Libbie in *Boots and Saddles.* "It was given in the public hall of the town [Stone's Hall], which, being decorated with flags and ornamented with all the military paraphernalia that could be used effectively, was really very attractive."

The local band and its conductor, Felix Vinatieri, particularly impressed the general. Custer asked them to become the regiment's band, and Vinatieri soon signed up for his third hitch with the army. After the ball on the 24th, Custer and the officers of the Seventh wrote a glowing "Adoption

Personal Battle: Who's in Charge Here?

Colonel Sturgis commanded the Seventh Cavalry and the camp in Yankton had his name, but where was he?

Sturgis and Custer had previously served together in Texas and had a professional working relationship. That changed in 1869 when Sturgis was bumped up to full colonel and succeeded Andrew J. Smith in command of the Seventh Cavalry. This outraged Custer, who had trained the regiment and assumed it would be his.

The two rarely saw eye to eye and were never friendly. General Sheridan remedied this by keeping Custer in the field with the regiment and Sturgis at department headquarters, which didn't sit well with Sturgis. This arrangement continued with the activation of the Seventh for service in Dakota and carried awkward overtones in Yankton. Perhaps to embarrass Sturgis, Custer named the new post "Camp Sturgis," after him, surely knowing people would ask "Where is Colonel Sturgis?" (The camp at Fort Hays was also called Camp Sturgis.)

The conflict between the officers can be seen in the local newspaper of the day, the *Dakota Herald*. "Col. Samuel D. Sturgis is the first officer of the regiment and sustains a good reputation as a soldier," it wrote, immediately adding "Gen. G. A. Custer, who has a war record which has given him a national reputation of being a brave, daring and chivalrous cavalry general, won during the 'late unpleasantness,' by dint of personal merit, and not through political influence, is the Lt. Col. of the regiment, will have command of the ten companies

of Complimentary Resolutions" to the townspeople, published in the Yankton newspaper.

Rain and snow storms continued to delay departure, but Custer decided he could wait no longer and struck camp on May 7. The townspeople lined the streets to wish them luck, and Custer and the troops gave the city and territorial governor John Burbank a review down Third Street. They headed west on the Sioux City–Fort Randall Military Road as the steamer *Miner* followed on the river, carrying the officers' wives, baggage, and other supplies.

After Custer

Yankton continued to grow, but suffered some losses that affected its prosperity. Its riverboat traffic was all but destroyed in 1881 when an ice jam on the Missouri burst, damaging or sinking many of the boats. In 1883, Yank-

at this place and while on the expedition on the Yellowstone the coming summer." Custer–or whoever gave the interview with the newspaper–left no doubt as to who was in charge in Dakota.

Apparently aware of the public relations snafu, Sturgis came to town a week before the Seventh left to assume command, but then issued only one order stating that all previous orders from Custer were still in effect. He visited with local dignitaries while Custer continued to issue orders and prepare the regiment for its march. The two stayed out of each other's way and Sturgis returned to Fort Snelling and department headquarters in Minnesota.

Sturgis was in St. Louis at the time of the Battle of Little Bighorn. His son, Lt. James G. Sturgis, was killed with Custer and his men and Sturgis blamed Custer for both the loss of the battle and of his son.

Colonel Sturgis came to Fort Abraham Lincoln in March 1877 to command the Seventh for the first time in person since 1872. He oversaw the regiment's move to Fort Meade in the Black Hills, and it was there he had a role in ending the career of Maj. Marcus Reno (see page 200).

Samuel D. Sturgis. LIBRARY OF CONGRESS

ton lost the title of territorial capital to Bismarck. It hoped to regain the capital in 1889, when the territory was split into North and South Dakota, but lost that race to Pierre. In 1905, the state fair went to Huron, South Dakota.

The Site Today

Yankton hasn't hung on its losses—it's one of the most historic towns in South Dakota and among its most beautiful. There are an amazing number of stately, well-tended homes from its early history throughout the city, making it worth the trip if you're interested in nineteenth-century architecture alone.

Camp Sturgis, of course, is gone, but if you've stopped at the Yankton Chamber of Commerce and Visitor Center offices on the east entrance to town, you're practically standing on it. The unmarked camp was to the

Visiting Yankton

How to Get There: Yankton is located in southeast South Dakota in Yankton County, on the Missouri River border with Nebraska. From Exit 26 of Interstate 29, take SD 50 west for thirty-seven miles to the city.

north of Highway 50 where commercial and industrial buildings are now located. To the west, the laundresses' tents were between you and the creek, now known as Milne Creek.

There are several other sites of note from Custer and the Seventh's month in Yankton. Stone's Hall, where Custer and his officers were feted, was at the northeast corner of Third and Capital (it's now a parking lot). There's a Custer connection across the street at 301 Capital; this red stone building housed the federal courtroom where Jack McCall was tried, convicted, and hanged in December 1876 for murdering Wild Bill Hickok in Deadwood. Hickok, of course, was once a Custer scout and friend. A historical plaque that tells the story is on the building's Capital Street side. (McCall is buried in an unmarked site at the city cemetery, and Hickok fans who know where it is sometimes dance a jig over the grave.)

Farther west on Third at its intersection with Broadway is the Yankton County Government Center; its front lawn contains a stone DAR marker commemorating the Yankton Stockade, where citizens took protection during the Sioux Uprising of 1862. North of here was Stetson's Hotel, in which George and Libbie Custer were billeted after the blizzard.

Related Sites and Attractions

An excellent gateway to the region's Custer-era history is the Dakota Territorial Museum at 610 Summit Street. The museum has plenty of territorial and local history, but there are two areas of interest to Custerphiles. One is the display on Felix Vinatieri. He and his band enlisted and accompanied the Seventh into the Dakota Territory and to Fort Abraham Lincoln, but they did not follow the troops to Little Bighorn, as Custer did not want the band engaged in battle. The display includes several musical instruments and a band uniform once owned by the conductor; part of the display also covers Vinatieri's great-great-grandson Adam, a Yankton native and five-time Super Bowl placekicker.

The second area of interest is the story of the steamer *Far West.* Its captain, Grant Marsh, made his home in Yankton. In rushing the survivors of Little Bighorn seven hundred miles back to Bismarck, Marsh guided the *Far West* through sandbars and other obstacles within fifty-four hours. It was one of the most remarkable feats ever achieved in river steamboating and passed the captain and his ship into legend. The museum hosts a large model of the *Far West*, a detailed painting, and an actual fork from the ship's service, with "Far West" engraved into its handle. Who knows? Maybe Custer used it. *Address:* 610 Summit Street, Yankton, SD 57078. *Hours:* May through September: Monday through Friday, 10 A.M. to 5 P.M.; Saturday and Sunday, noon to 4 P.M. October through April: open daily from noon to 4 P.M. or by appointment. *Admission:* Free. *Phone:* (605) 665-3898. *E-mail:* dtmuseum @iw.net. *Website:* www.dakotaterritorialmuseum.org.

There's a statue of Marsh in Riverside Park between downtown and the river (along with a replica of the Territorial Capitol) and his home still stands at 513 Douglas Avenue. Built in 1877, the two-story redbrick now serves as offices for a nearby church, and former NBC newscaster Tom Brokaw once rented it when he worked at the local television station.

Another home with a Custer connection is the Cramer-Kenyon Heritage Home at 509 Pine Street. Available for tours and special occasions, the interior of the Queen Anne home includes a small corner table purportedly hand-carved by members of the Seventh as a gift of appreciation to the women of Yankton. Atop the table is a candlestick made from the plume socket of an 1870s-era soldiers' helmet, also made by the troops. *Address:* 509 Pine Street, Yankton, SD 57078. *Hours:* Memorial Day through Labor Day, Wednesday through Sunday, 1 P.M. to 5 P.M. *Admission:* Adults $5, Students under twelve $2. *Phone:* (605) 665-7470.

Yankton was the territorial capital of the Dakota Territory when Custer was here; a replica of the capitol building now stands in the city's Riverside Park.

Six unknown soldiers of the Seventh—at least according to local legend—are buried at the Bon Homme Cemetery.

There is one more link to the Seventh Cavalry outside of Yankton: the graves of six unknown soldiers. No deaths were recorded by the regiment when they camped west of the city on May 8–11, 1873, but area residents noted the appearance of a mass grave after the troops left. Were they soldiers, or were they teamsters or some other civilians who followed the Seventh? Local legend and the tombstone inscriptions hold that they were soldiers, but muster rolls and regiment returns indicate they weren't. In any event, the graves were moved to the Bon Homme Cemetery in 1893, with a tombstone made for the new resting place in 1922.

The cemetery is about twenty miles west of Yankton on Highway 52. Take the highway to its intersection with Highway 50 and turn south toward Lewis and Clark Lake and the Missouri River. Turn right (west) at the memorial to the Dakota Territory's first schoolhouse and after a mile you'll find the cemetery on a bluff overlooking the river. The graves are relatively easy to find—walk straight back with your eye to the left. The large concrete monument reads "In memory of six unknown soldiers buried here."

Recommended Reading

The Sioux City to Fort Randall Military Road 1856–1892, Revisited by Maxine Schuurmans Kinsley (Pine Hill Press).

Fort Randall

Pickstown, South Dakota

Lewis and Clark camped in the area that later became Fort Randall, noting the abundance of wood at this bend in the Missouri. So much timber grew here, in fact, that several decades later there were quite a few "woodhawks" who made a living here selling fuel to steamboats on the river.

By the time emigrants and settlers moved into the country, this was the Nebraska Territory. Gen. William Harney selected this site on the river's west bank to protect those people in 1856. His troops built the new Fort Randall (named for a deputy paymaster general) of cottonwood logs; as the fort's importance grew, one- and two-story frame buildings replaced the deteriorating log structures. Randall became part of the Dakota Territory during the 1861 realignment of boundaries.

During Custer

Fort Randall was a large fort, garrisoned by three hundred men, by the time Custer and the Seventh arrived on May 14, 1873. Barracks, a hospital, a commissary, and a guardhouse surrounded the parade ground,

Fort Randall in the 1860s. STATE ARCHIVES OF THE SOUTH DAKOTA STATE HISTORICAL SOCIETY

along with offices, officers' quarters, and an ordnance depot and powder magazine.

The Seventh camped on the east bank at White Swan village, a small settlement consisting of a post office, stage station, a few saloons, boardinghouses, and a ferry landing. Custer and other officers used the *Miner* to cross the Missouri to the fort during their two-day stop to prepare the troops and animals for their long march. The column and the steamboat left the area on May 15.

After Custer

In the years to come, Fort Randall became one of the most sought-after assignments on the northern plains. Many of the officers and enlisted men had their families there, leading to amenities like summer picnics, winter skating, flower gardens, and a library. The men and local citizens even built a church from local sandstone.

Most of the Indian tribes were on reservations by the 1880s, and Fort Randall was one of the few posts still open. Soldiers counted routine maintenance and road repair among their duties. Fort life got a little more exciting with the incarceration of Sitting Bull from 1881 to 1883, bringing the nuisance of celebrity hounds coming to see him and get an autograph.

The Fort Randall chapel ruins as they stand today on the U.S. Army Corps of Engineers grounds.

Visiting Fort Randall

U.S. Army Corps of Engineers
Fort Randall Project, U.S. Hwy 281/18, P.O. Box 199
Pickstown, South Dakota 57367-0199
(605) 487-7847, ext. 3223
www.nwo.usace.army.mil/html/Lake_Proj/fortrandall/welcome.html

How to Get There: Located in Charles Mix County in southeast South Dakota, twelve miles west of Wagner on South Dakota Highway 46; or twenty-five miles northeast of Spencer, Nebraska, on U.S. Highway 281.

Hours: Visitors center open daily from Memorial Day through Labor Day, 8:30 A.M. to 6 P.M.

Admission: Free

Amenities: Historical and interpretive markers, restrooms, and water are available at the fort site. Restrooms, displays, staff, picnic tables, and water are available at the visitors center. Camping is available at nearby Randall Creek Recreation Area, including 132 electrical sites, four camping cabins, showers, and boat ramp; and at North Point Recreation Area, which has 111 electrical sites, six camping cabins, showers, swimming beach, trails, and a boat ramp. Tours of the Fort Randall Dam are available; call for information.

Special Events: Although the soldiers' remains were removed to Fort Leavenworth National Cemetery, a Memorial Day service is conducted by the First U.S. Infantry of Fort Randall every year to remember the frontier soldiers, family members, and unknowns who lie buried in the post cemetery.

Fort Randall closed in 1892, with its buildings and surplus equipment sold at a public auction. Soldiers buried in the cemetery were moved down the Missouri to Fort Leavenworth while the church, still holding services, remained for a number of years.

The Site Today

Fort Randall is a rarity among Dakota forts in that its grounds are still there. Flood control efforts of the 1950s and '60s resulted in the damming of the Missouri, and its waters covered the grounds of many of the forts built on its banks. Fort Randall just missed that fate by having a dam being built immediately upstream from it—the old fort now stands at the foot of its namesake, the Fort Randall Dam.

Well, "stands" may be a generous term, as there is only one building there and it's not really a building. The ruins of the Fort Randall Church are all that survive, beaten down by nature and time. The U.S. Army Corps of Engineers, which operates the site, built a substantial covering for the church, which seems to have slowed its erosion.

Like Custer, you can walk the parade ground of the old fort. The corps has signage around the grounds to identify each building location and you'll get a good idea of what was around when the general visited in 1873. You may also want to visit the corps' visitors center, across the dam at Pickstown. It has a great view of the lake created by Fort Randall Dam—Lake Francis Case—along with information on the fort and the wildlife of the area.

Recommended Reading

Fort Randall on the Missouri, 1856–1892 by Jerome A. Greene (South Dakota State Historical Society Press).

Up the Missouri

South Dakota

Since Lewis and Clark, the Missouri River has served as the great transportation and communication route through the north central United States. Canoes, keelboats, mackinaws, and bullboats were the first to navigate its broad, shallow channels, but by the time the surrounding land became the Dakota Territory, the steamboat was king. Steamboats had been on the river since 1831, but by the 1860s they were hauling passengers and vast amounts of supplies to farmers, miners, ranchers, and trappers, and to the forts along the Missouri. They also brought back furs, hides, and gold dust.

The season was short, running from April to late June, as the Missouri required the spring runoff from the Rocky Mountains to give it enough depth for the riverboats. Custer, the Seventh, and the *Miner* made their advance in the middle of that season. The route would take the Seventh up the Missouri River on its east bank, across the river from the Great Sioux Reservation.

During Custer

The Seventh and the *Miner* left Fort Randall on May 15, 1873, making for the river post of Fort Thompson, closed two years earlier. The troops and the steamboat maintained visual contact when possible over the river bluffs.

The undulating ground and stream crossings were, in the words of Lt. Charles W. Larned, "rendering the march vexatious and tiresome." Custer had his men draw three days of rations from the *Miner* when they got to the fort on May 18. The steamboat moved onto the north on May 21 and the column departed shortly after that.

The land became more desolate past Fort Thompson, but those on the trail and the river looked forward to the next post, Fort Sully. Commonly called "New" Fort Sully to differentiate it from the post it replaced, the seven-year-old fort was modern, at least as far as forts went. It had wood-frame buildings, picket fences, gardens, and livestock, and kept in active touch with the civilized world through telegraph and regular mail service. They even had an icemaking machine, and fort denizens ran the treat out to the soldiers as they approached. The commander of Fort Sully, Col. David S. Stanley, would also command the Yellowstone Expedition and head the Twenty-Second Infantry.

Fort Sully in 1878, five years after the Seventh Cavalry's visit.

The Seventh set up camp about a half mile from the fort. While there, Custer convened a general court-martial for numerous desertions and other cases. He wanted the court at the campsite, preferring to keep the Seventh's problems within the regiment. The officers who made up the court, however, were able to exert their power and transfer the court to the more comfortable fort buildings.

Fort Sully was also the site of a new conflict between Custer and Frederick Benteen. The captain apparently violated Custer's tightly drawn rules on alertness and efficiency and Custer called him on it. Benteen used his word skills to their best, however, effectively deflating Custer's charges. He no doubt felt he had put his commander in his place but he also took himself out of any meaningful role in the forthcoming Yellowstone campaign.

The column and the *Miner* left Fort Sully on May 30 and continued upriver. They reached the mouth of the Cannonball on June 6, and Custer made plans to cross the Missouri south of the fort. He flagged down the riverboat *DeSmet* and made an agreement with its captain to ferry the entire command. Custer announced that his wagon master would load the boat but the captain insisted that he would direct the loading. An argument began; when Custer threatened to arrest the captain, the man excused himself to make preparations in the pilothouse. Once there, he began backing the boat away from the shore, forcing the already loaded officers to scramble back to the bank.

The column marched on, up the east bank to Fort Rice.

After Custer

The Yellowstone Expedition played a large part in ending steamboat traffic on the Missouri. The expedition helped advance the construction of the Northern Pacific Railroad, and as the railroad's fingers spread across the northern plains, its speed, affordable rates, reliability, and year-round service quickly replaced the steamboat.

Steamboats once paddled the Missouri for 2,285 miles from St. Louis to Fort Benton in present-day Montana. The damming of the Missouri for flood control, irrigation, and recreation by the Corps of Engineers has since made it a series of elongated lakes rather than a free-flowing river.

The Sites Today

The Seventh's passage up the Missouri's east side was long and difficult; the Custer traveler will find it equally tough to find visible historical sites. Fort Thompson, about two miles south of the town named for the fort, is

Depending upon drought conditions, the Fort Sully site is occasionally exposed. The concrete block once held a historical marker, which is now at the Sully County Courthouse in Onida.

now under Lake Francis Case. Fort Sully, which closed in 1894, is now under Lake Oahe. The Sully site is occasionally exposed during drought but it is very difficult to reach and restricted by the Corps of Engineers. A marker once stood at the fort site but is now at the Sully County Courthouse in Onida; it was moved when the river started rising above it after damming.

Related Sites and Attractions

The Akta Lakota Museum & Cultural Center is on the campus of the St. Joseph's Indian School in the town of Chamberlain, South Dakota, two miles north of exit 263 of Interstate 90. This is what is called a "living museum," where contemporary issues receive as much attention as past battles. There are displays on life on the plains before Euro-American contact; the early contact with explorers, missionaries, traders, and settlers; conflict with the U.S. government and the loss of lands; and adaptation to a new way of life and preserving traditions and heritage. There's also an art museum with creations by Lakota artisans and a substantial gift shop with native crafts. *Address:* 1301 North Main Street, Chamberlain, SD 57325.

Hours: May through October (including holidays): Monday through Saturday, 8 A.M. to 6 P.M.; Sundays, 9 A.M. to 5 P.M. November through April: Monday through Saturday, 8 A.M. to 5 P.M. Closed Sundays and national holidays. *Admission:* Free, donations accepted. *Phone:* (800) 798-3452. *E-mail:* aktalakota@stjo.org. *Website:* www.aktalakota.org.

A great stop is the South Dakota Cultural Heritage Center in the capital city of Pierre. Nestled into a bluff north of the capitol, the center tells the history of the state through many displays and artifacts. The Indian Wars enthusiast will probably take greatest note of displays on Fort Pierre and Fort Sully, featuring equipment and clothing typically used by soldiers posted to Dakota forts. Another display covers conflicts in the Dakotas, with weapons and other artifacts. *Address:* 900 Governors Drive, Pierre, SD 57501. *Hours:* Memorial Day through Labor Day, Monday through Saturday: 9 A.M. to 6:30 P.M.; Sundays and holidays, 1 P.M. to 4:30 P.M. The museum closes at 4:30 P.M. in the off-season and is closed New Year's Day, Easter, Thanksgiving, and Christmas. *Admission:* Adults $4, Seniors (60 and over) $3, Children (17 and under) free. *Phone:* (605) 773-3458. *E-mail:* sdshsweb master@state.sd.us. *Website:* history.sd.gov.

Farther upstream is the city of Mobridge, South Dakota, where the first bridge across the river was built in 1906 ("Mobridge" being a contraction for "Missouri Bridge"). The Klein Museum here has a fine collection of early Indian beadwork, headdresses, clothing, tools, and early photographs. *Address:* 1820 West Grand Crossing, Mobridge, SD 57601. *Hours:* Open from April 15 to October 15, Monday through Friday, 9 A.M. to noon and 1 P.M. to 5 P.M.; Saturday and Sunday, 1 P.M. to 5 P.M. Closed Tuesdays in April, May, and October. *Admission:* Adults $3, Student $2, preschool free. *Phone:* (605) 845-7243. *E-mail:* klein museum@westriv.com. *Website:* www.mobridgeklein museum.com.

Two great Sioux leaders—and final adversaries of Custer—are buried in the vicinity of Mobridge on the Standing Rock Indian Reservation. The grave of Gall is in St. Elizabeth Episcopal Cemetery overlooking the town of Wakpala, eleven miles

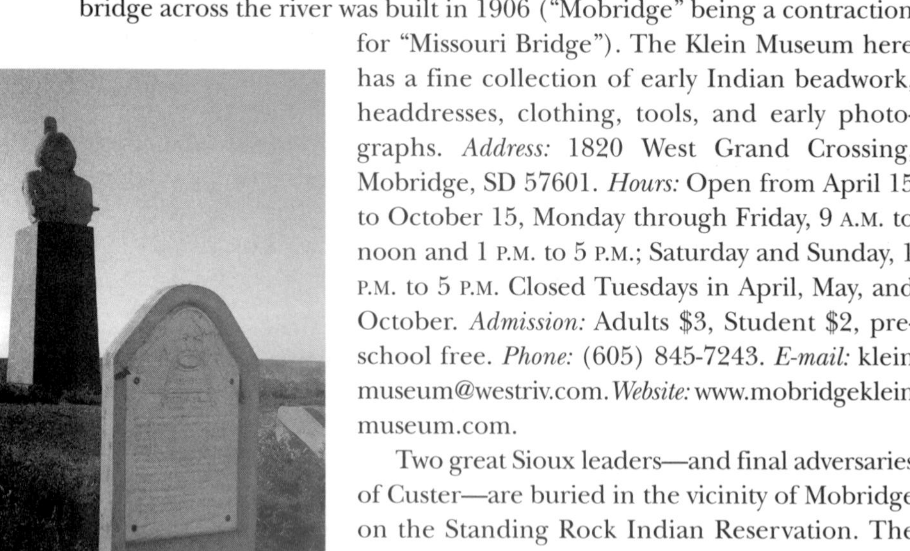

Sitting Bull's burial site, from its bluff overlooking the Missouri River.

north of Mobridge on Highway 1806. Gall settled on the reservation after his surrender in 1881 and promoted the education of Indian children. He was also a judge on the reservation's Court of Indian Offenses before his death in 1895.

After crossing the Missouri River and driving four miles south of the junction of State Highway 1806 and U.S. Highway 12, you'll reach Sitting Bull's burial site . . . or *one* of his burial sites . . . or maybe he isn't there at all.

In 1890, tribal police shot and killed Sitting Bull when the chief resisted arrest at his home. He was taken fifty miles north to Fort Yates in North Dakota and buried there. In 1953, seeing the economic potential of the remains, a few residents of Mobridge and distant relatives of the chief actually raided Sitting Bull's grave, dug up the remains, and brought them to his ancestral homeland near the Grand River's confluence with the Missouri. They dug a new grave on the bluff site and buried him under tons of concrete and steel to ensure Sitting Bull would stay there.

The problem is that they may have dug up someone else. A survey of the site by the state of North Dakota indicated that Sitting Bull—or at least most of him—is still in his original grave under a historical marker at Fort Yates. The nonprofit organization that administers the South Dakota reburial site concedes that only "local accounts" say that it is the true grave and asks that both sites be protected, preserved, and honored.

Fort Rice

Fort Rice, North Dakota

Gen. Alfred Sully established Fort Rice in July 1864 during his punitive expedition against the Sioux following the Dakota Uprising in Minnesota. Named for Civil War general James Clay Rice, the fort was made up of rough cottonwood huts built with earth-covered roofs on the west bank of the Missouri.

The fort was too small for the several hundred stationed there, and living conditions were poor; in fact, it almost lost more men in the first year than in all of its following years combined. In that time, eighty-one men died—thirty-seven of scurvy, twenty-four from chronic diarrhea, three of typhoid, ten of other diseases, and seven from Indian attack. More substantial buildings went up in 1868 and the soldiers planted a vegetable garden to improve nutrition.

Detail from Seth Eastman's painting of Fort Rice. U.S. ARMY CENTER OF MILITARY HISTORY

Fort Rice was highly active in the 1860s and early 1870s. Sully used it as a base for two campaigns and the government held several important Indian councils here from 1866 to 1868, including a great council with area Sioux that led to the 1868 Fort Laramie Treaty ending the Red Cloud War. The 1871 Whistler Expedition and Colonel Stanley's 1872 expedition both originated from here.

During Custer

Custer and the Seventh reached the bank opposite Fort Rice on June 9, 1873; from there, they could see army tents and Indian tepees spreading out from the fort to the south, west, and north.

Gen. Alfred Terry got to the fort on June 12 to go over the expedition's final plans. Meanwhile, the Custers and other officers got bad news, learning that most of the baggage and personal items brought upriver on the *Far West* had suffered severe water damage. "I endured everything," wrote Libbie, "until my pretty wedding dress was taken out, crushed and spotted with mildew." Unfortunately for her and other wives who hoped to stay at Fort Rice during the expedition, there was no room at the fort and the commander didn't want them there—they would have to return to family or friends. Libbie went back to Monroe.

Prior to a formal review of the Seventh by Terry on the 15th, Custer ordered the arrest of his brother Capt. Tom Custer and Lt. Charles Varnum for neglect of duty and disobedience of orders. The men were ordered confined to quarters and to ride to the rear of their troops during the expedition. Although they were later released from arrest during the march, it was clear that Custer wanted to tell the members of his regiment that their task was serious.

The great Yellowstone Expedition of 1873 finally left the fort on June 20, and it stretched for miles, consisting of nineteen infantry companies, ten companies of the Seventh Cavalry, more than 250 wagons, six hundred head of cattle, and nearly two thousand horses and mules. The Yellowstone Valley lay ahead.

After Custer

Although Custer never returned to the post, four of Fort Rice's Seventh Cavalry companies traveled with him on his 1874 Black Hills expedition and two of the companies fought at Little Bighorn. Captain Benteen was assigned to the post by Custer, likely to keep distance between the two.

With the construction of Fort Abraham Lincoln to the north in 1872 and Fort Yates to the south in 1874, Fort Rice lost its significance and was abandoned in 1878. The State Historical Society of North Dakota obtained

The Fort Rice State Historic Site today includes foundation markings and many prairie dogs.

Visiting Fort Rice

How to Get There: Located in Morton County in south central North Dakota. Fort Rice is on Highway 1806, nearly a mile south of the town of Fort Rice, twenty-two miles south of Fort Abraham Lincoln, or twenty-nine miles south of I-94 at Mandan.

Hours: Open year-round.

Admission: Free.

Amenities: Historical and interpretive markers, picnic grounds.

the grounds of the fort in 1913, and blockhouses were reconstructed at the site in the 1930s to help tell the story of Fort Rice.

The Site Today

Walking on the grounds of the Fort Rice State Historic Site today, it may seem impossible to believe that thousands of soldiers once swarmed the site, along with hundreds of horses, mules, cattle, wagons, tents, and tepees.

This is probably one of the least visited of North Dakota state historic sites. The reconstructed blockhouses were torn down years ago due to rot and neglect. The picnic grounds are still there, but the restrooms have been closed. If you go to the site today, you'll find foundation markings, historical and interpretive markers, a cannon, and acres of prairie dogs.

The 1873 Yellowstone Expedition

North Dakota and Montana

The Northern Pacific Railroad was first proposed in 1864 as a link between the Great Lakes and Puget Sound. The route would travel through Sioux territory. The tribe was hostile after having seen the devastating effect of the rail on the buffalo, and so the army would be essential in protecting the company's survey crews.

The first military expedition for that purpose was made in 1871, when Maj. Joseph Whistler accompanied surveyors searching for the best route through the Dakota Territory into Montana. Col. David Stanley took six hundred infantry on another route in 1872 in an attempt to avoid the Badlands; he found a way that was even worse. Now, in 1873, he would follow the Whistler route with two thousand men—including George Custer and the Seventh Cavalry—and drive even deeper into the Montana Territory along the Yellowstone River Valley.

Custer with a large bull elk killed during the Yellowstone Campaign. NATIONAL ARCHIVES

During Custer

In spite of arresting his own brother to show the seriousness of the expedition, it was a great vacation for Custer. He was its designated "chief huntsman" and led daily hunting parties to find antelope, elk, and deer for the troops. He practiced two new hobbies as well: taxidermy and paleontology. He would work on mounting the animals late into the evening in his tent and while in the Badlands collected many samples of fossils and petrified wood. By the end of the summer, he shipped crates of stuffed animals, heads, hides, horns, and prehistoric flora and fauna to museums back east.

Additionally, he had a friend to travel with. At the Muddy River, he met with Thomas Rosser, survey chief with the Northern Pacific Railroad and a West Point friend and Civil War adversary as a Confederate general. Both were thrilled to see each other again and the pair spent a great deal of time together.

It was a rough trip through the Badlands, however. Many times the column traveled in single file through the narrow rocky valleys, and single streams were bridged a number of times before they were finally passed. There was cactus everywhere and the soldiers cleared the ground of it for their horses to lay down before doing the same for their tents.

The column reached the Yellowstone River on July 15. They built a temporary fortified supply camp named "Stanley's Stockade," about eight miles south of the mouth of Glendive Creek in present-day eastern Montana. Two companies of cavalry headed by Capt. Frederick Benteen and a company of infantry were left to guard the post.

On August 4, Custer had his chance to show he could still fight Indians. He and two companies of cavalry, totaling about ninety men, were attacked while resting on the north side of the Yellowstone opposite the mouth of the Tongue River. It was a small group of raiders—only about half dozen mounted Sioux attempting to drive off the cavalry's horses—but they succeeded in drawing out Custer, his brother Tom, Capt. Myles Moylan, and twenty troopers for the pursuit.

After a two-mile chase, Custer and his men found themselves surrounded by a much larger group of about three hundred Sioux. They held them off while the rest of the cavalry closed in. Regimental veterinarian Dr. John Honsinger, sutler Augustus Balirian, and Pvt. John Ball were ambushed and killed when they broke off from the main group. The Sioux warrior Rain-in-the-Face took Honsinger's gold watch in the killing, which had later repercussions (see page 178).

Custer continued the advance with all eight companies of the Seventh and the Arikara scouts. After a forced march of thirty-six hours, they ended

Personal Battle: An Independent Streak Versus a Drinking Streak

Stanley and Custer quickly realized they would butt heads on the Yellowstone Expedition: Custer despised Stanley's drinking problem and Stanley was angered by Custer's tendency to act on his own.

After eight days on the trail, Stanley wrote to his wife that "I have had no trouble with Custer and will try to avoid having any, but I have seen enough of him to convince me that he is a cold-blooded, untruthful and unprincipled man. He is universally despised by all the officers of his regiment excepting his relatives and one or two sycophants." Custer likewise wrote to Libbie that "General Stanley is acting very badly, drinking, and I anticipate official trouble with him. I should greatly regret this, but fear it cannot be avoided."

Stanley's drunkenness led to stops for days at a time, but also gave Custer more free time. Custer pushed his luck by marching fifteen miles away from the train without consulting Stanley, sending the commander a note requesting rations and forage. Stanley had Custer arrested for presuming to take command, but Custer wrote Libbie that Stanley apologized within forty-eight hours of the arrest after sobering up and offered to apologize before the officers of the column as well. "Genl. Stanley, when not possessed by the fiend of intemperance," wrote Custer to Libbie, "is one of the kindest, most agreeable and considerate officers I ever served under."

Stanley also had an ongoing feud with another of Custer's foes, Col. William Hazen. It started in 1862 at the Civil War Battle of Shiloh, where Stanley accused Hazen of cowardice, and continued in 1879 when Stanley accused him of perjury in the 1876 Belknap impeachment case. Hazen charged Stanley with slandering a fellow officer, for which Stanley was court-martialed and found guilty.

David S. Stanley. LIBRARY OF CONGRESS

up on the north shore of the Yellowstone about three miles away from the mouth of the Bighorn. On the morning of August 11, warriors opened fire on the troops from the south shore as others crossed the river to the left and right of the camp. Furious gunfire was exchanged while the cavalry saddled up to return the attack, which was broken off by the Sioux when Stanley's infantry came up. The Seventh successfully held off at least 500 Sioux with its 450 cavalrymen, inflicting forty casualties by Custer's guess; his losses were four killed and four wounded in the fight known as the Battle of the Yellowstone.

The regiment saw the Sioux once more on the expedition, on August 16 at Pompeys Pillar, a 150-foot butte sandstone landmark first documented by Lewis and Clark in 1806. The Seventh was camped at the river across from the pillar when a half-dozen Sioux fired on troopers swimming and bathing. A mad scramble for clothing and cover resulted in no casualties, and the Indians left the site.

Custer and his troops marched as far north as the Musselshell River before getting orders on August 29 directing the Seventh to the new Fort Abraham Lincoln. They arrived at the fort on September 21, with Stanley and the infantry following at a much slower pace; Stanley eventually returned to Fort Sully.

Word of Custer and the Seventh's exploits on the expedition made its way east. As the regiment marched into Fort Abraham Lincoln, Custer got

Pompeys Pillar and the Yellowstone River, as photographed in 1873 during the expedition. Today, trees block most of the river view of the landmark. NATIONAL ARCHIVES

Visiting Pompeys Pillar

How to Get There: Pompeys Pillar National Monument is about twenty-five miles east of Billings, Montana, easily accessible from Exit 23 of Interstate 94 or from State Highway 312.

Hours: Open May 4 through May 22 from 9 A.M. to 4 P.M.; May 23 through Labor Day from 8 A.M. to 8 P.M.; and from Labor Day through October 9 from 9 A.M. to 4 P.M. Walk-in traffic is permitted in the off-season.

Admission: $7 per vehicle per day, $100 per bus or group. Admission is free with National Park Service Golden Age, Golden Access, and Golden Eagle Passports.

Amenities: Visitors center, museum, gift shop, restrooms, trails, historical and interpretive markers, picnic area.

Phone: (406) 875-2400 or (406) 896-5013.

Special Events: The Pompeys Pillar Historical Association, in conjunction with the Bureau of Land Management, hosts "Clark Days" the last weekend of July each year. River floaters reenacting Captain William Clark's 1806 canoe voyage on the Yellowstone River arrive at the monument during the afternoon. A buffalo barbecue, entertainment, living history demonstrations, and interpretive activities are included.

a telegram from General Sheridan welcoming him home. Newspapers praised his successes, making him one of the most recognized and hailed commanders on the Great Plains.

After Custer

As spectacular as the adulation was for Custer upon his return, the practical results of the expedition just weren't there. The 1873 collapse of the banking house funding construction of the Northern Pacific put the railroad into bankruptcy and halted its construction beyond Bismarck for six years.

The Sites Today

The North Dakota Badlands are where Custer collected prehistoric specimens to ship back east, and also where he was treated to some of the most spectacular scenery he'd see on the 1873 expedition and again in the 1876 Little Bighorn campaign. A great site to see what Custer saw is the National Park Service's Painted Canyon Visitor Center on I-94 (Exit 32), seven miles east of Medora. Watch for buffalo as you pull into the parking lot, as the monarchs of the plains are allowed to roam here. After enjoying the spectacular view of the colorful land formations, you may be inspired to take in nearby Theodore Roosevelt National Park. If you're on a Custer mission, definitely ask for a copy of the Custer Trail Auto Tour. This free map will guide you through one- and two-hour tours of the area, highlighting four Custer camps from 1873 and 1876 as well as Sully's 1864 "Battle of the Badlands." (For more details on Custer in the Badlands, see "The Dakota Trail of 1876" on page 205.)

The site for the August 4 battle—sometimes known as the Battle of Honsinger's Bluff for its most prominent casualty—is across the Yellowstone from Miles City, Montana. Once you cross the river on Highway 59 and come into the vicinity of the Miles City Airport and Sunday Creek, you're in the area of the unmarked battle site.

The Battle of the Yellowstone site is unmarked as well, but located in west Treasure County along Pease Bottom Road on private land. The easiest site to see is that of the final conflict of the expedition at Pompeys Pillar National Monument, administered by the Bureau of Land Management and open to the public. To view the Seventh's encampment and where the skinny-dipping soldiers took gunfire from the Sioux, make the climb to the top of the monument. At the top, you'll have a view of the Yellowstone River, obscured by trees growing along its banks; if you look past the iron bridge crossing the river, you're looking at the site of the Seventh's camp.

The Badlands in North Dakota. Custer would again travel through this terrain three years later on the Little Bighorn Campaign.

View of Custer's camp looking north from the summit of Pompeys Pillar. The Seventh's men were bathing at the north shore when they received fire from Sioux at the base of the pillar.

Directly across the river from you is where the soldiers were swimming, and an interpretive marker helps depict the scene. (While taking the stairs to the summit, you'll also pass William Clark's signature in stone, the only remaining physical evidence of the Lewis and Clark expedition.)

The monument is open year-round, but go during the travel season to enjoy the visitors center and museum, which includes a J. K. Ralston painting of the attack on the Seventh's swimmers.

Related Sites and Attractions

Interstate 94 follows much of the 1873 route; if you follow the highway to Glendive, Montana, you won't see any evidence of Stanley's Stockade, but you can at least see the land surrounding it six miles southwest of the town on Route 335. It's here that you'll also find Makoshika State Park, Montana's largest state park at more than 11,000 acres. Custer likely found fossils in this region as well—the rock exposed here is much older than the badlands of the Dakotas. Makoshika (Lakota for "land of bad spirits") includes modern facilities and a visitors center with a gift shop. *Address:* 1301 Snyder Avenue, Glendive, MT 59330. *Hours:* Daily from Memorial Day to Labor Day, 10 A.M. to 6 P.M.; daily from Labor Day to Memorial Day, 9 A.M. to 5 P.M. *Admission:* $5 per vehicle, $3 per person. *Phone:* (406) 377-6256. *Website:* makoshika.org.

While in Miles City, don't leave without stopping at one of its most interesting attractions, the Range Riders Museum. This privately owned museum contains one of the most amazing collections of the Old West, including firearms, Indian artifacts, Charles Russell artwork, and much, much more. The Custer fan will be impressed to find an original letter from Libbie Custer to Nelson Miles, commander of nearby Fort Keogh, in which she sent him one-inch squares of Custer's famous red neckerchief, and the surrender table and truce flag from Appomattox. *Address:* 435 LP Anderson Road, Miles City, MT 59301. *Hours:* Open daily from April 1 through October 31, 8 A.M. to 5:30 P.M. *Admission:* $5. *Phone:* (406) 232-6146. *Website:* rangeridersmuseum.org.

Recommended Reading

The Custer Story: The Life and Letters of General George A. Custer and His Wife Elizabeth, edited by Marguerite Merington (University of Nebraska Press); *The Custer Companion: A Comprehensive Guide to the Life of George Armstrong Custer and the Plains Indian Wars* by Thom Hatch (Stackpole Books); *Ten Years with Custer: A 7th Cavalryman's Memoirs,* edited by Sandy Barnard (AST Press); and *Jay Cooke's Gamble: The Northern Pacific Railroad, the Sioux, and the Panic of 1873* by M. John Lubetkin (University of Oklahoma Press).

Fort Abraham Lincoln

Mandan, North Dakota

The Northern Pacific approached Bismarck in 1872 and needed a fort for protecting its work crews. A site was selected across the Missouri and downstream from the town on a bluff overlooking the river. It was named Fort McKeen for Col. Henry McKeen, killed at the Civil War battle of Cold Harbor.

General Sheridan visited the fort later that year and didn't like the site selected. He ordered further development to take place on the flats below the bluff and called for cavalry to become a major part of the fort. Finally, he renamed the post Fort Abraham Lincoln in honor of the nation's assassinated president.

When completed, the Northern Pacific would be the second transcontinental route after the Union Pacific, but it was going into unexplored territory that hosted aggressive tribes who were more resistant to the white man. The army would play a major role in the construction of the route and Fort Abraham Lincoln became its home on the northern plains.

Fort Abraham Lincoln in 1876, as viewed from the site of Fort McKeen.

During Custer

Custer and the Seventh got to Fort Lincoln on September 21, 1873, and he soon left for Monroe and time with Libbie. He returned with her in November, greeted by the band playing "Home Sweet Home" and "Garryowen."

Fort Lincoln was known as "the Custer Post" for its commander. He kept six companies of the Seventh Cavalry at the fort, while four were at Fort Rice under Maj. Joseph Tilford with Captain Benteen and two at Fort Totten under Maj. Marcus Reno. With his "problem" officers elsewhere, Custer was thus surrounded by friends and enjoyed a happy winter at Fort Lincoln.

Still, fort life was probably not nearly thrilling enough for Custer. Poor insulation caused his quarters to burn to the ground in February 1874; they were rebuilt to Custer's specifications that spring and became the only real home he and Libbie had on the plains. Excitement came in April when an Indian raid drove off a herd of mules at the fort. Custer leapt into action and rode off in pursuit with all six companies of cavalry, incredibly leaving the fort undefended. Tensions were high among the women and the few remaining men at the fort throughout the day, fearing that the mule stampede could be a diversion. Custer and the cavalry returned after dark with mules but no Indians.

Custer learned in June that he would lead an expedition from Fort Lincoln into the Black Hills, presumably to scout for a fort site in the area but also to check out rumors of gold in the hills. He was gone from the fort for two months on the excursion; after his return, the Custers spent nearly two months in Monroe before returning to winter at Fort Lincoln.

During that winter, while visiting the Standing Rock Agency south of Fort Rice, scout Charley Reynolds overheard Sioux warrior Rain-in-the-Face

Custer in his study at Fort Lincoln, November 1873.

Visiting Fort Abraham Lincoln

Fort Abraham Lincoln State Park
4480 Fort Lincoln Road, Mandan, ND 58554
(701) 667-6340 • falsp@state.nd.us
www.parkrec.nd.gov/Parks/FLSP.htm and www.fortlincoln.com

How to Get There: Located in Morton County in south central North Dakota, Fort Abraham Lincoln State Park is eight miles south of I-94 and seven miles south of Mandan on North Dakota Highway 1806.

Hours: Grounds open year-round from sunup to sundown. Visitors center is open from Memorial Day weekend to Labor Day weekend, 9 A.M. to 7 P.M.; May and September, from 9 A.M. to 5 P.M., and late April and in October from 1 P.M. to 5 P.M. Interpretation of site available by appointment only to groups of five or more during off-season; call (701) 667-6380 or e-mail info@fortlincoln.com.

Admission: Vehicle entrance fee, $5. Interpretive passes (adults $5, children $3) are required in addition to the vehicle entrance fee for those touring the Custer House, the historic fort buildings, and the Mandan Village.

Amenities: Visitors center, museum, historic buildings, concessions, tours, historical and interpretive markers, camping, hiking, fishing, horseback riding, bike trails, water, restrooms, picnicking, snowmobiling.

Special Events: The American Legacy Exposition takes place over one weekend in late July or early August and covers the Fur Trader's Rendezvous, Nu'Eta (Mandan Indian) Corn & Buffalo Festival, and the Frontier Army Days historical reenactment at the cavalry square.

take credit for killing Dr. Honsinger and Augustus Balirian at the Tongue River fight during the Yellowstone Expedition. Hearing this report, Custer ordered Rain-in-the-Face's arrest and sent his brother Tom, Capt. George Yates, and two contingents of fifty men each. They arrested the warrior on December 15 at the agency after a struggle, and brought him back to Fort Lincoln through eighteen inches of snow. In the fort guardhouse, Custer interrogated Rain-in-the-Face until he confessed to the murders. He never faced justice, however; a break-in to free another prisoner allowed Rain-in-the-Face to escape. An unproven story said he vowed to cut out Tom Custer's heart and eat it when given a chance.

Custer's narrative, *My Life on the Plains,* came out while he was at Fort Lincoln. Instantly a best seller, the book had the effect of making Custer an

Rain-in-the-Face

expert on the tribes, even though his views differed little from those of his fellow officers.

Custer allowed himself to become embroiled in politics while at Fort Lincoln (and during visits to the East Coast in 1875 and '76). He snubbed William W. Belknap during the secretary of war's visit in early September 1875, seeing Belknap as a prime recipient of kickbacks from post traders. It may have been hypocritical, as Custer's men had long suspected him of making money from the Seventh's contractors and sutlers.

While plans were made for a spring campaign against the Indians, Custer was subpoenaed at Fort Lincoln in March 15, 1876, to testify in the secretary's impeachment trial. He went to Washington and testified against Belknap and the Grant administration; for that, an angered President Grant held up Custer's return to Fort Lincoln and ultimately removed him from command of the campaign.

General Terry was able to free up Custer to return to his post, but under Grant's condition that Terry would command the spring campaign. Terry and Custer arrived together at Fort Lincoln on May 10 to complete the preparations for the campaign. A week later, on Wednesday, May 17, 1876, George Armstrong Custer led troops out to the field for the last time.

After Custer

Fort Abraham Lincoln continued as a major post of the northern plains. After returning from Little Bighorn, Terry organized a force of about twelve hundred at the fort, including remnants of the Seventh, to continue punitive efforts against the Plains Indians. Colonel Sturgis finally joined his regiment to command it and participated in the 1877 Nez Perce War in Montana.

Fort Lincoln supplied the troops to protect Northern Pacific Railroad work crews when construction resumed in 1879. The crews completed work in 1883, reducing the need for the fort, and in 1891, Fort Abraham Lincoln was decommissioned. Once the soldiers moved out, local settlers stripped the fort of its buildings.

The fort reservation was deeded to the state in 1907. In 1934, the Civilian Conservation Corps (CCC) built a museum, earth lodges, blockhouses,

Personal Battle: More Hazing from Hazen

The Great Plains were immense, but not so large that a previous adversary, Col. William B. Hazen, wouldn't have the opportunity to butt heads once again with George Custer.

Hazen, of course, had conflicts with Custer while the two were at West Point in 1861 and later at Fort Cobb in the winter campaign of 1868–69 (see page 96). The colonel's ability to pick fights ultimately led to his banishment to remote Fort Buford at the confluence of the Missouri and Yellowstone Rivers in the northwest Dakota Territory.

After reading a promotional brochure from the Northern Pacific that praised the farming potential of the Dakota and Montana territories, Hazen wrote a letter to the *New York Tribune* in 1874 calling the region barren and not worth "a penny an acre." Custer was a great friend of the railroad and its chief engineer Thomas Rosser; he happily wrote a rebuttal to Hazen's claim in the *Minneapolis Tribune*, which the Northern Pacific reprinted and circulated.

Hazen wasn't done. He wrote more articles condemning the area's prospects, published a book called *Our Barren Lands* about the territory, and put out his own brochure that heavily criticized Custer's *My Life on the Plains.*

Custer ignored Hazen at that point and instead enjoyed the favor of the Northern Pacific, receiving free rail passes for himself and Libbie.

shelters, and roads, and placed cornerstones to mark former buildings. The site became part of the North Dakota Parks & Recreation Department in 1965.

The Site Today

Fort Abraham Lincoln State Park is one of the most popular of the North Dakota state parks, and definitely the one most steeped in Custeriana.

The showpiece of the fort grounds and its reconstructed buildings is the Custer House, rebuilt to the original specifications of the home once occupied by the general and Libbie. If you want to take a tour of the home, meet at the welcome sign at the north end of the parking lot reading "The Year is 1875." Once you pass the sign with the costumed tour guide, you are back in the final year of Custer's life at the post. The home is furnished

The reconstruction of the Custer House. The Seventh Cavalry passed between the hills in the background on its way to Little Bighorn.

as it would have been in that year, but none of the furniture belonged to the Custers. Curtains in the main parlor and a serving plate in the kitchen were theirs, and Custer's field desk is in his office.

Additional reconstructions around the original parade ground are the post granary (which hosts productions of the Fort Abraham Lincoln Melodramatic Association), barracks (equipped as if the Seventh Cavalry is still there), stable (with displays on the horses of the regiment), and the post commissary, which also houses the park's gift shop. Operated by the Fort Abraham Lincoln Foundation, the commissary store is a great source for books on Custer—if it's not here, it's probably not in print.

The Fort McKeen site includes three reconstructed blockhouses with a spectacular view of the Missouri River Valley, including upstream to the capital city of Bismarck. The former fort cemetery is also nearby, accessible by a short walk.

You should probably give yourself four hours for your visit to the fort: Keep in mind that there is more history at Fort Lincoln than the just the post itself. The ruins of the On-A-Slant Village (so named because of its slope toward the river) mark the village location of Mandan Indians from

1575 to 1781, with eighty-five round earth lodges standing here at one point. Lewis and Clark passed through the abandoned village on their way up the Missouri in 1804 and made note of it in their journals. Several of the lodges are part of the interpretive tour, as is a visitors center that houses a fine museum of the site's history and interesting exhibits on frontier military life.

Related Sites and Attractions

Camp Hancock State Historic Site marks the site of a U.S. infantry post from 1872 to 1877, and a quartermaster depot/signal office from 1877 to 1894. The post protected the rail crews and later served as a storage facility and reporting station for transmitting military messages and weather reports. The former officers' quarters serves as a small museum. *Address:* 101 E. Main Street, Bismarck, ND 58501. *Hours:* Open from May 16 through September 15, Wednesday through Sunday from 1 P.M. to 5 P.M. *Admission:* Free. *Phone:* (701) 328-2666. *Website:* www.state.nd.us/hist/.

A must-see stop adjacent to the capitol building in Bismarck is the state historical society's North Dakota Heritage Center, which tells the history of the state with an outstanding collection of artifacts and displays, as well as a fine exhibit on the military forts of North Dakota. *Address:* 612 East Boulevard Avenue, Bismarck, ND 58505. *Hours:* Monday through Friday, 8 A.M. to 5 P.M.; Saturday and Sunday 10 A.M. to 5 P.M. *Admission:* Free. *Phone:* (701) 328-2666. *Website:* www.state.nd.us/hist/.

St. Mary's Cemetery (23rd Street and East Avenue D in Bismarck) has the grave of Capt. Grant Marsh of the steamer *Far West* and some veterans of the Seventh Cavalry.

Recommended Reading

Boots and Saddles or, Life in Dakota with General Custer by Elizabeth B. Custer (University of Nebraska Press); *I Go with Custer: The Life and Death of Reporter Mark Kellogg* by Sandy Barnard (Bismarck Tribune); *Shovels & Speculations: Archaeology Hunts Custer* by Sandy Barnard (AST Press); *Ten Years with Custer, A 7th Cavalryman's Memoirs,* edited by Sandy Barnard (AST Press).

Custer and his Yellowstone Expedition scouts, including his favorite, the Arikara-Sioux Bloody Knife (at Custer's side, pointing). The Northern Pacific Railroad tent was a gift to Custer from the company. This photo is often linked to the 1873 Yellowstone Expedition, but the Colt Model 1873 revolvers seen weren't issued until just before the Black Hills Expedition. NATIONAL ARCHIVES

1874
The Black Hills Expedition

Around two hundred million years ago, the land that is now the Black Hills was part of a shallow inland sea. The seas retreated and advanced and landforms developed and eroded. About fifty million years ago, volcanic pressures pushed up into the land, creating the Rocky Mountains and the Black Hills.

Rising like a giant dark dome from the plains, the Black Hills were sacred and mystical to the Indians. They featured plenty of game, sheltered valleys, and firewood, making them perfect for winter camps. Many tribes occupied and passed through the Black Hills before the Sioux came to the region in the 1700s and forced out the Kiowa. The U.S. government granted the hills and surrounding lands to the Sioux as part of the Fort Laramie Treaty of 1868.

The Sioux occasionally made raids and other threats from the hills into settlements in northwest Nebraska, leading to the establishment in 1873 of Camp Robinson (later Fort Robinson) at the Red Cloud Agency and Camp Sheridan at the Spotted Tail Agency to the south of the Black Hills. General Sheridan felt that a fort on the north side of the Black Hills near the heart of the Great Sioux Reservation would further subdue the tribe—if they attacked white settlements, the army could easily bring retribution to Sioux villages.

Officially, the Black Hills Expedition of 1874 was to find a site for that fort; unofficially, the expedition would confirm reports of gold in the hills. An approach from the south to explore the hills would surely enflame the Sioux at their Nebraska agencies. If it came from the north, however, it was less likely to rile them. Suitably, Custer and the Seventh Cavalry got the assignment.

The Black Hills

Preparations began at Fort Abraham Lincoln for the expedition. Included were engineers, topographers, and other specialists required to map the land and identify a fort site. Custer also added a couple "practical miners" who knew gold when they saw it. Three journalists representing Bismarck, Chicago, and New York newspapers went along, as did photographer William Illingworth. Sheridan assigned two observers, Maj. George ("Sandy") Forsyth and Lt. Col. Fred Grant, the son of President Grant.

Finally, Capt. William Ludlow, the chief engineer for the Department of Dakota, was there. He had a history with Custer: Back at West Point in 1861, Cadet and Officer of the Guard Custer allowed Cadet Ludlow and another cadet to fight. When Officer of the Day William Hazen came along, he had Custer arrested and court-martialed.

With the ten companies of the Seventh, two infantry companies, sixty-one Indian scouts and interpreters, and a train of 110 wagons, more than one thousand people were part of the historic expedition. They left Fort Lincoln on July 2, 1874.

During Custer

The column reached the northwest corner of the Black Hills on July 22 after a 227-mile march. After climbing Inyan Kara (see page 189), Custer moved into the Black Hills themselves. The regiment was immediately struck by the green forests, the lush grass, the cold, clear streams, and the abundance of game animals and fish—all in stark contrast to the sun-parched plains they had just crossed.

They had no resistance from Indians; they surprised a small village of Sioux and ended up taking an old chief as a guide/hostage, but he was the

The Black Hills Expedition's wagons are seen snaking their way through the hills down Castle Creek Valley. NATIONAL ARCHIVES

last Sioux found. Without warfare, Custer immersed himself fully in the Black Hills. He not only commanded the column, but blazed the trails, did much of the hunting, collected scores of animal and mineral specimens for eastern museums, wrote reports and long letters to Libbie, and authored a forty-five-page article for a New York magazine—all on about two or three hours of sleep a night. He even fulfilled a longtime dream of shooting a grizzly bear (although it's likely Ludlow helped down it).

On July 30 came the discovery of small bits of gold in French Creek. While the prospectors continued to pan the stream the next day, Custer went mountain climbing at Harney Peak. After they found more gold, he set up a "permanent camp" during the first week of August and sent word of the discovery to Fort Laramie via scout Charley Reynolds.

The Black Hills Expedition on the return to Fort Abraham Lincoln. Custer is widely presumed to be in front, left of center. NATIONAL ARCHIVES

The excursion continued through the rough terrain to the north and east through the hills with difficulty, especially for the wagons. They finally found an opening that led to the plains on August 14 and began the 355-mile, fifteen-day return to Fort Abraham Lincoln.

After Custer

Custer's report of gold in the Black Hills electrified the country. Government officials tried to protect the reservation boundaries amid the frenzy. President Grant prohibited all citizens from the area and General Sheridan let it be known that trespassers in the hills would be arrested and their wagons burned.

Despite the initial exuberance, some doubted the mining potential of the Black Hills, including some members of the expedition. Newton Winchell, the chief geologist of the expedition, even suggested that the miners planted the gold they found. An authoritative expedition was planned for the next year to prove the mineral's existence and if it was there, to establish a value for the Black Hills.

Custer and many others assumed he would lead this 1875 expedition, but the command was instead assigned to Gen. George Crook, the head of the Department of the Platte and a West Point classmate and friend of Sheridan. Sheridan feared Custer was a little too close to mining interests by that point and wanted no politics in the trip.

The 1874 expedition's official purpose of finding a fort site resulted in the establishment of Fort Meade near Bear Butte in 1878. The federal government reserved the public forest lands of the Black Hills of South Dakota and Wyoming in 1897.

Featured Sites

Following are some of the most prominent and historic sites available to modern-day Black Hills visitors. They vary greatly in difficulty to reach by foot, but all are at least visible from the road.

Inyan Kara

Army explorers G. K. Warren and W. F. Raynolds identified the mountain as Inyan Kara in 1859, which more likely should have been called Inyan Kaga—"inyan" meaning stone and "kaga" meaning to make or form, and thus "made of stone" to refer to its hard rock center. This is probably one

Rising 1,600 feet above the surrounding plains, Inyan Kara is a mountain within a mountain.

of the most unusual mountains you'll ever see; sometimes called a mountain within a mountain, it has a horseshoe-shaped rim surrounding a large center dome.

Inyan Kara, along with Devil's Tower and Bear Butte, is one of the sacred outlying mountains from the Black Hills often visited by the Sioux, Cheyenne, and other tribes. Mysterious rumblings were reported from the mountain on calm days and nights by both Indians and the earliest white explorers. No mention was made after 1833 of the rumblings, which have since been attributed to the escape of hydrogen from underground beds of burning coal.

Custer's column reached Inyan Kara on July 22, 1874, establishing camp four miles east of the mountain along Inyan Kara Creek. Just before sundown, services were held for two men of the Seventh: John Cunningham of H Company, who died the night before of chronic diarrhea, and George Turner of M Company, killed by gunshot in a quarrel with another soldier.

The expedition didn't move the next day as Custer, the scientific party, and companies L and M went to the mountain. The companies were left at the foot while Custer, Forsyth, Ludlow, and three others climbed to the summit. It was reported that Forsyth also led his horse to the top, a very dangerous action given the steepness of the grade, the looseness of the stones, and the weight of the horse. At the summit, either Forsyth or Lud-

The graves of John Cunningham and George Turner of the Seventh Cavalry, with Inyan Kara on the horizon.

The "74 G Custer" carving at the top of Inyan Kara (outlined with water for ease of reading).

low (newspaper accounts differ) chiseled "74 G Custer" into the rock. The men spent about two hours at the summit, no doubt resting up from their climb, admiring the view, and looking for a route that would lead them into the Black Hills. Smoke blocked the view to the south, which Ludlow wrote was caused by a fire lit by the Sioux.

Aside from considerably more trees than in Custer's day, Inyan Kara is virtually unchanged since his visit. There is no development, not even a trail on the mountain, making this the most pristine of Custer sites.

Make plans before you go—you can't drive up to Inyan Kara and hike to its summit without prior arrangements. The mountain is managed by the U.S. Forest Service and is open for hiking, but the surrounding land is private property. Some landowners do allow

Visiting Inyan Kara

Black Hills National Forest
Bearlodge District Ranger Office
121 South 21st Street, PO Box 680, Sundance, WY 82729
(307) 283-1361 • r2_blackhills_webinfo@fs.fed.us

How to Get There: Located in Crook County in northeast Wyoming. Take Exit 187 off of Interstate 90. Drive fifteen miles south on Highway 585 until you reach the state historical marker on the east side of the road for the "Custer Expedition." You'll have a view of Inyan Kara to the west (although you will have seen it long before your stop).

Related Site: Behind the Custer Expedition marker on Highway 585 and up the hill, you'll notice a small cemetery surrounded by a picket fence; this encloses the graves of John Cunningham and George Turner, or what are assumed to be their burial sites (it's not known for sure). You are permitted to drive up the gravel road and walk to these two Seventh Cavalry graves.

passage but, as land ownership changes and some landowners just are not interested in helping out a Custer aficionado, it's best to contact the Forest Service office in Sundance and ask them to identify helpful landowners and their contact information.

Even with permission, hiking Inyan Kara is a very difficult task. Again, there are no trails. This is rough terrain with fallen trees, loose stones, heavy grass, and steep climbing. Trees block views of reference points and it's easy to get lost or injured. To top it off, rattlesnakes are common in the warmer months. If you're not a seasoned hiker, it's at least a two-and-a-half-hour strenuous climb to the summit. Excellent hiking shoes, water, and a hiking stick are essential. It's definitely not for the faint of heart.

If you *do* make it to the top, however, you won't regret it. There are spectacular views of the surrounding land and on ideal days you'll see Montana, North Dakota, and South Dakota in addition to Wyoming and Devils Tower forty miles away. Plus you'll see of one of few tangible signs that George Armstrong Custer was here.

Harney Peak

Warren named this mountain for Gen. William S. Harney, who led the first war against the Sioux in Nebraska in 1855 and was one of four U.S. generals at the beginning of the Civil War. Climbing Harney Peak, the highest mountain between the East Coast and the Rockies, was always Custer's objective. On July 31, he, Ludlow, some of the scientists, and a company of cavalry began

Visiting Harney Peak

Black Hills National Forest
Supervisor's Office
1019 N. 5th Street, Custer, SD 57730
(605) 673-9200 • r2_blackhills_webinfo@fs.fed.us

How to Get There: There are a number of trails that lead to the top of Harney Peak, but the shortest, easiest, and most popular route (which won't feel short or easy if you're not a regular Black Hills hiker) is Trail No. 9, Harney Peak South, from the Sylvan Lake day-use area. From Hill City, take U.S. Highway 16/385 south to Highway 87 and Sylvan Lake. Park in the day use area to begin the three-and-a-half-mile hike (and 1,200-foot ascent) through the Black Elk Wilderness.

The abandoned lookout tower on Harney Peak. The ashes of Valentine McGillycuddy, who found the true summit of the peak in 1875, are behind the bronze plaque at the foot of the stairs.

their climb to become the first whites to reach the summit (Indians had climbed the mountain for years, and this is where the Oglala Sioux holy man Black Elk had his "Great Vision" as a boy).

They started on horseback, but it was a long and winding climb during which they were often unsure of which way to go because summit views were blocked. They climbed the last two hundred feet on foot and were at the top by midafternoon. Custer fired his rifle three times to signal the success and they made their return to the base.

Today, with several trails to the top, Harney Peak is one of the Black Hills' most popular hiking sites, with thousands making the climb every year to see what Custer saw. It takes a couple hours to get there, but it is worth it.

The Harney Peak lookout tower gives a commanding view of the Black Hills. The tall rock at center is the false summit reached by Custer's climbing party.

The summit is graced by a large stone lookout tower built by the U.S. Forest Service. Just before making the final climb to the lookout tower, however, you'll pass a flat area with steps leading to it (site of a former concessions cabin); to your right are two massive granite spires with a gap between them that the Custer party believed to be the summit. Make the climb to the gap to be in Custer's footsteps.

Advancing to the lookout tower, and at the foot of its stairs, you'll notice a bronze plaque. Behind this plaque are the ashes of Valentine McGillycuddy, who climbed Harney Peak a year after Custer and discovered its true summit. From the top of the tower, you'll have a truly incredible view of the Black Hills. There are no interpretive signs to identify the various peaks and formations (including Custer Peak and Terry Peak, which were named by the Custer party), so bring a good map of the hills if you want to identify the more well-known sites. You've seen the faces of Mount Rushmore plenty of times, but it's here you'll view the seldom-seen back side of the national monument.

Permanent Camp, August 1–5

This is where the expedition spent the better part of a week mining, exploring, and taking photographs. There was plenty of grass for the horses and fishing for the men. Custer made his mark here after climbing to the top of the granite knob in the camp, where he (or someone) carved "GC U.S. 7" into its surface.

There are several indications that Custer and the Seventh were here (besides the large sign for the campground that reads "Camp Here—Custer Did!") For one, there is the state highway historical marker in front of the campground's café commemorating the expedition. Behind the campground, on Heller Road, there is a second marker built of native stone and a plaque with a typo: "General Custer Camped Here, July 1874"—of course, he camped here in August. (The grave of Pvt. John Pommer, who died of chronic diarrhea while campaigning with Crook in 1876, is next to the marker.)

Custer's inscription is still here, on Granite Knob across the highway from the restaurant. It takes some hiking and climbing to reach it and the mark is very faint; an attempt to clean the lichen away only succeeded in making the pink granite easier to spot.

Visiting the Permanent Camp

How to Get There: The Permanent Camp is three miles east of present-day Custer, South Dakota, on U.S. Highway 16 at the site of today's Wheels West RV Park and 7th Cavalry Café.

The site of the Permanent Camp, three miles east of Custer, South Dakota, viewed from the rock outcrop on which Custer's initials were carved.

This is part of Custer State Park and the only public approach to this site is from County Road 342, about a half mile east of the restaurant. Park at the Annie Tallent historical marker (she was the first white woman to enter the Black Hills) and hike about a half mile west on the abandoned road. Before reaching the knob, you should see a trail that veers southwest. Take the trail and work your way to the top of the knob; on its northwest face is the carving (look for pink granite). If you're unable to find the carving, take comfort in knowing that you are walking in Custer's footsteps and enjoy the great view of the Permanent Campsite.

The August 13 Camp and Trooper King's Grave

Searching for an exit from the Black Hills, the expedition found a plateau that provided a view of the plains outside. They made camp here as pioneer crews cleared a path and built a road. To commemorate their

A group photo was made with officers and civilian members of the Black Hills Expedition at the August 13 camp. No conclusive identification has been made of all in the photo; the following is the best estimation made by Ernest Grafe and Paul Horsted in their book, Exploring with Custer: The 1874 Black Hills Expedition, *after reviewing ten sources. The photo is interesting in that many of the men here were also with Custer (reclining at center) at Little Bighorn.*

1. *Capt. William Ludlow*
2. *Capt. George Yates*
3. *Lt. Tom Custer*
4. *Lt. George Wallace*
5. *Lt. James Calhoun*
6. *Lt. Henry Harrington*
7. *Dr. A.C. Bergen, asst. surgeon*
8. *Boston Custer or Capt. Thomas French*
9. *Lt. Donald McIntosh*
10. *William Curtis, Chicago Inter-Ocean*
11. *Luther North, assistant to Grinell*
12. *George Bird Grinell, naturalist*
13. *Aris Donaldson, botanist*
14. *Lt. Algernon Smith (see 31)*
15. *Maj. John Williams, asst. surgeon*
16. *Maj. George "Sandy" Forsyth*
17. *Bvt. Maj. Gen. George Custer*
18. *Lt. Thomas McDougal*
19. *Bloody Knife, chief scout*
20. *Maj. Joseph Tilford*
21. *Lt. Col. Frederick Grant*
22. *Capt. Thomas French*
23. *Lt. Charles Varnum*
24. *Capt. Myles Molan*
25. *Lt. Julius Gates (?)*
26. *Capt. Verling Hart*
27. *Capt. Lloyd Wheaton*
28. *Newton Winchell, geologist*
29. *Lt. Edward Mathey*
30. *Lt. Benjamin Hodgson (?)*
31. *Capt. Louis Sanger or Lt. Algernon Smith (resembles 14)*
32. *Capt. Owen Hale*
33. *Lt. George Roach*
34. *Lt. Julius Gates (?)*
35. *Lt. Joseph Chance or Lt. Hodgson*
36. *Capt. Frederick Benteen*
37. *Lt. Edward Godfrey*
38. *Lt. Frank Gibson*

Visiting Trooper King's Grave

How to Get There: From Rapid City, travel west on West Chicago Street from its intersection with I-90. After .7 miles, you'll make a slight right onto South Canyon Road/Nemo Road; follow this for seven miles until the road levels off on the hilltop. This is the site of the encampment (you'll notice street signs for "Seventh Cavalry Road" and "Garry Owen Drive"). At the north end of this flat area, in a pasture to the left, is the burial site of Trooper King; you'll see the flagpole and gravestone. Make local inquiries to access the site.

The grave of James King from Company H. While Custer marched on, Frederick Benteen read for the trooper's services.

expected last day in the Black Hills, the officers and civilian members took a group photo.

Unfortunately, the regiment lost another man. Like Cunningham at Inyan Kara, Pvt. James King died of chronic diarrhea while here. He was very popular and the men of Company H widely blamed his death on the expedition doctors. They buried King near the camp the next morning with Captain Benteen reading the services while Custer and most of the column moved out.

The August 14–15 Camp

After three weeks in the Black Hills, the expedition finally emerged onto the plains early on the morning of August 14. Custer and the Seventh made excellent speed, marching twenty-six miles that day, more than the previous four days combined. That was not to say the men were in a hurry to leave the Black Hills. Custer's brother-in-law, Lt. James Calhoun, wrote "(W)hen we move for days upon an open prairie beneath a burning sun, with nothing but warm alkali water to quench our thirst, we will be reminded of the many cold springs of pure water which flowed sweetly from the mountain side, and often will we turn round and cast a wistful dire toward these prominent hills."

Visiting the August 14–15 Camp

How to Get There: To reach the site from Sturgis, take exit 30 of Interstate 90 and drive east on Highway 34 for 5.3 miles; turn right (south) onto 131st Avenue and drive another two miles to reach Cattail Place and the site of the camp and its historical marker.

The August 14–15 campsite, the first out of the Black Hills.

They made camp that afternoon near Bear Butte, which to the men appeared small after the Black Hills. Custer didn't climb the butte—perhaps even he was beat after Inyan Kara and Harney Peak—but several of the men did. He did make the decision to spend two nights at the site before returning to Fort Abraham Lincoln.

Related Sites and Attractions

In Custer

While at the permanent campsite, you can also visit the reconstruction of Gordon's Stockade, a half mile east of the campground's restaurant on Highway 16. The original structure was built by prospectors joining John Gordon in December 1874 in search of Black Hills gold. They built the stockade for protection and began panning for gold, but a few were unsuccessful and left the stockade. They were captured by the cavalry and forced to reveal the location of their camp. The whole party was taken to Fort Laramie and released; some of them came back to prospect again.

The 1881 Courthouse Museum in Custer largely covers community history but readers of this book would be interested in the display on the 1874 Expedition. Artifacts on display include a rifle used by Custer to hunt antelope at Fort Hays, his shoulder epaulets, a first edition of *My Life on the Plains,* items found at the campsite west of town, a fan given to a friend by the Custers, and the remains of a tree carved by an expedition member. Across the street from the museum is an impressive monument to Horatio Ross, the discoverer of gold on French Creek. *Address:* 411 Mount Rushmore Road, Custer, SD 57730. *Hours:* Times vary throughout the year; contact for current hours. Museum closed from October to May. *Admission:* Adults $5, Seniors $4, Students $1, under twelve free. *Phone:* (605) 673-2443. *Website:* www.1881courthousemuseum.com.

Ten minutes north of Custer on U.S. 16 is the spectacular Crazy Horse Memorial, planned as the world's largest mountain carving. Sculptor Korczak Ziolkowski began work in 1948 on this 563-foot tall monument of the Oglala Sioux chief on horseback. The face is completed and carvers and blasters are now blocking out the horse's head (there's no completion date scheduled). While admiring the mountain, there's much more to see at the memorial, including the Indian Museum of North America, with art and artifacts; and the Native American Educational & Cultural Center, where you can visit with and purchase artwork from native artisans.

Of course, in connection with General Custer, Crazy Horse was in the attack on Last Stand Hill at Little Bighorn and it was the Black Hills Expedition that led to that final battle. And, yes, there's just a little irony that this imposing monument overlooks the trail blazed by Custer into the hills. *Address:* 12151 Avenue of the Chiefs, Crazy Horse, SD 57730-8900. *Hours:* Visitors complex open daily Memorial Day weekend to mid October, 8 A.M. until dark; off-season, 8 A.M. to 5 P.M. *Admission:* Adults $10, children under six free; carloads $27. Motorcycles $5 a rider. Walkers and bicyclists $5 each. *Phone:* (605) 673-4681. *E-mail:* memorial@crazyhorse.org. *Website:* www.crazyhorsememorial.org.

In Rapid City

The Journey Museum comprises four major prehistoric and historic collections; the Minnelusa Pioneer Collection has a decent display about the Black Hills Expedition, including a number of artifacts found on the trail through the hills and a complete set of the Illingford photographs taken during the expedition. The collection also includes personal effects of Sitting Bull, Crazy Horse, Gall, and others. *Address:* 222 New York Street, Rapid City, SD 57701. *Hours:* Memorial Day through Labor Day, 9 A.M. to 6 P.M. Winter: Monday through Saturday, 10 A.M. to 5 P.M. and Sunday 1 P.M. to 5 P.M. Closed Thanksgiving, Christmas Day, Easter Sunday, and January 1–15 (annual cleanup). *Admission:* Adults $8, Seniors $6.90; Students $5.75; Children 10 and under free. *Phone:* (605) 394-6940.

In Sturgis

On the way to the campsite, you drove past the Veterans Administration Health Care System's Fort Meade campus; you'll definitely want to make a stop here. Fort Meade was the home to the Seventh Cavalry after Fort Abraham Lincoln and there's considerable regimental history to be found here. For example, Capt. Keogh's horse Comanche continued his retirement and regimental mascot status here as the "sole survivor" of Custer's Last Stand. This is also where the career of Maj. Marcus Reno came to an end via court-martial. Already awaiting trial on charges stemming from a drunken brawl in the officer's club, Reno made the mistake of peeping into the window of Sturgis's quarters to spy on the colonel's daughter. Both of these stories and many others are told at the Fort Meade Museum in the fort's former headquarters building at the north end of the parade ground. Fort Meade is one mile east of Sturgis. Mailing *Address:* PO Box 164, Fort Meade, SD 57741. *Hours:* Open daily from May 15 to September 15, 9 A.M. to 5 P.M. *Admission:* Adults $3, children 11 and under free. *Phone:* (605) 347-9822. *Website:* www.fortmeademuseum.org.

Even though Custer didn't hike Bear Butte, Indian leaders like Red Cloud, Crazy Horse, and Sitting Bull did. You can too. Besides a trail to the summit (featuring a view of four states), Bear Butte State Park also has a visitors center, interpretive displays, camping, lakeside activities, and a buffalo herd roaming the base of the mountain. *Address:* 20250 Highway 79, Sturgis, SD 57785. *Hours:* Visitors center open May through September,

8 A.M. to 6 P.M. Two-mile trail to summit open until 7 P.M. *Admission:* $4 per person or $6 per vehicle. *Phone:* (605) 347-5240. *E-mail:* BearButte@state.sd.us. *Website:* gfp.sd.gov/state-parks/directory/bear-butte.

Recommended Reading

Exploring with Custer: The 1874 Black Hills Expedition by Ernest Grafe and Paul Horsted (Golden Valley Press) is indispensible. The book not only retraces the expedition through the hills with maps, directions, and GPS readings, but Horsted's stunning photography recreates Illingworth's photos from 1874. Journal and newspaper accounts from the expedition also accompany Grafe's narrative, adding to the adventure. A second book from the team, *Crossing the Plains with Custer,* covers the return trip to Fort Lincoln.

Also recommended are *Custer's Gold: The United States Cavalry Expedition of 1874* by Donald Jackson (University of Nebraska Press) and *Report of a Reconnaissance of the Black Hills of Dakota, Made in the Summer of 1874* by William Ludlow (University of Michigan).

One of the last known photographs of Custer, taken in March 1876.

1876
Prelude to the Little Bighorn

War was all but guaranteed after the Black Hills Expedition. The government failed to negotiate a settlement for the hills with the Sioux, nor could it convince the warring tribes of the northern plains to report to reservations. In November 1875, Indian Inspector Erwin C. Watkins wrote a report that encouraged a winter campaign against the "wild and hostile bands." This was fine with the military; it was likely that Generals Sheridan and Crook—Civil War acquaintances of Watkins—told him what to put in his report.

The Interior Department had to sign off on the plan. Interior Secretary Zachariah Chandler delayed approval until December, when he issued an ultimatum that the tribes come in to the reservations by the end of January 1876. That gave the army scant time to prepare for a winter war against Sitting Bull's bands. Crook said he was ready to march from Fort Fetterman in eastern Wyoming as soon as he got word, but General Terry put off plans until Custer returned to Fort Abraham Lincoln from the east on February 15. It was obvious the winter campaign would become a spring campaign.

Alfred Terry. LIBRARY OF CONGRESS

Terry quickly determined his best strategy was to give Custer and the Seventh free rein against the tribes while supplying them from a base on the Yellowstone. He planned to strike out from Fort Lincoln on April 6, but two forces—weather and politics—combined to prevent that from happening.

A March blizzard made Crook's advance impossible and delayed Custer's arrival at Fort Lincoln. Almost as soon as Custer got there, a telegraph arrived requiring him to come to Washington and testify in Congressional hearings on corruption in the post trader system. Custer thought he could avoid it and Terry, an attorney, gave his legal opinion that he could be excused, but Custer decided to go anyway.

Unfortunately for Custer, he openly consorted with the Democratic leadership while testifying against Grant's Republican administration, even implicating the president's brother in the trader scandal. Grant retaliated by delaying Custer's return to Fort Lincoln and told Terry to find another commander.

Grant refused to see Custer in Washington, and when Custer got to St. Paul, Minnesota, and learned that he could not lead the campaign, he tearfully begged Terry to help him return to command. Pleading from Sherman and Terry, along with pressure from newspapers against the administration, made Grant relent. On May 8, he sent word that Custer could lead the Seventh but under only Terry's direct supervision.

A jubilant Custer ran into Captain Ludlow in St. Paul. He told Ludlow of the reversal and vowed that once on the plains, he would cut loose from Terry at his first opportunity.

The Dakota Trail of 1876

North Dakota

Many things were working against the Seventh Cavalry during its 1876 campaign. Much of the land ahead had never before been seen by whites. There was no real knowledge of the distances they would face and many of the rivers and streams were dotted lines on a map, as no one knew their courses or origins. Their opponents, the Sioux and Cheyenne, already knew the land very well.

Training, or the lack of it, was an issue. Major Reno, in charge of the Seventh while Custer was in Washington, neglected to go through the fundamentals, including target practice. New soldiers came in to fill gaps in the companies of the Seventh, but most had no training and some had never ridden a horse. Many of the horses were green and untrained in battle.

Additionally, the Seventh was also missing many of its officers. Besides Col. Sturgis in St. Paul, there were two majors, four captains, and seven lieutenants who were on leave or detached service. The few officers who did remain, including Major Reno and Captain Benteen, were assigned men that they didn't know that well.

There were two more Custers among the civilians on the campaign: George's nephew Armstrong Reed, along as a herder, and his youngest brother Boston Custer, serving as forage master. In reality, both were along for the adventure.

Terry and Custer arrived at Fort Lincoln on May 10. They were now against the wall for embarking on a spring campaign and Custer had virtually no time to provide further training. The 1876 campaign would begin in one week, no matter what.

During Custer

The column left Fort Lincoln on the morning of May 17, 1876. They marched across the parade ground to reassure the women, but it was said there was still a feeling of dread for the troops. A mist that had covered the ground, began to lift as the troops marched out, and their reflections were seen in the rising haze, a strange vision of the soldiers walking both on the ground and in the sky.

It had to have been a magnificent sight, despite the gloom. There were about 1,200 men, more than 1,700 horses and cattle, and scores of wagons,

Visiting the Dakota Badlands Trail of '76

The trail starts at the Painted Canyon Visitor Center overlooking Theodore Roosevelt National Park on Interstate 94, east of Medora, North Dakota (a map of the tour route is available at the visitor center). From the overlook (exit 32 on I-94), turn south on Forest Road (FR) 739A onto FR 739, and then turn south onto FR 762 to Easy Hill and the Easy Hill Campsite. It was here that Custer climbed the hill and searched for landmarks he'd recognize from the 1873 Stanley Expedition.

Continue west on FR 762 to FR 740 and follow it northwest to Initial Rock. Here is where two privates with the Seventh Cavalry, Frank Neely and William C. Williams, paused on May 28, 1876 to carve their names into a sandstone bluff while on rearguard duty. Both men survived Little Bighorn, serving under Reno. The names are still there today and are protected under glass. There are restrooms and picnic tables here.

Backtrack on FR 740 to FR 762 and follow it to its junction with FH 3. Take a brief side trip on FR 742-1 from FH 3 to the Bully Pulpit Golf Course, the

Initial Rock (in foreground) became the name of the May 28, 1876, campsite after two privates from Custer's army left their names behind.

The trailhead to Custer's Snow Camp, site of the unexpected June blizzard.

location of a Seventh Cavalry campsite on the Little Missouri River. The regiment spent a couple days here to take advantage of the fresh water, and there's a small marker on the clubhouse deck commemorating the campaign. Continue north on FH 3 to the town of Medora.

The second leg of the trail starts from Medora and travels west on State Highway 10 to I-94. Go west to exit 23, then south on SH10 to West River Road (FR 745), then FR 750. Turn northwest on FR 750-1 to Sully's Waterhole and continue on FR 7054 to the Battle of the Badlands site near Square Butte.

The battle site and the waterhole were the only sites of conflict in the area from Sully's 1864 campaign, but the hilltop provides a great view of the draws and ridges in which the fighting took place, along with interpretive markers. There's also a marker for Custer's Snow Camp with a view toward that valley; visiting that site requires a two-mile cross-country hike. You can either backtrack to Medora from this point or take the scenic drive on FR 750, FR 748, and County Road 11 to Sentinel Butte and then I-94 (exit 10).

stretching two miles in length. The Seventh had two wings, the right commanded by Reno and the left by Benteen. Custer commanded the advance guard while two battalions rode with Terry for constructing bridges and roads as needed.

Libbie traveled with Custer on the first day's march, accompanying him to their encampment on the Heart River. She never saw him again after they parted on the morning of the 18th. The troops headed straight west across the plains of the northern Dakota Territory, traveling at a slow pace over ground softened by spring rains; wagons were often mired up to their axles and much time was spent pushing and pulling them out.

Ten days after leaving Fort Lincoln, the column reached the Badlands. Terry was certain the Indians would be found here along the Little Missouri River, a favorite winter camp for the Sioux. Marching through the rough terrain was extremely difficult, and they crossed Davis Creek ten times over a single eight-mile stretch. Mosquitoes constantly annoyed the men and animals, and cactus and rattlesnakes were everywhere; those factors, along with the fear of encountering Indians in such close quarters, had the men on edge. They reached the confluence of the creek and Little Missouri River on May 30.

Custer, a dozen scouts, and four cavalry companies thoroughly scouted the land for signs of Indians but found nothing, forcing the realization that the Seventh would be marching farther west and probably into the summer. They moved on and were hit by an unexpected winter storm on the first of June. Two feet of snow and a lack of firewood and grazing brought emphasis to the name "badlands." The Arikara scouts with the column saw the storm as a sign of pending disaster as they headed into the Montana Territory.

After Custer

The route cut by Custer and the Seventh through the Dakota Territory was largely followed by the Northern Pacific Railroad, and in modern days by Interstate 94. Settlement of the southwestern part of the state led to farming and ranching, but a great swath of land—more than one million acres—was reserved by the federal government as the Little Missouri National Grassland.

The Trail Today

Most of the Terry and Custer encampments in North Dakota are now on private farm and ranch land, inaccessible to the general public. There are also sites on public land that you can visit, particularly in the North Dakota

Badlands within today's Little Missouri National Grassland and its Custer Trail Auto Tour (see page 206).

Related Sites and Attractions

While in the North Dakota Badlands, spend some time in Medora. This is a quaint little town thoroughly steeped in the Old West and there are numerous shops and attractions to occupy your attention. The headquarters of Theodore Roosevelt National Park is here, as is the Chateau de Mores State Historic Site; it's the latter that has something of interest to Custer fans. After touring the museum and mansion of the cattle baron who once made his home here, head down to the coach house. Within the building are the wheels and axle of a wagon found decades ago buried in nearby Davis Creek, documented as abandoned by the Seventh Cavalry when stuck in the creek. Medora is also home to one of the best western Americana bookstores, the Western Edge (425 4th Street, Medora, (701) 623-4345). If you can't find it here, it's probably not in print.

Recommended Reading

An indispensible guide is *Following the Custer Trail of 1876* by L. J. Chorne (Trails West). The book provides specific locations, routes, current photographs, and daily observations made by the men of the Seventh, from Fort Lincoln to Rosebud Creek. Also recommended are *Custer's Luck* by Edgar I. Stewart (University of Oklahoma Press), *Centennial Campaign: The Sioux War of 1876* by John Gray (University of Oklahoma Press), and *Traveler's Guide to the Great Sioux War* by Paul L. Hedren (Montana Historical Society Press).

The Montana Trail of 1876

Montana

Previously part of the Nebraska Territory and Dakota Territory, the Montana Territory was created out of the Idaho Territory by an Act of Congress in 1864. The discovery of gold at Camp Bannack, Alder Gulch, and other sites in the early 1860s brought a flood of prospectors and speculators to the western part of the territory.

The military in the southeast portion of the territory in the 1870s was there primarily for the protection of Northern Pacific Railroad survey crews. By 1876, the railroad's construction was on hold because of a depression; the army's mission in southeast Montana became one of searching out hostile Indians and forcing them onto reservations.

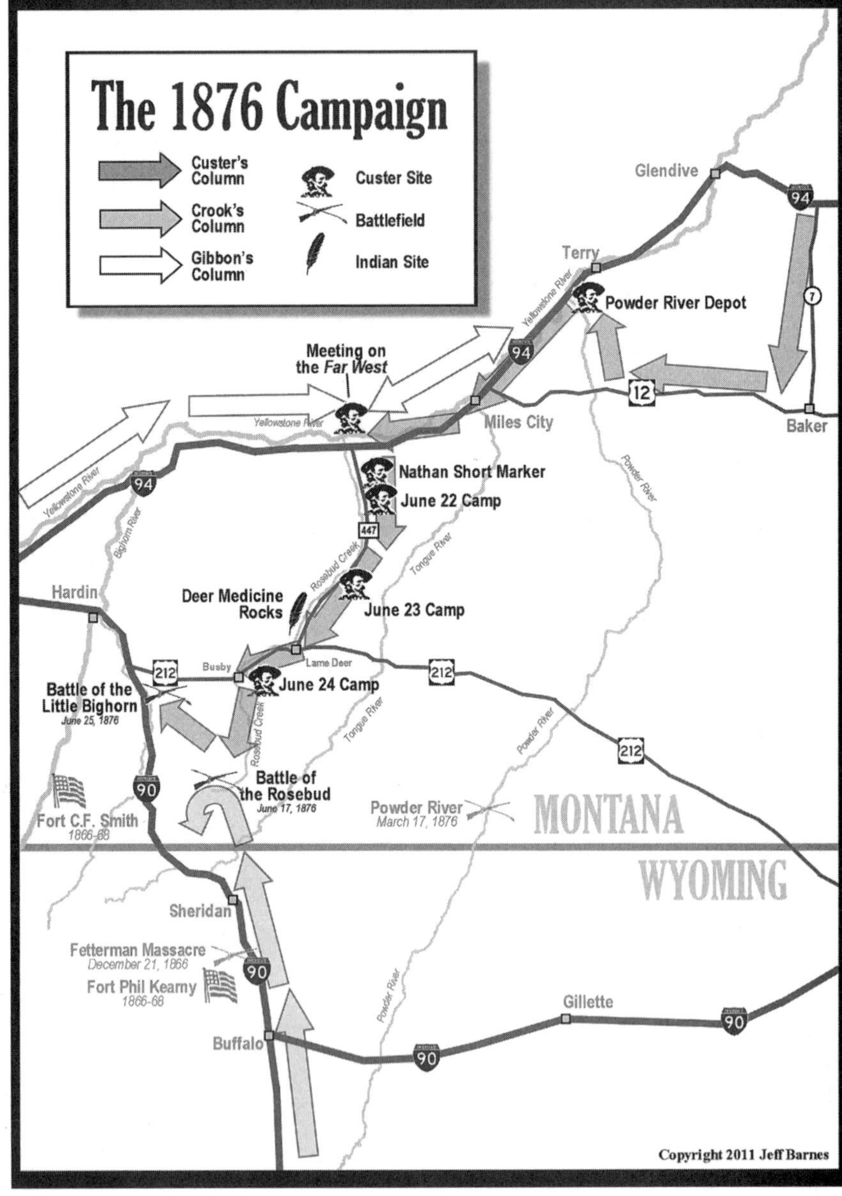

During Custer

The column crossed into the Montana Territory on June 3, 1876. During the day, messengers from Col. John Gibbon's command out of Fort Ellis (near present-day Bozeman) reported that a large number of Sioux were south of the Yellowstone; they also received word that the steamers *Far West* and *Josephine* had brought supplies to the former Stanley Stockade. Terry decided, based on the information, to march west to the Powder River and build a supply post at its confluence with the Yellowstone. He sent word to Gibbon to halt and await further orders.

The column marched on through the southeast Montana Territory, seeing land never before encountered by white men. The ground was rough and the scenery was barren. Scrub brush, cactus, and rattlesnakes were common and the heat was so bad that Terry suffered sunstroke.

They reached the Powder on June 7. Described by one eastern writer as "the filthiest stream in America," the Powder got its name from a grayish sediment along its banks that resembled gunpowder. Terry decided to hold up for a few days to rest the troops and plan; scouts were sent downstream the following day.

The scouts returned the next day with mail and a report that Gibbon had been driven back by hostiles. Terry decided to go on to the mouth of the Powder, about twenty miles away. He left with two companies and then took the *Far West* up the Yellowstone to meet with Gibbon between the mouths of the Powder and Tongue.

A scouting party of six troops headed by Major Reno was sent to explore the upper reaches of the Powder and Tongue Rivers to ensure no Indians were in the area before the main column proceeded further. Custer wanted to lead this scouting party, but Terry refused to let him go in order to avoid the appearance of favoritism.

Custer led the balance of the column up to the mouth of the Powder, where they made camp for several days and essentially stripped for speed. The infantry was to remain to guard the camp, the wagons were to remain, and the wagon mules were trained for use as pack mules, carrying only essentials. Officers and men gave up their sabers, packing them into storage crates, and even Custer's hunting dogs stayed.

John O. Gibbon. LIBRARY OF CONGRESS

The river steamer **Far West** *moored at the mouth of the Rosebud.*

Around one hundred men had marched from Fort Lincoln expecting to find horses waiting for them at the Powder River camp; there weren't any, so the men were left behind. Felix Vinatieri and his regimental band stayed here as well, and their horses were taken by soldiers needing them. When the Seventh departed the Powder River Depot on June 16, the band saluted the regiment from a nearby bluff by playing a number of songs, including "Garryowen."

The regiment marched up the Yellowstone, this time taking the south bank of the river as opposed to the north as during the 1873 Yellowstone Expedition. They arrived at the mouth of the Tongue River on June 17 and there found evidence of a cavalryman who had been tortured, burned, and killed—possibly the soldier who went missing during the 1873 expedition.

Word was received the next day that Reno was back on the Yellowstone from his scouting expedition, but he came out on the Rosebud rather than the Tongue, reporting that he'd found an Indian trail. Custer crossed the Tongue and Terry came up the Yellowstone—they and Gibbon and Reno all met below the mouth of the Rosebud at noon on the 21st. Reno was criticized by Terry for exceeding his orders and going to the Rosebud; Custer severely upbraided him for not pursuing the Indians once he saw them. Still, Reno gave them considerably more information than they had. It was obvious the Indians were at the head of the Rosebud or west in the valley of the Little Bighorn. (Unknown to all was that Crook's column was fighting the Indians on the upper Rosebud at the time of the Reno scout.)

On June 21, Terry met with Custer and Gibbon. Although Gibbon felt he and his infantry were deserving of the honor since they had tracked the Indians since February, Terry decided during this meeting that Custer would strike the blow against the tribes.

Terry gave his final, written instructions to Custer on the morning of the 22nd: He was to proceed south up the Rosebud to its headwaters before crossing west to the Wolf Mountains toward the Little Bighorn in pursuing the Indians whose trail Reno had found. The instructions also gave Custer considerable discretion, offering suggestions instead of orders. Terry and

Gibbon, meanwhile, would move west and be in the area of the mouth of the Bighorn River to cut off the Indians' expected escape route.

Custer's column, consisting of more than six hundred officers, soldiers, contractors, and civilians, moved out at noon toward the Rosebud, two miles away. Custer himself stayed behind for a short while waiting for further instructions and then goodbyes to his fellow commanders. Gibbon, in a semi-joke, told Custer "Don't be greedy—save some for the rest of us." "I won't," Custer replied, and rode off to join his regiment.

They marched up the Rosebud for the next three days, examining various abandoned Indian village sites. One of the campsites was near an unusual rock formation called the Deer Medicine Rocks, and there they found evidence of a sun-dance ceremony. The signs left behind indicated that the tribes could expect a great victory over the soldiers; unknown was that this vision came to the Hunkpapa Sioux chief Sitting Bull.

Custer made excellent time since leaving the Yellowstone and was twenty-four hours ahead of schedule when his contingent made camp on June 24. Although the men and horses were exhausted, Custer decided to make a night march when Crow scouts returned to camp and indicated the Sioux had gone east over the Wolf Mountains. Closing in on the Indians and probably nearing a meeting with Crook, in which case he would lose his command to the senior officer, Custer pressed on into the night.

After Custer

After Little Bighorn, the army concentrated its efforts in southeast Montana. Two months after the battle, the Cantonment on Tongue River was built at that stream's confluence with the Yellowstone, and replaced the following year with Fort Keogh. From this post, Col. Nelson Miles relentlessly pursued the hostile tribes of the region until their surrender.

The Northern Cheyenne were forced to join their Southern Cheyenne brethren in Indian Territory (Oklahoma), but found the new land intolerable and left to return to Montana in 1878; the "Cheyenne Outbreak" resulted in sixty-four of their members being killed during their pursuit and in fighting. The tribe was eventually granted its own reservation on the Tongue River in Montana in 1884.

The Crow, friendly to the United States, already had their own reservation in Montana. Originally 38.5 million acres, it was reduced by the Fort Laramie Treaty of 1868 to eight million acres; subsequent acts of Congress and cessions reduced it to about three million acres, which still contained the battlefield at Little Bighorn.

Visiting the Montana Trail of 1876

Interstate 94 west takes you from North Dakota to Terry, Montana, and the Powder River encampment. To more closely follow the route of the Seventh, however, take exit 241 of I-94 at Wibaux, Montana, and drive forty-five miles south on State Highway 7 to Baker. From there, take U.S. 12 west for fifty miles to North Locate Road and then travel north along the road, which eventually becomes Ten Mile Road and leads into Terry. Most of this road is alongside the Powder River and it takes around an hour to get to Terry. *Note:* Many portions of this route are unpaved, so if you don't want to risk being stuck in bad weather, continue on U.S. 12 to Miles City and then double back on I-94 to Terry.

The Powder River Depot and encampment are about seven miles west of the town of Terry at the mouth of the Powder River and across from Sheridan's Butte. The site is commemorated with a historical exhibit created in cooperation with Montana State University, the Montana Stockgrowers Association, and the federal Bureau of Land Management. To reach the site, take exit 169 from I-94 and go a half mile north to State Highway 10; turn east and find the exhibits after .3 miles on the north side of the road.

Continue north along the highway; go underneath the railroad bridge, drive up to the bench overlooking the Yellowstone and take the dirt road north for 1.5 miles to the grave of Pvt. William George, who fought in the hilltop clash at the Battle of Little Bighorn and died of his wounds while returning on the *Far West*. The steamboat stopped here long enough for him to be buried. The grave's headstone was dedicated in 1975 and is surrounded by an iron fence (you'll have to pass through a gate to reach the grave). There is also a monu-

Interpretive markers overlooking the Yellowstone River and the Powder River Depot site.
SANDRA BROWN

The Nathan Short marker, dedicated to a presumed witness of Little Bighorn who didn't live to tell the tale. PAUL HEDREN

ment nearby dedicated to scout Wesley Brockmeyer, killed in a skirmish at the depot on August 2, 1876.

The confluence of the Yellowstone and the Rosebud—the site of the last meeting of Custer, Terry, and Gibbon—is found off of exit 102 of I-94. Turn north onto the Old Highway 10 and drive east to Highway 448; cross its bridge over the Yellowstone, then turn left (west) onto the Fishing Access Road. A marker at the access commemorates that meeting.

When traveling south from exit 102, you'll be on State Highway 447 (Rosebud Creek Road). About seven miles south of the exit, you'll reach the "Grave of Unknown Man," also known as the Nathan Short marker. Through incomplete evidence, a dead horse found near the Rosebud/Yellowstone confluence after the Battle of Little Bighorn was thought by some to belong to Short, a cavalryman with the Seventh who would have been at the battle. When human remains were found ten years later and seven miles away, still others assumed it was the body of Short despite its lack of anything that would identify him with the army. Nonetheless, the marker is part of Seventh Cavalry lore.

Nearly another four miles south of the Short marker on Highway 447 is a marker for Custer's camp on June 22; in another thirty-seven miles along the route, you'll reach a marker for the June 23 camp. Highway 447 eventually merges with Highway 39, which eventually takes you to Lame Deer. Four miles south of that junction (or about five and a half miles north of Lame Deer) is the site of the Deer Medicine Rocks and Sitting Bull's sun dance vision. Look for four vertical rocks about a half-mile west of the road. This is private land, so make local inquiry to visit the site.

From Lame Deer, drive west to Busby, site of the June 24 encampment and the final camp before the Battle of the Little Bighorn.

The Trail Today

As in North Dakota, most of the Terry and Custer encampments in Montana are now private farm and ranch land.

Related Sites and Attractions

The Prairie County Museum/Cameron Gallery offers a glimpse of an bygone era, featuring a homesteader's house, a restored Northern Pacific depot, a caboose, and a steam-heated outhouse. The gallery is home to many of the pictorial works of Lady Evelyn Cameron, an Englishwoman who homesteaded in Prairie County in 1889. *Address:* 101 S. Logan Avenue, Terry, MT. *Hours:* Open Memorial Day weekend through Labor Day weekend, Monday through Friday (closed Tuesday), 9 A.M. to 3 P.M.; Saturday and Sunday, 1 P.M. to 4 P.M. Open during the off-season by appointment. *Phone:* (406) 486-5598.

The town of Lame Deer grew up on the battlefield of the same name; the May 7, 1877, fight was one of the last of the Great Sioux War. Lame Deer is now the headquarters of the Northern Cheyenne Indian Reservation, and Northern Cheyenne chiefs Dull Knife and Lone Wolf are both buried in the Lame Deer Cemetery.

Twenty-four miles south of Busby on State Highway 314 is Rosebud Battlefield State Park. On June 17, 1876, just eight days before the Little Bighorn battle, troops led by Gen. George Crook were attacked by Sioux and Cheyenne led by Crazy Horse. Crook was supposed to close in on the tribes' summer villages along with Custer and Gibbon, but his stalemate here and subsequent withdrawal meant Custer was alone at the Little Bighorn. This is a beautiful and undeveloped park with primitive restrooms, picnic tables, and interpretive and historical markers. To be honest, the state of Montana doesn't do a lot to promote the battlefield—there are no highway signs directing you to the site, so unless you have a map you have to "know" where you're going. You'll eventually find it while heading south on Highway 314. Enjoy the scenery on the way. *Hours:* Open year-round. *Admission:* $5 for non-Montana residents. *Phone:* (406) 757-2219. *Website:* fwp.mt.gov/parks/visit/rosebudBattlefield/.

Recommended Reading

Custer's Luck by Edgar I. Stewart (University of Oklahoma Press); *Traveler's Guide to the Great Sioux War* by Paul L. Hedren (Montana Historical Society); *Following the Custer Trail of 1876* by L. J. Chorne (Trails West); *Our Hal-*

lowed Ground: Guide to Indian War Battlefield Locations in Eastern Montana by R. Kent Morgan (Author House).

The Little Bighorn and Custer's Last Stand

Crow Agency, Montana

Sitting Bull's people were originally camped on Rosebud Creek in early June 1876, moving out before Crook's troops arrived there on June 17. The successful block of Crook in the Battle of the Rosebud ensured their safe passage west, over the Wolf Mountains to the valley of the Little Bighorn.

They settled for the next six days in the bottomlands along the winding stream, finding plenty of cottonwood trees for shade and grass for the ponies. There was celebration for the apparent victory over Crook but also for the growing size of their village. More people had arrived for the summer hunt from the agencies, and not just from the five Sioux tribes: Cheyenne and Arapaho lodges were there as well. In just a few days, the village grew from four hundred lodges to almost a thousand, from three thousand people to nearly seven thousand, and from eight hundred braves to nearly two thousand.

It was one of the largest villages ever seen in the history of the plains tribes, a mile and a half long and a half mile to a mile wide. So large was the village, so convincing was the repulse of Crook, and so angry were the tribes over repeated violation of treaties, that they were more inclined to fight than run should they be attacked.

During Custer

A few hours after the Seventh made camp at sundown on June 24, Custer's Crow scouts found evidence of the village's movement from the Rosebud

Sitting Bull. LIBRARY OF CONGRESS

west over the Wolf Mountains and the Little Bighorn. Custer decided to reactivate his men for a march at midnight rather than wait for daylight. They made the ascent through the mountains in the dark and halted just before dawn on Sunday, June 25.

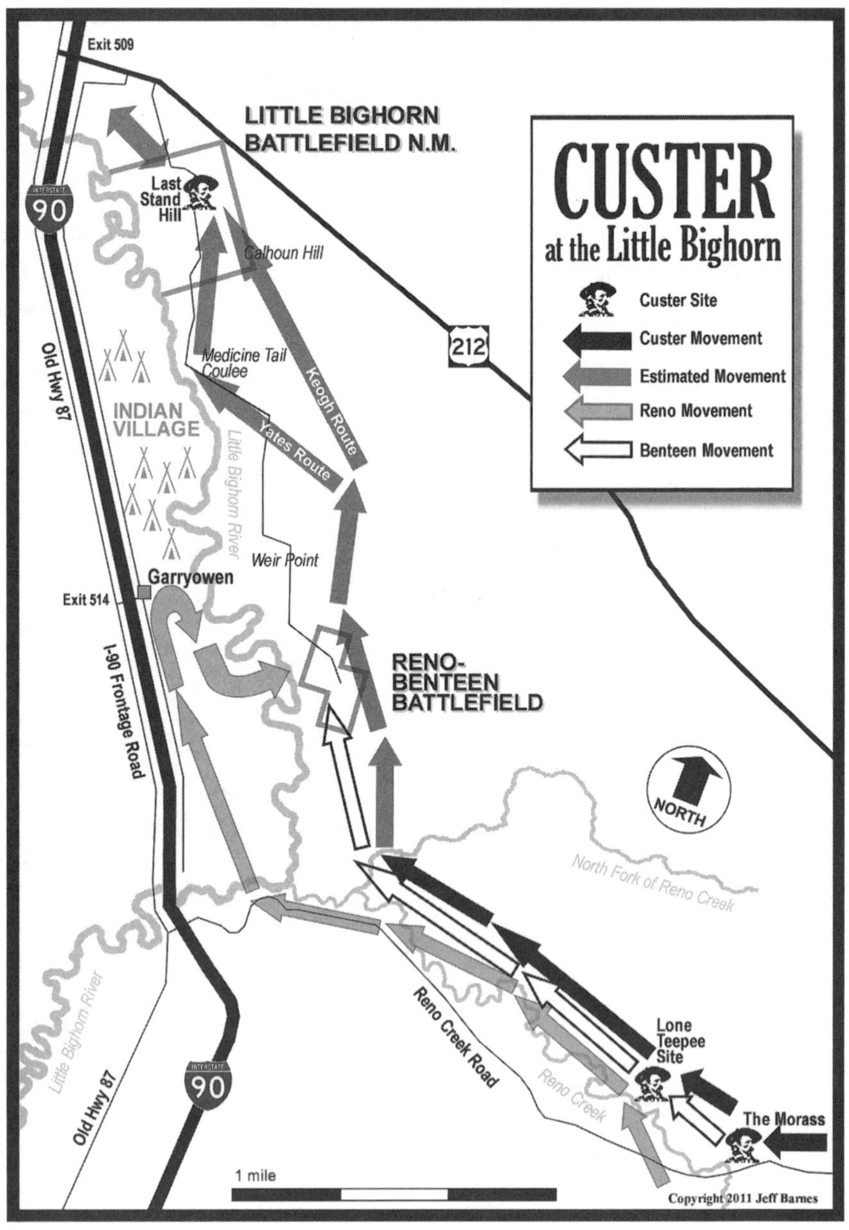

Crow and Arikara scouts posted on a large hill known as the Crow's Nest saw in the pre-dawn light the smoke and the pony herd from the massive village on the Little Bighorn. Custer climbed most of the way up the hill and scanned the valley with his fieldglass but saw nothing through the morning haze to tell him the same.

Before he returned to the column, word came that Sioux scouts had spotted the soldiers and were almost assuredly hurrying back to warn the village. Custer decided to find and hit the village as soon as possible before they could escape.

Shortly after noon, Custer stopped the column at a tributary of the Little Bighorn now known as Reno Creek. He decided the Seventh should be formed into battalions, with Major Reno commanding one of 140 men, Captain Benteen heading a second of 125, and Custer leading two battalions of 225, subdivided between Captains Miles Keogh and George Yates. Benteen was sent to the west and north to look for Indians and prevent their escape to the Bighorn Mountains; Custer and Reno, meanwhile, marched down the Reno Creek Valley toward the presumed site of the village.

They stopped to water their horses at a semi-swampy point in Reno Creek now known as the Morass. They rode on to a previous site of the village and found a lone tepee, containing the body of a warrior slain in the battle at the Rosebud; the tepee was torched and Custer moved on.

A party of about forty Sioux was flushed out and ran toward the river. Custer could see a cloud of dust over some bluffs and knew he had to attack immediately. Although he couldn't reach Benteen, he ordered Reno to pursue the small detachment of warriors and charge the village; Custer would be there with his support.

Reno chased the warriors while Custer continued with his 225-man battalion down Reno Creek to the confluence with its north fork. While stopped and watering their horses, the battalion received word that the Indians were coming to meet Reno rather than running. No one knows why, but based on this news Custer directed his troops north toward the tops of the bluffs overlooking the valley. After about a mile, he got his first view of the size of the village, and he also saw Reno's men fighting at the south end of it.

Custer briefly discussed the scene with his officers. They continued their march north, but not before sending back word to the tail of the column to bring up the pack train as fast as possible. The battalion continued into a large ravine that spilled toward the river and the village eventually widened into an area that became known as the Medicine Tail Coulee.

Custer turned into the coulee and sent word back to Captain Benteen to join in the fight and to bring up the ammunition that would certainly be

Custer's Last Rally *by John Mulvany, one of countless depictions of the general's final battle.*
LIBRARY OF CONGRESS

needed. The messenger was trumpeter (and Italian immigrant) John Martin. Fearing that Martin might not be completely understood by Benteen, Custer's adjutant William W. Cooke quickly wrote a note for Martin to carry, reading "Benteen. Come on. Big village. Be Quick. Bring packs. W. W. Cooke. P. bring pacs." Two companies under Captain Yates then went down the Medicine Tail Coulee and attempted to cross the river, while three companies under Captain Keogh went up the north slope of the coulee.

At this point, no one knows with certainty which contingent Custer accompanied, what he did, or what happened to him. If he went with Yates, then he too was repulsed by the fire and counter-charge from the village. There are those who contend that Custer was wounded or killed with Yates at the river and carried to the hill where his body was later found. Others believe he traveled with Keogh while Yates kept the Indians tied down, thinking that once Benteen joined them they could begin a final, decisive attack on the village.

In any event, the Indians began pouring across the ford at Medicine Tail, and Custer's battalion continued the offensive to higher ground. Keogh's companies held the rise now known as Calhoun Hill, firing on warriors crossing at Medicine Tail. Yates's companies, and likely Custer, moved north along a ridgeline.

The sheer number of Indians forced the fighting from Medicine Tail up to the ridge, while further downstream, braves led by Crazy Horse crossed the river and united with Gall to crush the troops on Calhoun Hill.

Custer was on the western slope of the ridge's north end, on a rise that became known as Custer Hill or Last Stand Hill. With him were his brothers, Capt. Tom Custer and Boston Custer, his nephew Autie Reed, Yates, Cooke, Lieutenants Algernon E. Smith and William Van W. Reilly, the men of Companies E and F, and survivors of other companies. "Custer's Last Stand" began about 4:30 in the afternoon and no one can guess when it ended. Benteen never arrived, and all of the men and their commander—Bvt. Maj. Gen. George Armstrong Custer—eventually lay dead on the hill.

After Custer

Reno, meanwhile, had fully retreated from the village attack and was now across the Little Bighorn and atop the bluffs with his survivors. Benteen's battalion eventually arrived and helped hold off the attack through the rest of the day and most of the next until the Indians withdrew, following the now packed-up village headed toward the Bighorn Mountains.

The disaster was discovered on Tuesday, June 27, with the arrival of Terry, Gibbon, and their troops. Half of the Seventh was dead or wounded: 210 were killed with Custer, and 53 were killed during the valley fight and Reno's hilltop defense. Most of the bodies were stripped and mutilated, some beyond recognition, but Custer was said to have escaped serious mutilation. Tom Custer, whom Rain-in-the-Face had vowed to kill and eat his heart, was mutilated beyond recognition (some contend it was by Rain-in-the-Face's hand, although this is unlikely). Reno's surviving men buried the bodies in shallow graves due to the hard soil.

In 1877, Fort Custer was built on a bluff overlooking the confluence of the Big Horn and Yellowstone to control the area Sioux, although most were already on reservations by that time. The army also returned to the battlefield that year to retrieve the remains of Custer and the other officers (he was reburied at the U.S. Military Academy at West Point, New York) and the battlefield was named Custer National Cemetery two years later. In 1881 a large granite monument was erected on top of Last Stand Hill and the remains of all enlisted men were transferred into a common grave at its base.

As the forts of the region closed, soldiers buried at the post cemeteries were reinterred at Custer National Cemetery. Gradually, more people were visiting the battlefield rather than the cemetery and stewardship was transferred from the War Department to the National Park Service in 1940. The site's name was changed to Custer Battlefield National Monument in 1946.

The Site Today

Renamed Little Bighorn Battlefield National Monument in 1991, the battlefield is without question the most visited site of the Plains Indian Wars, hosting hundreds of thousands of visitors a year.

You can stop at the visitors center and museum and visit with a ranger to ask any questions and pick up literature about the battlefield. The NPS brochure you're given at the gate recommends driving past Last Stand Hill and starting the tour 4.5 miles south on the park road at the Reno-Benteen Battlefield. In addition to the monument, the site features an interpretive trail (brochure available at trailhead) and sight poles where you can spot the Crow's Nest and the site of the lone tepee.

The drive back north is where you'll find interpretive markers at crucial sites including Custer's Lookout, where he saw Reno's attack in the valley; Weir Point, the farthest point of the Reno command's advance toward Custer before it was repulsed; and Medicine Tail Coulee and Medicine Tail Ford, where Custer's charge toward the village was turned back.

Custer's marker on Last Stand Hill.

The memorial shaft above the common grave on Last Stand Hill. It is conceivable that a portion of Custer's remains are here, as many graves were disturbed in the year following the battle and those that weren't identified as officers were interred together.

Of course, the most visible site is Last Stand Hill, where the general's body was found and originally buried. You've noticed the many marble markers around the battlefield; these are not graves, but rather markers where soldiers or warriors fell. The only occupied grave on Last Stand Hill is the mass grave under the memorial shaft. An iron fence surrounds the stones on the hill, with General Custer's marker shield blackened for easy identification.

Last Stand Hill is also where you see the biggest change in the landscape and philosophy of the memorial. Ground was broken on the east side of the hill in 2002 for the Indian Memorial, dedicated the following year to the Indian tribes that participated in the battle. Between the memorial shaft and the Indian Memorial is a marker and wayside exhibit for the horses sacrificed for the defense of the hill; their remains were discovered during the construction of the Indian Memorial.

If you have yet to stop at the visitors center and museum, do so. You'll find many military and Indian artifacts, artwork, dioramas, and audio-visual programs. Highlights include a buckskin jacket owned by Custer as well as his West Point and Civil War uniforms, his military commission, beaded moccasins purportedly owned by Sitting Bull, a Sioux war bonnet, and numerous artifacts uncovered in archaeological digs.

Finally, you must visit the Custer National Cemetery. Originally, when the dead from Forts Phil Kearny and Fetterman were reburied at the monument, they were buried next to Last Stand Hill. As more soldier remains came to the site, the cemetery was relocated to its current site north of the visitors center. The cemetery contains the final resting place of some well-known names from the battle, including Major Reno, reburied here in 1967, and Custer scouts Curly, Goes Ahead, White-Man-Runs-Him, and White Swan (whose name was given to the adjacent White Swan Memorial Library/Research Facility). Capt. William Fetterman, killed in the so-called Fetterman Massacre that prior to Little Bighorn was the army's greatest defeat, is also buried here.

Visiting Little Bighorn Battlefield

Little Bighorn Battlefield National Monument
P.O. Box 39, Crow Agency, MT 59022-0039
(406) 638-3217 • www.nps.gov/libi

How to Get There: Located in southwest Montana, in Big Horn County on the Crow Indian Reservation. From Interstate 90, take exit 510 and go east on U.S. 212 to reach the gate.

Hours: Memorial Day through July 31: visitors center and Last Stand Hill/ Indian Memorial, 8 A.M. to 7:30 P.M.; Reno-Benteen Tour Road and Deep Ravine Trail, 8 A.M. 7 P.M.; Custer National Cemetery, 8 A.M. to 9 P.M.; entrance gate closes at 9 P.M.

Open the rest of the year on the following schedule: August 1 through Labor Day, 8 A.M. to 8 P.M. September and October (ending on daylight savings time), 8 A.M. to 6 P.M. November through March, 8 A.M. to 4:30 P.M. The monument is closed Thanksgiving, Christmas, and New Year's Day.

Admission: Individuals (on foot, bicycle, or motorcycle) $5; private vehicles, $10; commercial sedans (one to six people) $25; commercial van/mini-bus, $40; commercial (charter) bus, $100. All National Park Service Passport passes (Annual, Senior, and Access) admit cardholder and accompanying passengers in a single private vehicle, but do not cover more than one private vehicle. Admission is free after 4:30 P.M.

Recommended Reading

Little Bighorn Battlefield: A History and Guide to the Battle of the Little Bighorn by Robert M. Utley (National Park Handbooks, 132); *Custer's Last Campaign: Mitch Boyer and the Little Bighorn Reconstructed* by John S. Gray (University of Nebraska Press); *Archaeology, History, and Custer's Last Battle* by Richard A. Fox (University of Oklahoma Press); *Stricken Field: The Little Bighorn Since 1876* by Jerome A. Greene (University of Oklahoma Press); *A Terrible Glory: Custer and the Battle of the Little Bighorn* by James Donovan (Little Brown).

Related Sites and Attractions

First of all and most importantly, remember that you are on the Crow Indian Reservation and to respect all property rights. Some key sites are on private land: the Crow's Nest and Reno's crossing site are not readily accessible to the traveler, for example. Organizations such as the Custer

Amenities: Visitors center, museum, gift shop and bookstore, restrooms, interpretive programs, research center, guided and self-guided tours, historical and interpretive markers.

Special Events: A Memorial Day service for veterans is held at Custer National Cemetery starting at 11 A.M. On the June 25 anniversary of the Battle of Little Bighorn, special speakers and activities are offered throughout the day and admission fees are waived.

Reenactments of "Custer's Last Stand" are not held at the national monument, but there are two privately run reenactments held during the anniversary. The first is held between Crow Agency and Garryowen at the battlefield on the actual site of the Sioux village across from the Medicine Tail Coulee. Hosted by the Real Bird Family, the reenactment is held at 1 P.M. on Friday, Saturday, and Sunday of the final full weekend of June. For more information, visit www.littlebighornreenactment.com.

The second reenactment is sponsored by the Hardin Chamber of Commerce as part of their annual Little Big Horn Days celebration. This reenactment, held six miles west of Hardin, encompasses more of the history of the area, beginning with Lewis & Clark's journey down the Yellowstone, through the periods of the mountain men and settlement, and ending with the climactic battle at the Little Bighorn. Held during the final full weekend of June. Contact the chamber at (888) 450-3577, or visit www.custerslaststand.org for ticket information.

Battlefield Historical and Museum Association offer member tours, however, and occasionally are able to secure visitation to this and other sites (see page 227 for a listing of organizations). The landowners of the Crow's Nest site have recently opened their land to paying customers. For $50 per person, descendants of original landowner Joe Mountain Pocket will escort you from Crow Agency, Montana, to the Crow's Nest to visit the historical marker there and take in Custer's view of the valley. Contact Tonya Lee Mountain Pocket Dust at P.O. Box 743, Lodge Grass, MT 59050 or (406) 665-5026 to make arrangements.

Two other sites related to events leading up to the battle are visible from the road. Drive three miles south of Garryowen on the I-90 Frontage Road; you'll cross the Little Bighorn and come to Reno Creek Road. Drive east on the road for about 5.5 miles and you'll cross Reno Creek; the north side of the road among the cattails is the conjectured site of the Morass where Custer, Reno, and (about an hour later) Benteen watered their horses before battle.

Above: ***The Morass where Custer and Reno, and later Benteen, watered their horses.*** **Left:** ***The Custer Memorial in Hardin.***

Retracing your route by about a mile on the way back toward I-90 (you're roughly following Custer's route to Little Bighorn at this point), you'll notice a homestead to your right, about .2 miles from the road. About halfway up the slope on the bluff behind the homestead is the location of the lone tepee investigated by Custer.

The Custer Battlefield Museum, off exit 514 of I-90 in Garryowen, is located on the site of Reno's initial attack on the Sioux village, and, as befits such a site, contains quite a few historical items. The museum's collection hosts an intriguing collection of cavalry and Indian artifacts, such as Little Wolf's war bonnet of golden eagle tail feathers (worn during the battle), and an Army pistol dropped on the Reno retreat route, still fully loaded. *Address:* Custer Battlefield Museum, Garryowen, MT 59031. *Hours:* Memorial Day through Labor Day, 8 A.M. to 7 P.M.; off-season, 9 A.M. to 5 P.M. Closed on major holidays. *Admission:* Adults $5, Seniors (65+) $4, Children 12 and under free. *Phone:* (406) 638-1876. *E-mail:* info@custermuseum.org. *Website:* www.custer museum.org.

Finally, a suitable end to the Great Plains Custer Trail is found in nearby Hardin. The city park at Third Street and North Crawford Avenue contains a large granite monument featuring a high-relief profile of Custer and a timeline of his life and military career.

Appendix: Custer-Related Organizations

There are a number of organizations related to the study of Custer, Little Bighorn, and the Indian Wars in general. Many have annual conventions that occasionally feature field trips to the forts, battlefields, and other sites involving Custer.

The **Custer Battlefield Historical and Museum Association** has been around since 1953. Its membership meets annually in Hardin, Montana, on the weekend closest to the anniversary of the battle. Besides the symposium, the weekend includes a field trip to sites outside the park boundaries, sometimes following the route of the Seventh Cavalry to the battlefield. Regular membership is $30/year. For more information, visit www.custerbattle field.org.

Little Big Horn Associates is a newer group (founded in 1967), and differs from the CBHMA in that it also takes an interest in Custer's life before the Great Plains. For that reason, the annual conference alternates between host sites east and west of the Mississippi River—recent host sites include Billings, Montana; Monroe, Michigan; and Oklahoma City. Regular membership is $40/year; visit www.thelbha.org for more information.

The **Order of Indian Wars** is the "spiritual" descendant of a veterans group of a similar name. Members meet annually at a site significant to Indian Wars history for presentations and tours by noted historians, scholars, writers, and preservationists. Annual assemblies have recently included Austin; Great Falls, Montana; and Salt Lake City. Regular membership is $30; additional information is at www.indianwars.com.

The **Custer Association of Great Britain** was formed in 2000 by British enthusiasts who had few opportunities to visit the American sites or attend related conferences but still wanted to meet and talk of Custer, Little Bighorn, and the Plains Indian Wars. They host full-day gatherings twice a year for presentations and discussions. Annual membership is £10 for residents of the United Kingdom, or £11 for those in Ireland or elsewhere in mainland Europe. For more information, visit www.westernerspublications.ltd.uk.

The **Friends of the Little Bighorn** was founded in 1996 to raise funds and promote programs and preservation of the Little Bighorn National Monument. Their website, www.friendslittlebighorn.com, offers books and related items on Custer and his last battle, as well as a live webcam of Last Stand Hill. Regular membership is $25.

The **Fort Abraham Lincoln Foundation** promotes the reconstruction, development, and interpretation of Custer's last post, today's Fort Abraham Lincoln State Park. Yearly membership is $40 and includes an annual pass to the state park and discounts at the park's commissary store and gift shop. Visit www.fortlincoln.com for more information.

Bibliography

Books

Barnes, Jeff. *Forts of the Northern Plains.* Mechanicsburg, PA: Stackpole Books, 2008.

Brill, Charles J. *Custer, Black Kettle, and the Fight on the Washita.* Norman: University of Oklahoma Press, 1938.

Burkey, Blaine. *Custer, Come at Once! The Fort Hays Years of George and Elizabeth Custer.* Hays, KS: Society of Friends of Historic Fort Hays, 1991.

Carmichael, Dr. John B., and Bob Rea. *Fort Supply: The Hub of the Military Roads and Trails of the Southern Great Plains.* Fort Supply, OK: Historic Fort Supply Foundation, 2001.

Carriker, Robert. *Fort Supply: Indian Territory.* Norman: University of Oklahoma Press, 1970.

Carroll, John M. *Custer in Texas.* New York: Sol Lewis/Liveright, 1975.

Chorne, L. J. *Following the Custer Trail of 1876.* Bismarck, ND: Trails West, 2001.

Custer, Gen. George A. *My Life on the Plains.* 1874. Reprint, Lincoln: University of Nebraska Press, 1966.

Custer, Elizabeth B. *Boots and Saddles: or, Life in Dakota with General Custer.* 1885. Reprint, Norman: University of Oklahoma Press, 1961.

———. *Tenting on the Plains: General Custer in Kansas and Texas.* 1893. Reprint, New York: Barnes & Noble Publishing, 2006.

Darling, Roger. *Custer's Seventh Cavalry Comes to Dakota.* El Segundo, CA: Upton & Sons, 1989.

Dary, David. *Comanche.* Lawrence: University of Kansas, 1976.

DeLano, Patti. *Kansas: Off the Beaten Path.* Guilford, CT: The Globe Pequot Press, 2001.

Donovan, James. *Custer and the Little Bighorn.* Stillwater, MN: Voyageur Books, 2001.

———. *A Terrible Glory: Custer and the Little Bighorn—the Last Great Battle of the American West.* New York: Little, Brown and Company, 2008.

Ellenbrook, Edward Charles. *Outdoor and Trail Guide to the Wichita Mountains of Southwest Oklahoma.* Lawton, OK: In-the-Valley-of-the-Wichita House, 1983.

Ellison, Douglas W. *Mystery of the Rosebud.* Medora, ND: Western Edge Books, 2002.

Faulk, Odie B. *Dodge City, the Most Western Town of All.* New York: Oxford University Press, 1977.

Federal Writers Project. *The WPA Guide to 1930s Kansas.* Lawrence: University Press of Kansas, 1984.

Frost, Lawrence A. *The Court-Martial of General George Armstrong Custer.* Norman: University of Oklahoma Press, 1987.

———. *The Custer Album: A Pictorial Biography of General George A. Custer.* New York: Bonanza Books, 1964.

———. *General Custer's Libbie.* Seattle: Superior Publishing Company, 1976.

Grafe, Ernest, and Paul Horsted. *Exploring with Custer: The 1874 Black Hills Expedition.* Custer, SD: Golden Valley Press, 2002.

Griffith, T. D. *South Dakota.* New York: Compass American Guides, 2004.

Gray, John S. *Custer's Last Campaign: Mitch Boyer and the Little Bighorn Reconstructed.* Lincoln: University of Nebraska Press, 1991.

Greene, Jerome A. *Fort Randall on the Missouri, 1856–1892.* Pierre: South Dakota Historical Society Press, 2005.

———. *Stricken Field: The Little Bighorn Since 1876.* Norman: University of Oklahoma Press, 2008.

Hart, Herbert M. *Old Forts of the Northwest.* New York: Bonanza Books, 1963.

———. *Old Forts of the Southwest.* New York: Bonanza Books, 1964.

———. *Tour Guide to Old Western Forts.* Boulder, CO: Pruett Publishing Company, 1980.

Hatch, Thom. *The Custer Companion: A Comprehensive Guide to the Life of George Armstrong Custer and the Plains Indian Wars.* Mechanicsburg, PA: Stackpole Books, 2002.

Hedren, Paul L. *Traveler's Guide to the Great Sioux War.* Helena: Montana Historical Society Press, 1996.

Heier, Vincent A. *Little Bighorn (Postcard History Series).* Charleston, SC: Arcadia Publishing, 2009.

Hoig, Stan. *The Battle of the Washita.* Lincoln: University of Nebraska Press, 1976.

Holmes, Louis A. *Fort McPherson, Nebraska. Fort Cottonwood, N.T. Guardian of the Tracks and Trails.* Lincoln, NE: Johnsen Publishing Company, 1963.

Hughes, J. Patrick. *Fort Leavenworth: Gateway to the West.* Topeka: Kansas State Historical Society, 2000.

Hutton, Paul Andrew, ed. *The Custer Reader.* Lincoln: University of Nebraska Press, 1992.

Jennewein, J. Leonard, and Jane Boorman, eds. *Dakota Panorama.* Sioux Falls, SD: Brevet Press, 1973.

Jackson, Donald. *Custer's Gold: The United States Cavalry Expedition of 1874.* Lincoln: University of Nebraska Press, 1966.

Juneau, Denise, and Julie Cajune, eds. *Montana Indians: Their History and Locations.* Helena: Montana Office of Public Instruction, 2009.

Katz, D. Mark. *Custer in Photographs.* New York: Bonanza Books, 1985.

Kinsey, Maxine Schuurmans. *The Sioux City to Fort Randall Military Road 1856–1892, Revisited.* Sioux Falls, SD: Pine Hill Press, 2010.

Mackintosh, Donald P., pub. *Brevet's South Dakota Historical Markers.* Sioux Falls, SD: Brevet Press, 1974.

———. *Brevet's North Dakota Historical Markers.* Sioux Falls, SD: Brevet Press, 1975.

McKale, William, and Robert Smith. *Fort Riley (Images of America)* . Charleston, SC: Arcadia Publishing, 2009.

McKale, William, and William D. Young. *Fort Riley: Citadel of the Frontier West.* Topeka: Kansas State Historical Society, 2000.

McNally, Jim. "A Romanoff Roams the Rockies in 1872." Paper, History Department, University of Colorado at Denver, 1984.

Michno, Gregory F. *Encyclopedia of Indian Wars: Western Battles and Skirmishes, 1850–1890.* Missoula, MT: Mountain Press Publishing Company, 2003.

Moeller, Bill, and Jan Moeller. *Custer: A Photographic Biography.* Missoula, MT: Mountain Press Publishing Company, 2003.

Morgan, R. Kent. *Our Hallowed Ground: Guide to Indian War Battlefield Locations in Eastern Montana.* Bloomington, IN: Author House, 2004.

Nye, Col. W. S. *Carbine and Lance: The Story of Old Fort Sill.* Norman: University of Oklahoma Press, 1937.

Oliva, Leo E. *Fort Dodge: Sentry of the Western Plains.* Topeka: Kansas State Historical Society, 1998.

———. *Fort Harker: Defending the Journey West.* Topeka: Kansas State Historical Society, 2000.

———. *Fort Hays: Frontier Army Post.* Topeka: Kansas State Historical Society, 1980.

———. *Fort Hays: Keeping Peace on the Plains.* Topeka: Kansas State Historical Society, 1996.

———. *Fort Larned: Guardian of the Santa Fe Trail.* Topeka: Kansas State Historical Society, 1997.

———. *Fort Wallace: Sentinel on the Smoky Hill Trail.* Topeka: Kansas State Historical Society, 1998.

Prucha, Francis Paul. *Atlas of American Indian Affairs.* Lincoln: University of Nebraska Press, 1990.

Scott, Douglas O., Peter Bleed, and Stephen Damn. "Custer, Cody, and a Grand Duke: Historical Archaeology of Camp Alexis, the Royal Buffalo Hunt Site in Nebraska." Unpublished manuscript, 2011.

Schuler, Harold H. *Fort Sully: Guns at Sunset.* Vermillion: University of South Dakota Press, 1992.

Sherman, Lt. Gen. P. H. *Outline Descriptions of the Posts in the Military Division of the Missouri.* Bellevue, NE: The Old Army Press, facsimile edition 1969

Stewart, Edgar I. *Custer's Luck.* Norman: University of Oklahoma Press, 1955.

Utley, Robert M. *Cavalier in Buckskin: George Armstrong Custer and the Western Military Frontier.* Norman: University of Oklahoma Press, 1988.

———. *Encyclopedia of the American West.* New York: Wings Books, 1997.

Van de Water, Frederic F. *Glory-Hunter: A Life of General Custer.* Lincoln: University of Nebraska Press, 1934.

Waldman, Carl. *Atlas of the North American Indian.* New York: Facts on File, 1985.

Walton, George. *Sentinel of the Plains: Fort Leavenworth and the American West.* Englewood Cliffs, NJ: Prentice-Hall, 1973.

Wishart, David J., ed. *Encyclopedia of the Great Plains.* Lincoln: University of Nebraska Press, 2004.

Wright, Muriel H., et al. *Mark of Heritage: Oklahoma's Historic Sites.* Norman: University of Oklahoma Press, 1976.

Magazines and Journals

"Custer's Texas Home," *Texas Highways* magazine, February 1986: 42–47.

Dvoracek, Fran. "Another Custer Mystery? Six Unknown Soldiers Buried at Bon Homme Cemetery, South Dakota." Paper presented at Annual Symposium of the Custer Battlefield Historical & Museum Association, June 21, 2002.

Hammer, Lawrence Charles. "A History of Fort Zarah." *Collections* 3, no. 1 (Spring 2004): 10–43.

Wright, Muriel H. "A History of Fort Cobb." *Chronicles of Oklahoma* 34, no. 1 (1956): 53–71.

Government Publications

Utley, Robert M. *Little Bighorn Battlefield: A History and Guide to the Battle of the Little Bighorn.* Washington, DC: National Park Service, 1988.

Utley, Robert M., et al. *Soldier and Brave: Historic Places Associated with Indian Affairs and the Indian Wars in the Trans-Mississippi West.* Washington, DC: National Park Service, 1971.

Miscellaneous Publications, Guides, Brochures, Pamphlets, and Maps

Barton County (Kansas) Historical Society Museum and Village.

Blackburn, Col. Forrest R. *Cantonment Leavenworth, 1827 to 1832.* Fort Leavenworth Historical Society (Reprint from *Military Review,* Dec. 1971).

Custer National Cemetery. Tucson, AZ: Southwest Parks & Monuments Association, 1994.

Custer Trail Auto Tour. USDA Forest Service.

Ellsworth County Historical Society.

Fort Harker Museum Complex. Ellsworth County Historical Society.

Fort Hays State Historic Site. Kansas Historical Society.

Fort Larned Official Map and Guide. National Park Service. Washington, DC: Government Printing Office: 1984.

Fort Riley's Historic Buildings. The U.S. Cavalry Museum.

Fort Riley 2007 Guide and Telephone Directory. Anchorage, AK: AQP Publishing, 2007.

Fort Riley 2008 Installation Map. Anchorage, AK: AQP Publishing, 2008.

Fort Wallace Memorial Museum. Fort Wallace Memorial Association.

Historic Custer House, Quarters 24, Fort Riley, KS. U.S. Cavalry Museum and the Fort Riley Historical and Archaeological Society.

Historic Main Post Walking Tour, Fort Riley, Kansas. Museum Division, Fort Riley, Kansas.

Little Bighorn Battlefield National Monument Official Map and Guide. Washington, DC: Government Printing Office: 1994.

Little Bighorn National Monument. Tucson, AZ: Western National Parks Association, 1996.

Reno-Benteen Entrenchment Trail. Tucson, AZ: Western National Parks Association, 2002.

Santa Fe Trail Center Historical Museum & Library.

Santa Fe Trail Official Map and Guide. Washington, DC: Government Printing Office: 2004.

Self-Guided Tour of Fort Leavenworth, the Gateway to the West. Fort Leavenworth Historical Society.

Shoemaker, Col. John O. *The Custer Court-Martial.* Fort Leavenworth Historical Society (Reprint from Military Review, Oct. 1971)

Washita Battlefield National Historic Site Trail Guide. Tucson, AZ: Western National Parks Association.

Washita Battlefield Official Map and Guide. Washington, DC: Government Printing Office: 2009.

Up Pawnee Fork. Fort Larned Old Guard.

Index

Page number in *italics* indicates illustrations and sidebars.